ALEXANDRE DUMAS

LE VICOMTE DE BRAGELONNE
(The Man in the Iron Mask)

Alexandre Dumas

Portrait reproduced by kind permission of Iconographie d'Alexandre Dumas père, Editions Champflour, Marly-le-Roi, 1991.

ALEXANDRE DUMAS

LE VICOMTE DE BRAGELONNE
(The Man in the Iron Mask)

A Critical Study

A. Craig Bell

By the same author:
  Alexandre Dumas: A Biographical Study
  Byron: His Achievement and Significance
  Charades: a 3-act play
  A Guide to the Novels of Trollope
  The Novels of Anne Brontë
  Stories from A Yorkshire Dale
  Fritz Kreisler remembered
  Learn English — and die!

Dumas works translated by the present author:
  La Route de Varennes
  Impressions de Voyage — En Suisse
  Mes Mémoires (abridged)
  Histoire de mes Bêtes
  Fernande: the story of a courtesan
  Parisiens et Provinciaux

©A. Craig Bell, 1995
First published in Great Britain 1995

Published by Merlin Books Ltd.
Braunton, Devon, England

British Library Cataloguing in Publication Data.
A catalogue record for this book is available from the British Library.

ISBN 0 86303 694–5

Printed in England by Orchard & Ind Ltd., Gloucester

Upon his acceptance of the office of President of the Dumas Association, Jean Cocteau communicated the following message to the General Secretary:

> 'I thank you once more for the great honour you confer on me. I have always considered Alexandre Dumas to be a great historian — the prince of the truer than the truth . . .'

The original message is reproduced in facsimile on this page.

The name of Alexandre Dumas is more than French, it is European; and it is more than European, it is universal.
VICTOR HUGO

I love and admire you, for you are a force of nature.
MICHELET

You have done more to teach the people history than all the historians put together.
IBID.

Excellent heart and brilliant genius. In him the novelist and the dramatist are thoroughly at one.
SWINBURNE

The most living dramatic genius since Shakespeare.
D. G. ROSSETTI

He speaks with heart to heart, and is understood and applauded.
HEINE

When I am unwell, upset, sad, tired or discouraged, I find Dumas's books the best antidote to all mental or physical ills.
GEORGE SAND

Dumas was what Gounod called Mozart — a summit of art. Nobody ever could, or did, or will improve on Dumas's romances and plays.
G. BERNARD SHAW

This statue, which would be of solid gold if every reader of Dumas contributed only a centime, is that of a great jester who, in his wit and gaiety, hid more good sense and wisdom than is to be found in all of us here. It is the image of a breaker of rules who gave the lie to rules, of a man of pleasure who could serve as a model for all workers . . . It is the likeness of a prodigal who, after squandering millions in his careless generosity, left without knowing it, a king's heritage . . .

From the speech of Edmond About at the unveiling of
Dumas's statue in the Place Malesherbes, Paris, 1883

Facsimile of the first page of Chapter XLIX 'La première apparition de Colbert' reproduced from the holograph by kind permission of the John Rylands University Library, Manchester (MS).

It is the privilege of historical romancers to create characters who annihilate those of the historians; the reason being that the historians are content to invoke phantoms, while historical romancers create people of flesh and blood.

Dumas: 'In search of a sequel to *Monte-Cristo.*'
(*Les Garibaldiens*)

PREFACE

Dumas and the Historical Novel

It was Dumas's declared ambition to 'write the history of France'; and what with the novel, the play, the *chronique* and straight history he all but accomplished it. From the era of Ancient Rome right up to his own day he covered the time-spectrum. The sheer quantity alone is staggering, and an achievement without parallel in the range of historical fiction. The mere list would have made Scott blench.

Reign or Era	Title
Nero (57–68)	Acté
354–1328	Gaule et France
Philip VI (1328–50)	La Comtesse de Salisbury
Charles V (1380–1422)	Isabelle de Bavière
Charles IX (1560–74)	La Reine Margot
	Henri III et sa Cour
	La Dame de Monsoreau
	Les Quarante-Cinq
Louis XIII (1610–43)	Les Trois Mousquetaires
Louis XIV (1643–1715)	Vingt Ans Après
	Le Vicomte de Bragelonne
	Louis XIV et son Siècle
	La Jeunesse de Louis XIV
Regency & Louis XV (1715–74)	Le Chevalier d'Harmental
	Une Fille du Régent
	Olympe de Clèves
	Joseph Balsamo
	La Régence
	Louis XV et sa Cour
Louis XVI (1774–93)	Le Collier de la Reine
	Ange Pitou
	La Comtesse de Charny
	Le Chevalier de Maison-Rouge
	Louis XVI et la Révolution
	Le Drame de '93
	La Route de Varennes

Directoire & Consulate (1775–1804)   Les Blancs et les Bleus
First Empire (1804–15)   Le Trou de l'Enfer
Louis XVIII (1824–30)   Le Comte de Monte-Cristo
Charles X (1824–30)   Les Mohicans de Paris
Louis-Philippe (1830–48)   Le Dernier Roi des Français
Second Empire (1852–70)   Les Garibaldiens
    La Terreur prussienne

But let us, for general interest, ask what it is that makes an author want to write historical novels, and to set his narrative in bygone times. The answer one supposes must be a fascination, a passion for the past, for its significance, its effect on and linkage with the present, and perhaps above all the spell of certain personalities. One can well understand the fascination of a writer for such as Julius Caesar, Nero, Cromwell, Henry VIII, William the Conqueror, Hereward the Wake, Henry of Navarre, Richard III, Robert the Bruce, Napoleon, the string-pullers of the French Revolution for men; and for women such wayward, intriguing, complex, baffling, fascinating characters as Joan of Arc, Catherine de Medici, Christina of Sweden, Anne Boleyn, Cleopatra, Catherine II of Russia, Mary Stuart, Elizabeth I — to name only a few of those figures and shapers of the past whose lives claim influence over the imagination of future ages and defy the oblivion of time.

    To take sides; to attack what he feels to have been a false interpretation; to support a seemingly lost cause; to try to solve a mystery; to revivify a favourite character — any of these facets will explain the appeal of history to the imagination of a serious writer, and have given Britain Shakespeare, Scott, Ainsworth, Lytton, Reade, Kingsley: France, Hugo, Vigny, Mérimée, and above all, Dumas.

    The mission of the historical novelist is at once easier and more testing than that of the contemporary social novelist: easier in that the characters and incidents are ready-made for him; more difficult in that what he makes of them is in competition against what history has already given us. Unless he can outgun bare fact and present a convincing picture the result must be failure. And this has nothing to do with so-called factual accuracy. Dumas himself got to the nub of this when he declared in his own trenchant way: 'One can violate history provided one has a child by her.' In other words, the picture of the fictional character presented by the novelist must be a convincing extension of the factual character. As examples of the failure and contrasting success of this, one has only to compare May Sinclair's simplified portrait of Henry of Navarre in her eponymous novel with the infinitely more subtle one in Dumas's *The Forty-five Guardsmen*.

    Finally: history is full of the material of biography and fiction since our interest in it depends on the portraits of the men and women in its pages; and it is more than a paradox to say that those given by such as Livy, Tacitus,

Holinshed, Shakespeare, Scott, Kingsley, Reade, Mérimée and Dumas are truer than the bare bones of history itself. Dumas is in the forefront of such creative fiction, as realized by Jean Cocteau when he wrote to the present writer on his acceptance of the office of President of the Dumas Association quoted on the frontispiece of this book. Or as Michelet, the great historian expressed the same thing in different words to Dumas himself: 'You have done more to teach the people history than all the historians put together.' For like those of Shakespeare, Dumas's figures are not just puppets dressed in old clothes, but living men and women, and the bare historical details of their characters and lives have become fused by his glowing imagination and stamped with the warm impress of very truth to give them the consummation of essential being.

PROLOGUE

British readers will be familiar with the novel — sequel to *Twenty Years After* and grand finale of the Musketeer cycle — through the various translations as a trilogy, viz. *Le Vicomte de Bragelonne, Louise de la Vallière, The Man in the Iron Mask*. But to read any one of these alone is to have a very fragmented idea of the whole. I have, of course, considered the novel as Dumas wrote and published it, with one exception, namely, that of the title itself. For this my excuse is, that after long and varied inquiry I was made aware that British readers in general, while expressing comparative ignorance of and indifference to the novel under its French title, showed knowledge of and interest in it when informed that it included *The Man in the Iron Mask*.

In a moment of weakness, then, and pandering to popular advice, I have added the better known title to the original one for which I pray forgiveness to the shade of Alexander the Greatest.

The monograph being intended for British readers, all the excerpts are given in English. Much as I would have liked to adjoin the original French, I feel this would have made the book a somewhat ponderous volume; but I have kept the expletives and colloquial apostrophes in the original, partly because there is no equivalent English for most of them, and partly to emphasize the overall French background. The translations are my own.

The fact that I have used so many excerpts and often at length, is deliberate, the reasons being (1) to give readers the satisfaction of savouring Dumas's own phraseology and the verve of his style* (2) to illustrate the verdicts I have passed and so present them with the luxury of either agreeing or disagreeing with me.

A final point. It may be asked why, from the vast gallery of 'Dumas' I have chosen *Le Vicomte de Bragelonne* for my subject. The answer is twofold. Firstly, I believe it to be not only the greatest of all Dumas's novels but the greatest of all historical novels. Secondly, it is my confutation of those critics and cavillers who, judging it by the same criteria as its more popular forerunners (viz. *The Three Musketeers* and *Twenty Years After*) regard it as less attractive and a lower level of achievement.

First among such commentators must (regretfully) come that delectable

---

*But one must always bear in mind Stevenson's perceptive comment: 'There is no style so untranslatable; light as a whipped trifle, strong as silk; wordy like a village tale; pat like a general's despatch; with every fault, yet never tedious; with no merit, yet inimitably right.'

creation of H. G. Wells, Mr Polly. Describing his hero's literary predilections, Wells informs us that 'Mr Polly ... liked all Dumas till he got to The Vicomte de Bragelonne.' This is a pity, though understandable. Mr Polly, young and brash, no doubt revelled in the cut and thrust, the hot blood, youth and heroics of the young d'Artagnan and Musketeers. What at his time of life he could not do was to realize and accept the fact that as the subsidiary title of the novel — 'Or Ten Years After' — proclaims, the Four are now in their fifties. The morning of *The Three Musketeers* and the afternoon of *Twenty Years After* are left behind. The scenario is now enacted in the mellow sunlight of evening. The light is subdued, the voices lowered, the wheels running down, the shadows of twilight encroaching. Here is the last act of the drama. Another ten years have added their tally, and the sense of an end shortly to be pervades everything. You turn the pages, and the pictures invoked, the figures passing before you, are of men who are ageing, who move more slowly than formerly, with more care, introspection and dignity. Though firm and active still, their heads are grey, they do not hold themselves so upright, and they watch the king and court and youth of a younger generation with the tolerance of age and experience that have known more splendid things in the past, and for whom the future is only a short corridor with a door at the end waiting to open on the unknown. Where are the snows of yesteryear? Where are the Four who were One, the Inseparables of old? Now only a legend; four single, separate ageing men, each following his own destiny, seeing one another more and more rarely. Not for a single time does one of them draw his sword in a duel. Not once in the whole course of the narrative do the Four come together. That is significant. And d'Artagnan, setting out to find his friends, and relying on their devotedness for the carrying out of an idea wild enough to have come from the d'Artagnan of thirty years back, cannot trace them, and he is left to his own devices. These last ten years have seen the consummation and maturity of the promises and predictions of the earlier ones. Little, if anything, is left of the Athos we knew. Always the moralist, he has become a Puritan and very much a preacher, sinking his hopes, his personality and all but his life in his son, Raoul. Once and once only does the old Athos flash out: in that scene when, after defying the king, he breaks his sword over his knee.* Porthos, still the same in soul, honest, loyal, single-minded, devoted, is more than twenty stones corporeally. The Aramis of *Les Trois Mousquetaires*, the Abbé d'Herblay of *Vingt Ans Après*, is now the Right Reverend Bishop of Vannes, the counsellor and supporter of the falling Fouquet, the arch-plotter, inspired conspirator, General of the Jesuits and would-be Pope, fulfilling the portents of his youth when, even in those days, he had always some secret to conceal.

And d'Artagnan? He of *Vingt Ans Après* was a triumph; the d'Artagnan of *Le Vicomte de Bragelonne* is incomparable. Where else will you find a creature so fine, a being so human, so lovable in his very faults, a personality so rich in

---

*As Stevenson pointed out, Thackeray remembered this scene when writing *Henry Esmond*.

character, so full of subtle shades, as this d'Artagnan, Lieutenant-Captain of the king's Musketeers? For intimacy, for the sheer power of creation, the sense that there has been life, no male creation outside Shakespeare surpasses him. Every subtlety of creative art was used there. By friend and enemy, by king and valet, but above all by himself, by monologue surpassed only by Shakespeare before and no writer since, the man is made known: a man to be loved if ever a man was; to be admired and esteemed; to be censured and pardoned; to be taken to the heart at once and for ever. There is the central figure, the hinge on which everything turns. Almost every great scene, every touch of poetry and fancy, springs from him. Yes, of poetry and fancy. For while to the king he was simply 'the best soldier in France'; while to Fouquet he called himself 'a good trooper', Athos showed that he knew him better than did either the king or d'Artagnan himself when he said to him ' "You, whether you admit it or not, are a poet at heart" ' — d'Artagnan, if he is still the Musketeer and man of action, can vie with Hamlet for soliloquy, and it is by these shades that he becomes one of the outstanding and most memorable characters of fiction.

In case the reader should consider my words an overstatement, I call on that acute critic R. L. Stevenson for vindication. In his 'A Gossip On A Novel of Dumas's' in *Memories and Portraits* he writes:

> In so vast a mansion there were sure to be back stairs and kitchen offices where no one would delight to linger ... and until d'Artagnan sets out to seek his friends, I must confess that the book goes heavily enough. But, from thence forward, what a feast is spread! Monk kidnapped; d'Artagnan enriched; Mazarin's death ... Belle-Isle ... Aramis made General of the Jesuits; Aramis at the Bastille; the night talk in the forest of Sénart ... the death of Porthos; and last but not least, the taming of d'Artagnan, the untameable, under the lash of the young King. What other novel has such epic variety and nobility of incident? Often, if you will, impossible ... but yet all based in human nature... And once more, to make an end of recommendation, what novel is inspired with a more unrestrained or a more wholesome morality?... And it is in the character of d'Artagnan we must look for that spirit of morality which is one of the chief merits of the book... D'Artagnan has mellowed into a man so witty, rough, kind and upright, that he takes the heart by storm... I do not say there is no character as well drawn in Shakespeare; I do not say there is none I love so wholly... There is yet another point in the *Vicomte* which I find incomparable. I can recall no other work of the imagination in which the end of life is represented with so nice a tact... Upon the crowded, noisy life of this long tale, evening gradually falls; the lights are extinguished, and the heroes pass away one by one ... the young succeed them; Louis Quatorze is swelling larger and shining broader; another generation and another France dawn on the horizon; but for us and these old men whom we have loved so long, the inevitable end draws near and is welcome. To read this well is to anticipate experience. Ah, if only, when these hours of long shadows fall for us in reality and not in figure, we may hope to face them with a mind as quiet!...

Such is my retaliation to Mr Polly and his ilk. But while his error is excusable, he being young and foolish, the comments of the writers of the Introductions to the Collins edition of the novel are not. These, for sheer critical obtuseness, impercipience and misrepresentation beggar all description. Among other imbecilities one of them goes so far as to state that d'Artagnan, *the* triumph of the work, 'is only a shadow of his former self'. One despairs when one finds such judgements voiced by so-called literary critics. They are more heinous than the Mr Pollys in that they are examples of Kipling's aphorism 'But his own disciple shall wound him worst of all,' and an instance of 'save us from our friends'.

A last reason for my study is that I am hopeful it may prove a gauntlet-throwing reply to and opener of the eyes of those academic cult-conforming compilers of so-called 'histories of French literature' who, while snobbishly disposing of Dumas in a paragraph, devote pages to George Sand, Mme de Staël, Anatole France, the Goncourts, Feuillet, Daudet and Zola, and class lifeless failures like Flaubert's *La Tentation de Saint Antoine*, *L'Education Sentimentale* and *Salammbô* above novels which pulsate with life. I name no names, but we all know who they are, figuring as they usually do in the French Academy and the various English and French histories and encyclopaedias as authorities. In any case their assessments are made to look foolish when placed alongside the verdicts of those great names quoted on the first pages of this book. As these reveal, it is always the genius, the creative mind, who recognises genius and a fellow creative mind where mere talent, the critic, the literary dilettante, sees only an 'amuseur.' In answer to some typical academic belittler of his father's works Dumas *fils* retorted "My father is a river. Anyone can foul a river." After the tributes of the really great one can ignore the comments of the little foulers.

To come now to the novel itself which so far I have described only in general terms. I shall now write of it in detail. And as a first step I propose to tackle the complaint of Mr Polly and those others who lament the so-called slowness of the action, for there is a factor here which passes them by. As with Trollope, Dumas maintained that although his novels were first published in instalments, he had the complete material in his head before he began them. Then again similar to Trollope with his *The Last Chronicle of Barset*, he set out to make *Bragelonne* the last and crown of his d'Artagnan cycle. So it was that with this in mind and the multitudinous and vast canvas he contemplated painting, he deliberately fashioned his build-up, moving his pieces with the concentrated thought of the master chess player making his opening gambit with ultimate victory in mind. Seen in this light by the intelligent reader (*pace* Mr Polly!), and more especially when re-read, the opening chapters fall rightly into place like the pieces of a jigsaw.

The opening scene in Blois castle* exemplifies this, presenting us as it does with Louise de la Vallière (the heroine, if she can be regarded as such), her friend Aure de Montalais, and the eponymous hero, who has been in love with Louise ever since childhood. In answer to the plea of her would-be lover Louise has begun a difficult letter to him; but before she can finish it Raoul himself arrives as messenger announcing the unexpected visit of the king, the queen-mother, Cardinal Mazarin and members of the court. Montalais, the only one of the three to come alive as a character, seeing Raoul from the window, and full of mischief, energy and romance, waylays him on his way back and brings him up by the back stairs to Louise's room, explaining roguishly that by doing this she is saving Louise the trouble of finishing her letter now lying openly on the table. On learning what it is, each tries to snatch it, but Montalais wins, remarking as she slipped it into the bosom of her dress ' "M. Raoul is not likely to venture to take it from there!" ' To which Louise, confused like Raoul, remonstrates ' "Montalais, you are a madcap!" ' Only to receive the retort ' "And you, Louise, are so sensible you will never know what it is to fall in love!" ' Raoul, thinking only of the letter, and face to face with Louise, throws himself on his knees before her and rapturously kisses her hand.

The whole episode is astutely embryonic of the future. Raoul will continue in his error of believing that Louise loves him; Louise will give the lie to Montalais's association of her inability to love, which in view of her future relationship with the king is dramatic irony indeed. And in effect, the trio will meet together again in the not so distant future but with very different emotions and in very different circumstances.

After being pushed unceremoniously out of the room by the endearingly roguish Montalais, who has little sympathy with his too serious attitude to Louise (and will later put her feminine finger on his error) or with his known submission to parental discipline, the young vicomte dejectedly takes his way

---

* See Brief Biographies.

to his home near by where his father, the Comte de la Fère lives. The chapter 'Father and Son', raises expectations in the reader which can only disappoint. The Athos of *The Three Musketeers* and *Twenty Years After*, who was one of Thackeray's favourite characters, has all but disappeared, degenerating into an ageing moralist with religious overtones, and his relationship with his son* is an amalgam of old-world parental strictness and over-emotional affection which today's reader must find both repellently sentimental and improbable.

So now, after greeting Raoul with fatherly affection, learning that he has come from Blois and seen Louise, he repeats his stern command that he must not associate with the girl — an exaction for which no reason is ever given and will persist until the moment when, overcome by the young man's unhappiness, against his will he becomes for one brief triumphant occasion when he confronts the king to demand justice, something of his former self.

But if the characterization of Athos must be deemed a disappointment and a failure, a triumph of the novel and something of a compensation must surely be seen in the depiction of the gradual change of character in the young king Louis XIV from the timid merely nominal sovereign under the tutelage and shadow of Mazarin, uncertain of himself but secretly longing for the freedom and authority of kingship, to becoming the personification of royalty as the Sun King, the voluptuary and dictator who was to boast ' "*L'État c'est moi!*" ' His first appearance at Blois castle soon after Raoul's warning message is a perfect example of this. After the collation he reluctantly makes the expected rounds of the assembly with his aunt as a gesture of politeness for the hospitality shown him. Looking at the ceremoniously grouped maids of honour, Louis remarks to her on their outmoded provincial dress and hairstyles (as foreseen by the despairing Montalais in her earlier scene with Louise), but he excepts one who was wearing a simple white dress, adding ' "See what an artless figure she has, what gracious natural manners! That is a woman. The others are just so many dummies." ' The young woman so noticed and described is no less than Louise de la Vallière. Making the most of the moment, Madame beckons her and presents her formally to Louis, who smiles vaguely as she 'bowed with so much grace mingled with timidity and awe inspired by the presence of the king', and casually passes on his way. For him the meeting was merely one of many and instantly forgotten. To Louise it was a moment of destiny. The episode is one of intense dramatic irony. Soon, however, Louis begins to exhibit his youthful boredom with the whole proceedings by walking aimlessly about, fidgeting and stifling sighs and yawns and looks of longing towards the cardinal and his mother and the door, but to no avail — symptoms acutely observed by the eagle eye of the duty Musketeer officer 'leaning against the embrasure ... a figure with a weather-beaten face, an aquiline nose, a brilliant eye, grey hair but black moustache ... watching with folded arms and obvious apathy both the pleasures and ennuis of the scene'.

* By Madame de Chevreuse, as related in *Twenty Years After*.

Though not named, the reader at once recognizes d'Artagnan — a recognition verified by his reading and answering the king's mute desire by calling out in a sonorous voice ' "On the king's service!" ' thus enabling Louis to leave with due formality and protocol.

In this way is d'Artagnan brought on to the scene, and the reader may well anticipate that the action will now accelerate. It does: but not before the reader is faced with a strange (because rare) *longueur* much resembling those frequent ones of Balzac by giving an unnecessary and lengthy description and history of a hostelry in Blois merely because a new and mysterious character called by Dumas 'the Unknown' happens to be staying there. This turns out to be no less than Prince Charles of England, son of Charles I, roaming Europe in the forlorn hope of finding support for assisting him to gain the English throne. Desperate, he is driven to seek help from his brother-in-law, the young Louis XIV of France, like himself in Blois.

Thanks to the lucky chance that the Lieutenant of Musketeers happens to be on duty, by confessing his identity to him and from the latter's poignant recollections of the role he had played *vis-à-vis* the prince's father in England,* he finally succeeds in obtaining his unlikely audience. But to his chagrin Prince Charles learns from his brother-in-law that he can do nothing to help him.

> 'You ask me for a million, brother — me, who has never possessed a fraction of that sum. I possess nothing. I am no more King of France than you are King of England. I am a name, a cipher dressed in fleur-de-lis velvet, that is all, and my only advantage over you is that I am on a visible throne. I have nothing. I can do nothing... Look at this abandonment, this silence. Then look yonder. See the bustle, the lights, the homage. There is the real King of France, brother.'
> 'In the cardinal's apartments?'
> 'Yes, in the cardinal's apartments.'
> 'Then am I to be condemned?'

But in the end, moved by Charles's distress and ashamed of his own impotence to help, Louis declares he will present his request for either a million in money or two hundred gentlemen to the cardinal.

With the next two chapters the narrative gathers speed and smoothness, for Dumas is always in his element when bringing Mazarin into play. His character speaks in every word. By astute financial and political insight he proves to his royal but naïve pupil and ward that to assist in any attempt towards the restoration of Charles II would not only be to break the treaty France had made with Cromwell, but to antagonize England, now powerful under Cromwell's enigmatical successor, Monk. ' "You are the ally of England and not of Charles II," ' Mazarin explains, and in answer to the other's suggestion that they might ' "find means of assisting this poor king without compromising themselves," ' shows both his mastery of the political scene and his character with his reply:

---

* v. *Twenty Years After*.

'And that is precisely what I am not willing to do, my dear Sire. If I were directing English policy myself I could not hope for it to act in a different way. Governed as she is, England is a nest of contention for all Europe. Holland supports Charles II. Good! They are the only maritime powers. They will become hostile and fight. Good again! Let them destroy each other's navy. We can then construct our own with the wreck of theirs, and save money to buy the nails with.'

Powerless against this logic, Louis is forced to let his brother-in-law depart without hope of support. D'Artagnan lights the way out for him, saying to himself as he watches the poor prince disappear in the darkness:

'To him as to his father formerly, Athos would say "Salute to fallen majesty!" ' Then reascending the staircase 'Oh, the miserable service I follow!' he said at every step. 'Oh, my pitiful master! No generosity, no energy... It is decided. Tomorrow I throw my uniform to the nettles, *mordioux*!'

His witness next day of the king's timidity and failure to prove his feelings for Marie de Mancini, the cardinal's niece, only emphasized his determination, and on the king's return from their meeting he asks for audience. And it is now with the 14th chapter 'In which the king and the lieutenant give proofs of memory' that the reader's 'train' moves into full speed and bearing out R.L.S.'s 'From then on, what joy is spread!'

But before moving into fluent stride with d'Artagnan, it is worth remarking that while the preliminary chapters may seem to the recalcitrant Mr Polly and his ilk lacking in Dumasian fire, and to limp, nevertheless one of the triumphs of the novel is that it is by such degrees Dumas has skilfully depicted the transformation of the young monarch, at first under the rule of Mazarin timid and unsure of himself, making himself little by little after his minister's death 'the Sun King', and finally, at the height of his dictatorial power, able to leave to history his ' *"L'État, c'est moi!"* '

But to return to the Lieutenant of the Musketeers' requested audience of the king, destined to be the first of the four of such, each of which marks a highlight not only of the novel but of all fiction. The Musketeer opens by requesting his discharge from the king's service on the plea of age.

'I am getting old, Sire. I have worn harness now thirty-four or thirty-five years; my poor shoulders are tired; I feel that I must give place to the young. I don't belong to this age; I have still one foot in the old one; and in consequence everything is strange in my eyes, everything astonishes and bewilders me. In short, I have the honour to ask Your Majesty for my discharge.'

'Monsieur,' said the king, looking at the officer, who wore his uniform with an ease that would have awakened envy in a young man, 'you are stronger and more vigorous than I am.'

'Oh!' replied the officer with an air of assumed modesty, 'Your Majesty says so because I still have a good eye and a tolerably firm foot, because I can still ride a horse, and my moustache is black; but, Sire, vanity of vanities all that, illusions all that, — appearance, smoke, Sire! I have still a young air, it is true, but I am old at bottom; and within six months I feel certain I shall be broken down, gouty, impotent. Therefore, Sire — '

'Monsieur,' interrupted the king, 'remember your words of yesterday. You said to me, in that very place where you now are, that you were endowed with better health than any other man in France; that fatigue was unknown to you; that you cared not for passing whole days and nights at your post. Did you tell me that, or not? Exercise your memory, Monsieur.'

The officer breathed a sigh. 'Sire,' he said, 'old age is boastful; and it is pardonable for old men to sound their own praises when others no longer praise them. It is very possible I said that; but the fact is, Sire, I am very much fatigued, and request permission to retire.'

'Monsieur,' said the king, advancing towards the officer with a gesture at once full of address and majesty, 'you are not assigning me the true reason. You wish to quit my service, it may be true, but you disguise from me the motive for your retreat.'

'Sire, believe that — '

'I believe what I see, Monsieur; I see a vigorous, energetic man, full of presence of mind, the best soldier in France perhaps; and this person cannot persuade me the least in the world that he stands in need of rest.'

'Ah, Sire,' said the lieutenant with bitterness, 'what praises! Indeed, Your Majesty confounds me! Energetic, vigorous, brave, intelligent, the best soldier in the army! But, Sire, Your Majesty exaggerates my small portion of merit to such a point that, however good an opinion I may have of myself, in very truth I no longer recognize myself. If I were vain enough to believe only half of your Majesty's words, I should consider myself a valuable, indispensable man. I should say that a servant possessed of such brilliant qualities was a treasure beyond all price. Now, Sire, I have been all my life — I feel bound to say it — except at the present time, appreciated, in my opinion, much beneath my value. I therefore repeat, Your Majesty exaggerates.'

The king knitted his brow, for he saw a bitter raillery beneath the words of the officer. 'Come, Monsieur,' said he, 'let us meet the question frankly. Tell me, are you dissatisfied with my service? No evasions; speak boldly, frankly — I demand it.'

The officer, who had been twisting his hat in his hands with an embarrassed air for several minutes, raised his head at these words. 'Oh, Sire,' said he, 'that puts me more at my ease. To a question put so frankly, I will reply frankly. To tell the truth is a good thing — as much from the pleasure one feels in relieving one's heart as on account of its rarity. I will speak the truth, then, to my king, at the same time imploring him to excuse the frankness of an old soldier.'

Louis looked at his officer with anxious disquietude, manifested by the agitation of his gesture. 'Well, then, speak,' said he, 'for I am impatient to hear the truths you have to tell me.'

The officer threw his hat upon a table, and his countenance, always so intelligent and martial, assumed all at once a strange character of grandeur and solemnity.

'Sire, I have, as I have said, now served the house of France thirty-five years; few people have worn out so many swords in that service as I have, and the swords were good swords too, Sire. For five years together I was a hero every day — at least, so I was told by personages of merit — and that is a long period for heroism, trust me, Sire, a period of five years. Nevertheless, I have faith in what these people told me, for they were good judges. Such were M. de Richelieu, M. de Buckingham, M. de Beaufort, M. de Retz — a rough genius himself in street warfare — in short, king Louis XIII, and even the Queen, your august mother, who one day condescended to say, "Thank you." — I don't know what service I had had the good fortune to render her.* Pardon me, Sire, for speaking so boldly; but what I relate to you, as I have already had the honour to tell Your Majesty, is history.'

The king bit his lips, and threw himself violently into his armchair.

'I appear importunate to Your Majesty,' said the lieutenant. 'Eh! Sire, that is the fate of truth; she is a stern companion; she bristles all over with steel; she wounds those she attacks, and sometimes him who delivers her.'

'No, Monsieur,' replied the king; 'I bade you speak — speak then.'

'After the service of the king and the cardinal, came the service of the regency, Sire; I fought pretty well in the *Fronde* — much less, though, than the first time. Men began to diminish in stature. I have, nevertheless, led Your Majesty's Musketeers on some perilous occasions, which stand upon the orders of the day of the company. Mine was a beautiful lot then! I was the favourite of M. de Mazarin. Lieutenant here! Lieutenant there! Lieutenant to the right! Lieutenant to the left! There was not a buffet dealt in France of which your humble servant was not charged with the dealing. But they soon became not contented with France; Monsieur the Cardinal, he sent me to England on Cromwell's account — another gentleman who was not over gentle, I assure you, Sire. I had the honour to know him, and I was well able to appreciate him. A great deal was promised me on account of that mission. So, as I did in it quite contrary to all I had been bidden to do, I was generously paid, for I was at length appointed Captain of the Musketeers; that is to say, to the post most envied at court, which gives precedence before the marshals of France — and with justice; for when one mentions the Captain of the Musketeers he speaks of the flower of the soldiers and the king of the brave.'

'Captain, Monsieur?' interrupted the king; 'surely you are mistaken.' Lieutenant, you mean to say.'

'Not at all, Sire, — I make no mistake; Your Majesty may rely upon me in that respect. Monsieur the Cardinal gave me the commission himself.'

'Well?'

'But M. de Mazarin, as you know better than anybody, Sire, does not often give, and sometimes takes back what he has given; he took it back again as soon as peace was made and he was no longer in want of me. True, I may not have been worthy to replace M. de Tréville, of illustrious memory; but they had promised me, and they had given me; they ought to have stopped there.'

'Is that what dissatisfies you, Monsieur? Well, I will make inquiries. I love justice; and your claim, though made in military fashion, does not displease me.'

'Oh, Sire!' said the officer, 'Your Majesty has not understood me; I no longer claim anything now.'

'Excess of delicacy, Monsieur; but I will keep my eye upon your affairs, and hereafter — '

'Oh, Sire! what a word! — hereafter! Thirty years have I lived upon that promising word, which has been pronounced by so many great personages, and which your mouth has just pronounced. Hereafter! that is how I have received a

---

* A reference to the affair of the queen's diamond studs in *The Three Musketeers*.

score of wounds, and how I have reached fifty-four years of age without ever having had a louis in my purse, and without ever having met with a protector on my road — I, who have protected so many people! So I change my formula, Sire; and when any one says to me "Hereafter", I reply "Now". It is repose I solicit, Sire. That may be easily granted me. That will cost nobody anything.'

'I did not look for this language, Monsieur, particularly from a man who has always lived among the great. You forget you are speaking to the king, to a gentleman who is, I suppose, of as good a house as yourself; and when I say "Hereafter", it is a certainty.'

'I do not at all doubt it, Sire; but this is the end of the terrible truth I had to tell you. If I were to see upon that table a marshal's baton, the sword of constable, the crown of Poland, instead of "Hereafter", I swear to you, Sire, that I should still say "Now!" Oh, excuse me, Sire! I am from the country of your grandfather, Henry IV. I do not speak often; but when I speak, I speak all.'

'The future of my reign has little temptation for you, Monsieur, it appears,' said Louis haughtily.

'Forgetfulness, forgetfulness everywhere!' cried the officer with a noble air; 'the master has forgotten the servant, so the servant is reduced to forget his master. I live in unfortunate times, Sire. I see youth full of discouragement and fear; I see it timid and despoiled, when it ought to be rich and powerful. Yesterday evening, for example, I open the door of the King of France to a King of England, whose father, humble as I am, I was near saving, if God had not been against me, — God, who inspired his elect, Cromwell! I open, I said, the door, that is to say, of the palace of one brother to another brother, and I see — stop, Sire, that presses upon my heart! — I see the minister of that king drive away the proscribed prince, and humiliate his master by condemning to want another king, his equal. Then I see my prince, who is young, handsome, and brave, who has courage in his heart and lightning in his eye, — I see him tremble before a priest, who laughs at him behind the curtains of his alcove, where upon his bed he absorbs all the gold of France which he afterwards stuffs into secret coffers. Yes, I understand your looks, Sire. I am bold to madness; but what is to be said? I am an old man, and I tell you here, Sire, to you, my king, things which I would cram down the throat of any one who should dare to pronounce them before me. You have commanded me to pour out my heart before you, Sire, and I cast at the feet of Your Majesty the bile which I have been collecting during thirty years as I would pour out all my blood, if Your Majesty commanded me to do so.'

The moment of silence which followed this vehement outbreak represented for him who had spoken, and for him who had listened, ages of suffering. 'Monsieur,' said the king at length, 'you have pronounced the word forgetfulness. I have heard nothing but that word. I will reply, then, to it alone. Others may have forgotten, but I have not. And the proof is that I remember a day of riot — a day when the people, a mob, invaded the palace. And when I lay in bed and was told to pretend to be asleep, one man alone, sword in hand, hidden behind my curtains, watched over my life, ready to risk his own for me as he had already risked it a dozen times for the safety of my family. Was not that gentleman, whose name I asked for, called d'Artagnan?'*

* v. *Twenty Years After*, chapter LIV

'Your Majesty has a good memory,' replied the officer coldly.

'You see then,' continued the king, 'if I have such clear remembrances of my childhood, what power of remembrance I may acquire in age.'

'Your Majesty has been richly endowed by God,' said the officer in the same tone.

'Come, M. d'Artagnan,' Louis went on with agitation, 'can you not be as patient as I am, and do as I do? Say!'

'And what do you do, Sire?'

'I wait.'

'Your Majesty may do so because you are young. But I, Sire, have not time enough. Old age is at my door, and death looking into the very depths of my house. Your Majesty is beginning life. Its future is full of hope and fortune. But I, Sire, am at the far side of the horizon, and we are so far from each other that I should never have time to wait till Your Majesty caught up with me.' Louis made another turn in the apartment expressive of his emotion.

'Well, Monsieur,' he said then in a harsh voice, 'you desire your discharge. You shall have it. I will order your pension. Adieu, M. d'Artagnan. You are free.'

And the king, with a hoarse sob which was lost in his throat, passed quickly into the adjoining chamber. D'Artagnan took up his hat from the table on which he had thrown it, and went out.

The scene in its superb dialogue is more even than creation. It is divination. One senses that Dumas has become d'Artagnan, the creator the creation. Furthermore, the thought and speech of the Musketeer are touched with that magical blend of realism and poetry which is one of the glories of Homer and Shakespeare, and since caught only by certain Irish writers, notably Synge and O'Casey.

* * *

From this scene onwards the narrative makes amends for its low-key beginning. Prince Charles, wandering forlornly along the highway from Blois with the aged and faithful Parry, his sole attendant, happens to see Grimaud outside a garden gate waving goodbye to Raoul, now on his way back to Paris for military duty, and mutual recognition ensues. Learning that this is Athos's house and that he is at home, Charles goes in to greet him, and finding him, explains who he is and relates his tale of frustration. In return, consoling him, Athos remarks, ' "Sire, I have always believed that it is in the most desperate straits that the great turns of fortune have been made," ' and in response to the other's sad disbelief he then goes on to relate the grim details of his father's execution, ending with his historic, mysterious final word ' "Remember!" '

' "I was aware," ' Charles said in an agitated voice, "that it was the last word pronounced by my father. But why? And for whom?"'

Athos then goes on to explain that prior to the final stroke of the masked executioner, the king, stooping down and speaking to him (Athos) hidden beneath the boards and under the black cloth, confided that he has a secret buried under the vaults of Newcastle castle, and requested Athos to use it ' "when you think it can be of greatest service to my eldest son" '. And it was then as he placed his head on the block that he spoke the injunction to the unseen Athos: ' "Remember!" '

' "So you see, Sire," Athos concluded, "I have remembered." ' When Charles, enlightened but still despondent, asks how he alone, with Parry his only servant, can hope to obtain the buried gold with Monk and his army encamped on the very place, for answer Athos offers himself, and the chapter ends with the prince, Parry, Athos and the inevitable and trusty Grimaud leaving there and then for England on this adventitious and aleatory adventure, renewing for us something of the Athos of *Twenty Years After*.

But scarcely have they left when d'Artagnan appears on the scene. The ex-Musketeer, now, as we have seen, retired and free, 'at ease with himself and existence', has come on a search for his old comrades-in-arms to enlist their aid in an enterprise put into his mind by the sight of the natural heir to the English throne being turned away by his (d'Artagnan's) French masters, and by being a free man able to do as he pleases — an enterprise as yet unnamed but which, he told himself, would be a shared venture worthy of being put beside that of the famous Bastion St Gervais.*

His outstanding affection for Athos takes him to him first of the three; but Athos, he finds, has suddenly left and gone no one knows where. Though disappointed, the now-retired Lieutenant of the Musketeers, having reached the 'years that bring the philosophic mind', merely reflects ' "Athos gone on a journey? That is incomprehensible. Bah! It is all devilish mysterious. But then — no — he is not the man I want. I want one of a cunning, patient mind..." ' and that thought takes him on the way to Melun and 'a certain presbytery there', ironically unaware that Athos is already on his way to England with the same idea in mind.

But he is equally unfortunate with Aramis, who, he learns from 'the old pedagogue' Bazin, is now a bishop and in his diocese of Vannes, in Brittany — a bishopric awarded him by the all-powerful superintendent Fouquet. Whereupon he departs the next day from Melun as he had departed from Blois.

He is thus left only with Porthos. But on reaching Pierrefonds after three days' riding he finds only the portly hospitable Mousqueton of Musketeer memory, who informs him that his master had left following an urgent message from M. le Vicaire-Général d'Herblay to join him 'before the equinox'. So, after a good meal and a night in an excellent bed, d'Artagnan left Pierrefonds as he had left Melun and as he had left the château of the Comte de la Fère,

> empty-handed. With his head cast down, his eyes dull and fixed, his legs a hanging on each side of his horse, and saying to himself in that vague sort of reverie which sometimes reaches eloquence —

---

* v. *The Three Musketeers*.

'No more friends! no more future! no more anything! My energies are broken like the bonds of our ancient friendship. Oh, old age arrives, cold and inexorable; it envelops in its funereal crape all that was brilliant, all that was sweet in my youth; then it throws that pleasant burden on its shoulders and carries it away with the rest into the fathomless gulf of death.'

A shudder crept through the heart of the Gascon, so brave and so strong against all the misfortunes of life; and for some moments the clouds appeared black to him, the earth slippery and full of pits as that of cemeteries.

'Whither am I going?' said he to himself. 'What am I going to do? Alone, quite alone, — without family, without friends! Bah!' cried he, all at once. And he clapped spurs to his horse, who, having found nothing melancholy in the heavy oats of Pierrefonds, profited by this permission to show his best paces in a gallop which covered two leagues. 'To Paris!' said d'Artagnan to himself. And on the morrow he alighted in Paris. He had devoted ten days to this journey.

* * *

The scene is next set in the Rue des Lombards at the sign of the Pilon d'Or — in other words the shop of his former lackey Planchet, who welcomes him with all the pleasure expressive of his enduring affection and esteem for his one-time master. Planchet, in fact, now the owner of a prosperous grocery business, had become the retired Musketeer's banker, and had invested much of his little capital at seven per cent interest; and it is here and now that for the first time d'Artagnan reveals the nature of his seeming impossible plan. His explanatory chat with Planchet is one of the many highlights of the novel, proving as his resignation scene with the king had done that Dumas is most fascinating and his characterization most alive when no action is taking place, and it is only a matter of cross talk. The next three chapters (19–21) must be accounted among the most delightful of the many such. No discerning reader worthy of the name but will savour this supreme example of literary craft (consisting of three chapters of nothing but dialogue) with a literary gourmet's same thrill as the wine expert's gustatory palate over the Musketeer's favourite Anjou served him by Planchet. One can read and re-read these chapters over and over again, year in, and year out, and find the bouquet of their aroma only becoming more delicious.

To give the new reader the full impact one should quote them in full; but that not being possible within the limits of this book, one can do only the next best thing and select passages which (to resume the vinous simile) as a first glass give vindication of the rest of the bottle. Locked securely and privately in a room above the shop, and with food and wine on the table, d'Artagnan lets out by circumspect degrees that his proposition for a shared ' "investment with a profit of 400 per cent" ' is to be undertaken in England and could be reckoned a ' "restoration" '.

' "Of monuments?" Planchet queried.

"Yes, you might call it that," the ex-Musketeer replied. "Of Whitehall."

"But I know very little about architecture," ' Planchet confessed. But before enlightening the worthy grocer, fellow conspirator and partner *malgré lui* as to the kind of restoration he has in mind, d'Artagnan describes how he had seen Prince Charles come begging at the door of the young Louis XIV and been turned away unhelped by him and Mazarin, and been moved by his distress, failure and poverty.

' "Poor little seed of a king," I said to myself, "I will pick you up and cast you into good ground." '
'Good God!' said Planchet, looking earnestly at his old master as if in doubt of the state of his reason.
'Well, what is it?' said d'Artagnan; 'what hurts you?'
'Me? nothing, Monsieur!'
'You said "Good God!" '
'Did I?'
'I am sure you did. Can you already understand?'
'I confess, M. d'Artagnan, that I am afraid — '
'To understand?'
'Yes.'
'To understand that I wish to replace upon his throne this King Charles II, who has no throne? Is that it?'
Planchet made a prodigious bound in his chair. 'Ah, ah!' said he in evident terror, 'that is what you call a restoration!'
'Yes, Planchet; is not that the proper term for it?'
'Oh, no doubt — no doubt! But have you reflected seriously?'
'Upon what?'
'Upon what is going on yonder.'
'Where?'
'In England.'
'And what is that? Let us see, Planchet.'
'In the first place, Monsieur, I ask your pardon for meddling in these things which have nothing to do with my trade; but since it is an affair that you propose to me — for you propose an affair to me, do you not? — '
'A superb one, Planchet.'
'But as you propose to me an affair, I have the right to discuss it.'
'Discuss it, Planchet; out of discussion light is born.'
'Well, then, since I have Monsieur's permission, I will tell him that there is yonder, in the first place, the Parliament.'
'Well, next?'
'And then the army.'
'Good! Do you see anything else?'
'And then the nation.'
'Is that all?'
'The nation, which consented to the overthrow and death of the late king, the father of this, and which will not be willing to belie its acts.'
'Planchet,' said d'Artagnan, 'you reason like a cheese! The nation — the nation is tired of these gentlemen who give themselves barbarous names and sing psalms to it. Chant for chant, my dear Planchet; I have remarked that nations prefer singing a merry chant to a doleful one.'

'Well, I return, then, to the army and the Parliament.'

'I say that I borrow twenty thousand livres of M. Planchet, and that I put twenty thousand livres of my own to it, and with these forty thousand livres I raise an army.'

Planchet clasped his hands; he saw that d'Artagnan was in earnest, and, in good truth he believed that his master had lost his senses.

'An army! — ah, Monsieur,' said he with his most agreeable smile for fear of irritating the madman and rendering him furious, 'an army! — large?'

'Of forty men,' said d'Artagnan.

'Forty against forty thousand! That is not enough. I know very well that you, M. d'Artagnan, alone are equal to a thousand men; but where are we to find thirty-nine men equal to you? Or, if we could find them, who would furnish you with money to pay them?'

'Not bad, Planchet. Ah, the devil! You play the flatterer.'

'No, Monsieur, I speak what I think; and that is exactly why I say that in the first pitched battle you fight with your forty men I am very much afraid —'

'Therefore I will fight no pitched battles, my dear Planchet,' said the Gascon, laughing.

'It is plain,' replied he, 'that if your forty men conceal themselves, and are not unskilful, they may hope not to be beaten; but you propose to yourself some result, do you not?'

'No doubt. This then, in my opinion, is the plan to be proceeded upon in order to replace quickly His Majesty Charles II on his throne.'

'Good!' said Planchet, redoubling his attention; 'let us see your plan. But, in the first place, it appears to me we are forgetting something.'

'What is that?'

'We have set aside the nation, which prefers singing merry songs to psalms, and the army, which we will not fight; but the Parliament remains, and that seldom sings.'

'And does not fight, either. How is it, Planchet, that an intelligent man like you should take heed of a set of brawlers who call themselves Rumps and Barebones? The Parliament does not trouble me at all, Planchet.'

'Since it does not trouble you, Monsieur, let us pass on.'

'Yes, and arrive at the result. You remember Cromwell, Planchet?'

'I have heard a great deal of talk about him.'

'He was a rough soldier.'

'And a terrible eater, moreover.'

'What do you mean by that?'

'Why, at one gulp, he swallowed all England.'

'Well, Planchet, suppose that on the evening before the day on which he swallowed England, someone had swallowed Cromwell?'

'Oh, Monsieur, it is one of the first axioms of mathematics that the container must be greater than the contained.'

'Very well! You see our affair, Planchet.'

'But Cromwell is dead, and his container is now the tomb.'

'My dear Planchet, I see with pleasure that you have not only become a mathematician, but a philosopher.'

'Monsieur, in my grocery business I use much printed paper, and that instructs me.'

'Bravo! You know, then, in that case — for you have not learnt mathematics and philosophy without a little history — that after this Cromwell so great, there came one who was very little.'

'Yes, he was named Richard, and he has done as you have, M. d'Artagnan, — he has given in his resignation.'

'Very well said — very well! After the great man who is dead, after the little one who gave in his resignation, there has come a third. This one is named Monk. He is an able general, considering that he has never fought a battle; he is a skilful diplomatist, considering that he never speaks in public, and that having to say "Good-day" to a man he meditates twelve hours and ends by saying "Good-night" — which makes people exclaim "Miracle!" seeing that it falls pat. Well, this Monk, who has England ready-roasted on his plate, and who is already opening his mouth to swallow it, — this Monk, who says to the people of Charles II, and to Charles II, himself, "*Nescio vos*" — '

'I don't understand English,' said Planchet.

'Yes, but I do,' said d'Artagnan. ' "*Nescio vos*" means "I do not know you." This Monk, the most important man in England, when he shall have swallowed it — '

'Well?' asked Planchet.

'Well, my friend, I will go over yonder, and with my forty men I will carry him off, pack him up, and bring him into France, where two modes of proceeding present themselves to my dazzled eyes.'

'In the first place, we will set a ransom on him.'

'Of how much?'

'*Peste!* a fellow like that must be well worth a hundred thousand crowns.'

'Yes, yes!'

'You see, then, — in the first place, a ransom of a hundred thousand crowns.'

'Or else — '

'Or else — which is much better — I deliver him up to King Charles, who, having no longer either a general or an army to fear, nor a diplomatist to trick him, will restore himself, and when once restored will pay me the hundred thousand crowns in question. That is the idea I have formed; what do you say to it, Planchet?'

'Magnificent, Monsieur!' cried Planchet, trembling with emotion. 'How did you conceive it?'

'It came to me one morning on the banks of the Loire, while our beloved King Louis XIV was snivelling over the hand of Mademoiselle de Mancini.'

'Monsieur, I declare the idea is sublime. But — '

'Ah! there is a but?'

'Permit me! But this is a little like the skin of that bear, you know, that they were about to sell, but which it was necessary to take from the back of the live bear first. Now, to take Monk, there will be a bit of a scuffle, I should think.'

'No doubt; but as I shall raise an army — '

'Yes, yes, — I understand, *parbleu!* — an exploit. Yes, then, Monsieur, you will triumph, for no one equals you in that sort of adventure.'

'I certainly am lucky in them,' said d'Artagnan with a proud simplicity. 'You know that if for this affair I had my dear Athos, my brave Porthos and my cunning Aramis, the business would be settled; but they are all lost, it seems, and nobody knows where to find them. I will do it, then, alone. Now, do you find the business good, and the investment advantageous?'

'Too much — too much.'

'How can that be?'

'Because fine things never reach the point expected.'
'This is infallible, Planchet, and the proof is that I undertake it. It will be for you a tolerably pretty gain, and for me a very interesting stroke. It will be said, "Such was the old age of M. d'Artagnan"; and I shall hold a place in stories, and even in history itself, Planchet. I am greedy of honour.'

Planchet would have been quite satisfied with giving d'Artagnan a simple receipt for his share of the capital, but — typical of the Gascon's sense of fair dealing — the latter insists on a full deed of partnership, ' "in case I am killed by a musket ball, or" (adding with a touch of drollery) "I should burst with drinking beer." '*

The deed, drawn up by d'Artagnan, is full of the character of the man. Planchet naïvely suggests a 50/50 deal.

'Oh, the devil, no!' said d'Artagnan, 'the division cannot be made by half; that would not be just.'
'And yet, Monsieur, we each lay down half,' objected Planchet timidly.
'Yes; but listen to this clause, my dear Planchet, and if you do not find it equitable in every respect when it is written, well, we can scratch it out again:-
'Nevertheless, as M. d'Artagnan brings to the association, besides his capital of twenty thousand livres, his time, his idea, his industry, and his skin — things which he appreciates strongly, particularly the last — M. d'Artagnan will keep, of the three hundred thousand livres, two hundred thousand livres for himself, which will make his share two thirds.'
'Very well,' said Planchet.
'Is it just?' asked d'Artagnan.
'Perfectly just, Monsieur.'
'And you will be contented with a hundred thousand livres?'
'Peste! I should think so! A hundred thousand for twenty thousand!'
'Do you find it so? Let us sign it, then,' and both affixed their signatures.
'In this fashion,' said d'Artagnan, 'I shall have no obligations to any one.'
'But I shall be under obligations to you,' said Planchet.
'No; for whatever store I set by it, Planchet, I may lose my skin yonder, and you will lose all. Peste! — that makes me think of the principal and indispensable clause. I will write it:-
' "In the case of M. d'Artagnan succumbing in this enterprise, liquidation will be considered made, and the Sieur Planchet will give quittance from that moment to the shade of Messire d'Artagnan for the twenty thousand livres paid by him into the treasury of the said partnership." '
This last clause made Planchet knit his brows a little; but when he saw the brilliant eye, the muscular hand, the back so supple and strong, of his associate, he regained his courage, and without regret at once added another stroke to his signature. D'Artagnan did the same. Thus was drawn the first deed of partnership known; perhaps such things have been abused a little since, both in form and principle.

* * *

* Dumas animadverts more than once against the English climate and English beer swilling via the Musketeers in *Twenty Years After*.

With the next chapter we pass from duologue to monologue with the same ease and mastery. D'Artagnan, 'sitting up in bed, his elbow on his knee and his chin in his hand', meditates on the difficulties of his plan, and reverse of Falstaff with his men in Kendal green, gradually reduces his little army from forty to ten upon suddenly remembering the need for horses.

' "Ah, idiot that I am! Where the devil was my head when I forgot the horses? Thirty horses are ruinous." '

I quote this little example of his long and thoughtful calculations as yet another instance of Dumas's genius for putting himself into the mind and tongue of his characters. With a final ' *Mordioux*! what things patience and calculation are!" ' he brings himself down to ten men and horses — ' "a single corps, and that commanded by d'Artagnan!" ' After which he spends the next day and a half in scouring 'certain dens in Paris' in search of his malodorous recruits. These collected and a meeting place — Calais — arranged, he says goodbye to Planchet and 'prepares to travel for the House of Planchet and Co.'

Though it is of some length, I cannot resist quoting the final pages of the chapter. In reply to Planchet's reluctant ' "But suppose you should not return?" '

> 'That is possible, though not very probable. Then, Planchet, in case I should not return — give me a pen; I will make my will.' D'Artagnan took a pen and some paper, and wrote upon a plain sheet:-
>
> 'I, d'Artagnan, possess twenty thousand livres, laid up sou by sou, during thirty years that I have been in the service of His Majesty the King of France. I leave five thousand to Athos, five thousand to Porthos, and five thousand to Aramis, that they may give the said sums in my name or to my young friend Raoul, Vicomte de Bragelonne. I give the remaining five thousand to Planchet, that he may distribute the fifteen thousand with less regret among my friends. With which purpose I sign these presents. — d'Artagnan.'
>
> Planchet appeared very curious to know what d'Artagnan had written.
>
> 'Here,' said the Musketeer, 'read it.'
>
> On reading the last lines the tears came into Planchet's eyes. 'You think, then, that I would not have given the money without that? Then I will have none of your five thousand francs.'
>
> D'Artagnan smiled. 'Accept it, accept it, Planchet; and in that way you will only lose fifteen thousand francs instead of twenty thousand, and you will not be tempted to disregard the signature of your master and friend in seeking how to lose nothing at all.'
>
> How well our d'Artagnan was acquainted with the hearts of men and of grocers! They who have pronounced Don Quixote mad because he rode out to the conquest of an empire with nobody but Sancho his squire, and they who have pronounced Sancho mad because he accompanied his master in his attempt to conquer the said empire — they certainly will have no hesitation in extending the same judgement to d'Artagnan and Planchet. And yet the first passed for one of the most subtle spirits among the minds of the court of France. As to the second, he had acquired by good right the reputation of having one of the most astute heads among the grocers of the Rue des Lombards; consequently of Paris, consequently of France.

Now, to consider these two men from the point of view in which you would consider other men, and the means by the aid of which they contemplated to restore a monarch to his throne, comparatively with other means, the shallowest brains of the country where brains are most shallow must have revolted against the presumptuous madness of the lieutenant and the stupidity of his associate. Fortunately d'Artagnan was not a man to listen to the idle talk of those around him, or to the comments that were made on himself. He had adopted the motto, 'Act, and let people talk.' Planchet, on his part, had adopted this: 'Act — and say nothing.' It resulted from this, that, according to the custom of all superior geniuses, these two men flattered themselves, *intra pectus*, with being in the right against all who found fault with them.

As a beginning d'Artagnan set out in the finest of possible weather, without a cloud in the heavens — without a cloud on his mind, joyous and strong, calm and decided, great in his resolution, and consequently carrying with him a tenfold dose of that potent fluid which the shocks of mind cause to spring from the nerves, and which procure for the human machine a force and an influence of which future ages will render, according to all probability, an account more scientifically than we can possibly do at present. He was again, as in times past, in that same road fertile of adventures which had led him to Boulogne, and which he was now travelling for the fourth time.* It appeared to him that he could almost recognize the trace of his own steps upon the road, and that of his first upon the doors of the hostelries; his memory, always active and present, brought back that youth which had not, thirty years before, belied either his great heart or his wrist of steel. What a rich nature was that of this man! He had all passions, all defects, all weaknesses; and the spirit of contradiction, familiar to his understanding, changed all these imperfections into corresponding qualities. D'Artagnan, thanks to his ever-active imagination, was afraid of a shadow; and ashamed of being afraid, he marched straight up to that shadow, and then became extravagant in his bravery if the danger proved to be real. Thus everything in him was emotion, and therefore enjoyment. He loved the society of others, but never became tired of his own; and more than once, if he could have been observed when he was alone, he might have been seen laughing at the jokes he related to himself, or the tricks his imagination created just five minutes before ennui might overtake him. D'Artagnan was not perhaps so gay this time as he would have been with the prospect of finding some good friends at Calais, instead of that of joining the ten scamps there. Melancholy, however, did not visit him above once a day; and he received about five visits from that sombre deity before he got sight of the sea at Boulogne, and these visits were indeed but short. But when once d'Artagnan found himself near the field of action, all other feeling but that of confidence disappeared never to return.

* * *

Unknown to d'Artagnan, however, Athos is already in England and made himself known to Monk at Newcastle. Dumas opens the English scene with a chapter headed 'In which the author, very unwillingly, is forced to write a little

---

* v. *The Three Musketeers* and *Twenty Years After*.

history', and begins 'While kings and men were thus occupied with England, which just then governed itself alone, and which, it must be said to its praise, had never been more badly governed...' In fact his historical disquisition could serve as a model for any historical novel in that it sums up succinctly and with an exactitude surprising for a foreign writer the political situation at that moment of time. He rightly shows that the destiny of England lay in the mutually hostile hands of Monk and Lambert. Both generals had fought conspicuously for Cromwell against the king; but following his death and the anarchy caused by the resignation of Cromwell's son Richard, they had taken different courses: Monk supporting Parliament and republicanism, though at the same time, sensing the nation's growing wish for a restoration of kingship, not opposing this; Lambert, after dismissing the remains of the Rump Parliament, setting himself to govern the country with his officers under the title of the 'Committee of Safety'.

Such was the state of affairs when Athos and d'Artagnan came to England. Each acts according to his plan and character: the former not only by making himself known to Monk but by confessing the reason for his coming to England with the purpose of using the buried million in Prince Charles's cause. Persuaded by Athos's frankness and personality, Monk not only agrees to let him have the treasure but lends his assistance to discover and unbury it. With the treasure found, Dumas inspirationally makes Athos, in a long, emotive and characteristic speech, appeal to Monk to consider the anarchy of the country and to bring it to an end by a possible restoration, thereby earning for himself a niche of historical glory. Monk's response is not only a superb résumé of his own secretive politics but also a hint of a possible consideration of Athos's appeal.

> Athos bowed and prepared to absorb greedily the words which fell, one by one, from the mouth of Monk — words rare and precious as the dew in the desert. 'You spoke to me,' said Monk, 'of Charles II; but pray, Monsieur, of what consequence to me is that phantom of a king? I have grown old in war and in politics, which are nowadays so closely linked together that every man of the sword must fight, in virtue of his rights or his ambition, with a personal interest, and not blindly behind an officer, as in ordinary wars. For myself, I perhaps desire nothing, but I fear much. In the war of today resides the liberty of England, and perhaps that of every Englishman. How can you expect that I, free in the position I have made for myself, should go willingly and hold out my hands to the shackles of a stranger? That is all Charles is to me. He has fought battles here which he has lost; he is therefore a bad captain. He has succeeded in no negotiation; he is therefore a bad diplomat. He has paraded his wants and miseries in all the courts of Europe; he has therefore a weak and pusillanimous heart. Nothing noble, nothing great, nothing strong has been shown by one who aspires to govern one of the greatest kingdoms of the earth. I know this Charles, then, under none but bad aspects; and yet you would wish me to go and make myself gratuitously the servant of a creature who is inferior to me in war, politics and dignity. No, Monsieur. When some great and noble action shall have taught me to value him, I may perhaps recognize his rights to a throne from which we threw down the father because he lacked virtues which so far are wanting

also in his son... The Revolution made me a general; my sword will make me Protector, if I wish it ... Therefore, Monsieur, say no more about him. I neither refuse nor accept. I reserve myself. I wait.'

In reply to Athos's ' "Does not Your Honour fear to compromise yourself by allowing this money to be taken away for the service of your enemy?" ' Monk responds:

'My enemy, you say? Eh, Monsieur, I have no enemies. I serve the Parliament, which orders me to combat General Lambert and King Charles — its enemies, not mine. If the Parliament, on the contrary, were to order me to unfurl my standard in London, to assemble my soldiers to receive Charles II — '
'You would obey?' cried Athos joyfully.
'Pardon me,' said Monk, smiling. 'I was going — I, a grey-headed man — in truth, how did I forget myself? — I was going to speak like a foolish young man.'
'Then you would not obey?' said Athos.
'I do not say that either, Monsieur. The welfare of my country before everything... If Parliament were to order such a thing, I should reflect.'

It is with these last words of Monk that Dumas's subtlety in making d'Artagnan and Athos work together albeit unknowingly becomes apparent: the latter's words of appeal only serve to make Monk ' "reflect" '; the former's drastic action in turn make him finally act. Kidnapped by d'Artagnan and his pretended fishermen as he makes his way alone from the castle to his camp, and stowed away in a coffin-like box and shipped to Holland like so much cargo, Monk, believing that Charles had organized the plot with the purpose of forcing him to restore him to the throne, defies him to do his worst and refuses all words. But then, as the prince and d'Artagnan reveal their complete disassociation, and Charles orders the disappointed ex-Musketeer to take his prisoner back to England and set him free, moved in spite of himself by the Frenchman's incredible achievement and loyalty, and by Charles's generosity, Monk, on the dissolution of Lambert's army and its leader's obvious determination to make himself another Cromwell, marches to London, sounds Parliament and acting on its expressed wish and popular demand, invites the prince to return to his country and his father's throne. D'Artagnan's ' "restoration of Whitehall" ' is accomplished!

The sequel makes as delectable reading as does the conception of it in Planchet's shop. Meeting Athos among the crowds milling in the streets to welcome the new king, and sighing heavily, replying to Athos's query as to what the reason for his sighs might be he explains:

'I have ruined myself, *mon ami*, — ruined myself for the restoration of this young prince who has just passed, capering upon his dun horse.'
'The king does not know you have ruined yourself, *mon ami*; but he knows he owes you much.'
'And say, Athos, does that advance me in any respect? I do you justice — you

have laboured nobly; but I — I, who in appearance marred your combinations, — it was I who really made them succeed. Follow my calculations closely: you might not, by persuasion or mildness, have convinced General Monk, while I have so roughly treated this dear general that I furnished your prince with an opportunity of showing himself generous; this generosity was inspired in him by the fact of my fortunate mistake, and Charles is paid by the restoration which Monk has brought about.'

'All that, *mon cher ami*, is strikingly true,' replied Athos.

'Well, strikingly true as it may be, it is not less true that I shall return, — greatly noticed by M. Monk, who calls me "My dear Captain" all day long, although I am neither dear to him nor a captain; and strongly appreciated by the king, who has already forgotten my name, — it is not less true, I say, that I shall return to my beautiful country, cursed by the soldiers I had raised with promises of large pay, cursed by the brave Planchet, of whom I borrowed a part of his fortune.'

'How is that? What the devil has Planchet to do in all this?'

'Ah, yes, *mon ami*. This king, so spruce, so smiling, so adored, — M. Monk fancies he has recalled him, you fancy you have supported him, I fancy I have brought him back, the people fancy they have re-conquered him, he himself fancies he has negotiated so as to be restored; and yet nothing of all this is true; for Charles II, King of England, Scotland, and Ireland, has been replaced upon the throne by a French grocer, who lives in the Rue des Lombards, and is named Planchet. Such is grandeur! "Vanity!" says the Scripture, "vanity, all is vanity" '.

Athos could not help laughing at this whimsical outbreak of his friend. But then, while Athos is being philosophically resigned and d'Artagnan humorously bitter on being 'forgotten' by Monk and the king, a missive from Parry for the former giving him an appointment arrives, followed later by one for the latter from Monk with a similar message. At last and at least the shares of Planchet and Co. are rising to par, is d'Artagnan's reflection. Their audience is inimitably described. Monk conducts the two Frenchmen to the king's private room where His Majesty begins by telling d'Artagnan he wishes to reward him for ' "the great service" ' he had rendered him, and offers him ' "a post worthy of him near our person... say the command of my Musketeers" '.

But d'Artagnan can only regretfully refuse, explaining that although he had quitted the service of the King of France he had given him his word ' "never to serve any other king" '.

'We will say no more about it, then,' said the king, turning towards Athos, and leaving d'Artagnan plunged in the deepest pangs of disappointment.

'Ah! I said so,' muttered the Musketeer. 'Words! words! Court holy water! Kings have always a marvellous talent for offering us that which they know we will not accept, and in appearing generous without risk. Fool! — triple fool that I was to have hoped for a moment!'

The king then turns to Athos, whom he takes by the hand, and after expressing his gratitude creates him a Knight of the Golden Fleece, an honour enjoyed in France by the king alone.

'It is unaccountably strange,' said d'Artagnan to himself, while his friend, on his knees, received the eminent order which the king conferred on him, — 'it is almost incredible that I have always seen showers of prosperity fall upon all who surrounded me, and that not a drop ever reached me! If I were a jealous man, it would be enough to make me tear my hair, upon my word of honour!'

After which the king turns again to Monk to inform him that in addition to his dukedom, in order to keep him near him as ' "almost my brother" ', he makes him Viceroy of Ireland and Scotland.

'*Mordioux!*' grumbled d'Artagnan, 'there is the shower beginning again! Oh, it is enough to turn one's brain!' and he turned away with an air so sorrowful and so comically piteous, that the king could not restrain a smile.

But Charles has deliberately kept back a surprise for the ex-Musketeer. Reminding the new viceroy that he is theoretically the Frenchman's prisoner in that he is not yet ransomed he goes on ' "It was I who took you out of M. d'Artagnan's hands, and it is I who will pay your ransom." '

'D'Artagnan's eyes regained their gaiety and brilliancy. The Gascon began to comprehend.'

To comprehend to such an extent, in fact, that in return for his sword which Monk there and then surrendered to him, he came away with an order signed by the king for 300,000 livres as its price of purchase.

'You will come and see me before you go, chevalier?' the king said. 'I shall want to lay in a stock of gaiety now my Frenchmen are leaving me.'

'Ah, Sire, it shall not be with the gaiety as with the duke's sword,' replied d'Artagnan, whose feet scarcely seemed to touch the ground. 'I will give it to Your Majesty gratis!'

* * *

In the course of his farewell audience with the king, Charles requests him to make the acquaintance of his younger sister Henrietta, soon to marry Louis XIV's brother and to live in France, giving as his reason ' "My sister must know you, and at her need have you to depend on." ' So, led by Parry, the Gascon is taken along the canal to be introduced to the princess. They find her surrounded as usual by a bevy of courtier gallants, all seeking her favours, for she is not only a very beautiful young woman but a born coquette. The Duke of Buckingham and the Earl of Rochester are the main rivals for her heart and hand. Parry introduces d'Artagnan as ' "the man to whom His Majesty owes the restoration of his kingdom" '. After a few words with Buckingham and a reference to his father and the diamond studs, the Gascon makes a little speech to the princess, declaring that she is ' "a daughter of France" ', and he looks forward to seeing her again in Paris, all concluding with a respectful bow — on which 'she gave him her hand to kiss with a grace truly royal'.

' "Ah, Madam," said Buckingham in a subdued impassioned voice, "what must a man do to obtain such a favour from Your Highness?" ' To which he is given the reply ' "My lord, ask M. d'Artagnan. He will tell you." '

With such subtle strokes does Dumas enrich his tale and give character to his creations.

Before embarking, the two friends have a revealing conversation which brings out their different characters. Athos admits he has a commission from King Charles for King Louis which is secret and which he cannot reveal even to his best friend.

> The Gascon sighed. 'There was a time,' he said, 'when you would have thrown that order on the table saying "d'Artagnan, read this scrawl to Porthos, Aramis and me." '
>
> 'That is true enough. Oh, that was the time of youth, confidence, trust, the generous season when the blood commands and is warmed by feeling.'
>
> 'Well, Athos, allow me to tell you something. That delightful time, that generous season, that mastery of the warm blood, were all very fine things, no doubt, but I do not regret them at all. It is like the period of studies. I have met with fools who would boast of the days of impositions and crusts of dry bread. But I never loved all that. For my part, poor though I was, I would none the less have preferred the embroideries of Porthos to my threadbare cassock. *Mon ami*, I shall always mistrust him who pretends to prefer evil to good. Now, in times past, all was evil with me, — those times in which every month found a new hole in my cassock and in my skin, a gold crown less in my poor purse; of that execrable time of small beer and ups and downs I regret absolutely nothing, nothing but our friendship; for within me I have a heart, and it is a miracle that heart has not been dried up by the wind of poverty which passed through the holes of my cloak, or pierced by the swords of all shapes which passed through the holes in my poor body.'
>
> 'Do not regret our friendship,' said Athos; 'that will only die with ourselves. Friendship is composed, above all things, of remembrances and habits; and if you have just now made a little satire upon mine, because I hesitate to tell you the nature of my mission into France — '
>
> 'I? Oh, heavens! If you knew, *mon cher ami*, how indifferent all the missions of the world will henceforth become to me!' and he laid his hand upon the parchment in his vast pocket.
>
> Athos rose from the table and called the host in order to pay the reckoning.
>
> 'Since I have known you, *mon ami*,' said d'Artagnan, 'I have never discharged the reckoning. Porthos often did, Aramis sometimes, and you — you almost always drew out your purse with the dessert. I am now rich, and should like to try if it is heroic to pay.'

On reaching Boulogne d'Artagnan met up with his little army, paid them and disbanded them, but only after threatening them, and particularly their leader Menneville, with direct and drastic punishment if a single word of their adventure escaped any of them. Dumas, with tongue in cheek, then adds a delightful postscript to his chapter.

Menneville swore, as his comrades had sworn, that he would be as mute as the tomb. And yet someone must have spoken; and as to a certainty it was not one of the nine companions, and as equally certainly it was not Menneville, it must have been d'Artagnan, who as a Gascon, had an itchy tongue. for in short if it was not he, who could it be? And how can it be explained that the secret of the deal box pierced with holes should come to our knowledge, and in so complete a fashion that we have, as has been seen, related the history of it in all its most intimate details, — details which, besides, throw a light as new as unexpected upon that portion of the history of England which has been left, up to the present day, completely in the shade by our brother historians?

None the less, tongue in cheek though it may be, Dumas is absolutely correct in the two statements he makes apropos of our history at this period (1) the country had never been worse governed (2) its politics, the hesitations and decisions of Monk, Lambert, and the Rump Parliament have seemed dubious to and sketchily glossed over by our historians, and the end of the Protectorate and the return of Charles II to Whitehall something of a mystery. No historian has satisfactorily explained Monk's change of heart from being one of Cromwell's generals and then, after the latter's death, from one of the most ardent and powerful supporters of the Commonwealth to switching his allegiance to the exiled Charles. In his *A Short History of the English People* Green can only write: 'Monk ... while he accepted petitions for a "Free Parliament", entered London unopposed. From the moment of his entry the restoration of the Stuarts became inevitable.' And other historians are equally vague and elusive. Dumas saw his chance here and took it superexcellently. As with opera, if the music is great enough we are made to suspend belief in the librettos however incredible, so Dumas, by the sheer magic of his narrative power makes us accept his version of events. In short, if Monk's part in affairs remains unexplained by historians, why not Athos and d'Artagnan as the catalysts? Why not indeed? Who can believe the exploits of Odysseus? The Wooden Horse, the Cyclops, Circe, the Sirens, Scylla and Charybdis, the slaughter of the suitors — all figments of imagination and beyond credence. But Homer weaves his magic and we thrill to them. *Ipso facto*, if Homer, why not Dumas? Monk kidnapped and put in a wooden box, shipped out to Holland, dumped humiliatingly as a prisoner before the exiled Charles and so changing the course of British history? Impossible! But what superb impossibilities.

But there is to come a two-part epilogue which rounds off the whole of the English adventure so admirably: the first one involving d'Artagnan and Athos, the second d'Artagnan and Planchet. Once back in Paris the two friends separate, but not before a little mutual philosophizing about poverty and wealth, and a characteristic offer to his friend from Athos.

> 'Why not *au revoir* instead of *adieu*, for why can't you come and live with me at Blois? You are free; you are rich. I will purchase for you, if you like, a handsome property in the environs of Chiverny or of Bracieux. On the one side you will have

the finest woods in the world, which join those of Chambord; on the other, admirable marshes. You who love sporting, and who whether you admit it or not are a poet, *mon cher ami*, excursions on the water, to make you fancy yourself Nimrod and Apollo themselves. Awaiting the acquisition, you can live at La Fère, and we will fly our hawks among the vines, as Louis XIII used to do. That is a quiet amusement for old fellows like us.'

  D'Artagnan took the hands of Athos in his own. '*Mon cher comte*,' said he, 'I will say neither "Yes" nor "No". Let me pass in Paris the time necessary for the regulation of my affairs, and accustom myself, by degrees, to the heavy and glittering idea which is beating in my brains. I am rich, do you see; and from this moment till I shall have acquired the habit of being rich, — I know myself, — I shall be an unendurable animal. Now, I am not enough of a fool to wish to appear to have lost my wits before a friend like you, Athos. The habit is handsome, the habit is richly gilded, but it is new, and doesn't seem to fit me.'

So they separate, Athos to go to his temporary lodging and prepare himself for his secretive mission; d'Artagnan to Planchet's in the Rue des Lombards, where we are treated to the second episode of the epilogue which in its humour and lightness of touch belongs to Dumas alone among French novelists.

  At the moment when Planchet, according to his daily custom, with the back of his pen and uttering a sigh, was erasing another day, d'Artagnan kicked open the door, and the blow made his steel spurs jingle.

  'Oh, good Lord!' cried Planchet.

  The worthy grocer could say no more; he perceived his partner. D'Artagnan entered with a bent back and a dull eye; the Gascon had an idea with regard to Planchet.

  'Good God!' thought the grocer, looking earnestly at the traveller, 'he looks very sad.' The Musketeer sat down.

  'My dear M. d'Artagnan!' said Planchet with a horrible palpitation of the heart. 'Here you are! And your health?'

  'Tolerably good, Planchet, tolerably good!' said d'Artagnan with a profound sigh.

  'You have not been wounded, I hope?'

  'Pugh!'

  'Ah! I see,' continued Planchet, more and more alarmed, 'the expedition has been a trying one?'

  'Yes,' said d'Artagnan. A shudder ran through Planchet's whole frame.

  'I should like to have something to drink,' said the Musketeer, raising his head piteously.

  Planchet ran to the cupboard, and poured d'Artagnan out some wine into a large glass. D'Artagnan examined the bottle.

  'What wine is that?' he asked.

  'Alas! that which you prefer, Monsieur,' said Planchet; 'that good old Anjou wine, which was one day nearly costing us all so dear.'*

  'Ah!' replied d'Artagnan with a melancholy smile, 'ah, my poor Planchet! ought I still to drink good wine?'

---

* v. *The Three Musketeers*, chapter XLII

'Come, my dear master,' said Planchet, making a superhuman effort, while all his contracted muscles, his paleness, and his trembling betrayed the most acute anguish. 'Come! I have been a soldier, and consequently have some courage; do not keep me in suspense, dear M. d'Artagnan: our money is lost, is it not?'

Before answering, d'Artagnan made a pause which seemed an age to the poor grocer. Meanwhile he did nothing but turn about upon his chair.

'And if that were the case,' said he slowly, moving his head up and down, 'what would you say, my dear friend?'

Planchet, from being pale, turned yellow. It might have been thought he was going to swallow his tongue, so full became his throat, so red were his eyes.

'Twenty thousand livres!' murmured he. 'Twenty thousand livres, though!'

D'Artagnan, with his neck elongated, his legs stretched out, and his hands hanging listlessly, looked like a statue of discouragement. Planchet heaved a sigh from the deepest cavities of his breast.

'Well,' said he, 'I see how it is. Let us be men! It is all over, is it not? The principal thing is, Monsieur, that you have saved your life.'

'Doubtless, doubtless, life is something; but I am ruined!'

'*Cordieu*! Monsieur,' said Planchet, 'if it is so, we must not despair for that. You shall become a grocer with me; I will make you my partner, we will share the profits; and if there should be no more profits, well then we will share the almonds, raisins, and prunes, and we will nibble together the last quarter of Dutch cheese.'

D'Artagnan could hold out no longer. '*Mordioux*!' cried he with great emotion, 'you're a brave fellow, on my honour, Planchet! You haven't been playing comedy, have you? You haven't seen the pack-horse with the money-bags under the shed yonder?'

'What horse? What money-bags?' said Planchet, whose trembling heart began to suggest that d'Artagnan was mad.

Why! the English money-bags, *mordioux*!' said d'Artagnan all radiant and quite transfigured.

'Ah, good God!' articulated Planchet, drawing back before the dazzling fire of his eyes.

'Imbecile!' cried d'Artagnan, 'you think me mad! *Mordioux*! on the contrary, never was my head more clear or my heart more joyous. To the money-bags, Planchet, to the money-bags!'

'My God! what money-bags?'

D'Artagnan pushed Planchet towards the window. 'Under the penthouse, yonder, don't you see a horse?'

'Yes.'

'Don't you see how his back is laden?'

'Yes, yes!'

'Don't you see your lad chatting with the postilion?'

'Yes, yes, yes!'

'Well, you know that lad's name because he is yours. Call him.'

'Abdon! Abdon!' vociferated Planchet from the window.

'Bring the horse!' prompted d'Artagnan.

'Bring the horse!' Planchet echoed.

'Now give ten livres to the postilion,' said d'Artagnan in the voice he would have used in commanding a manoeuvre. 'Two lads to bring up the first two sacks, two for the last two. And move, *mordioux*! Look alive!'

Planchet rushed down the stairs as if the devil were at his heels. A moment after the lads ascended the staircase, bending beneath their burdens. D'Artagnan sent them off to their garrets, carefully closed the door, and turned his attention to Planchet, who was beginning to look a little wild.

'Now we are by ourselves,' he said, 'get to work, Planchet.' After he had spread a large cover over the floor he emptied the first sack over it; Planchet did the same with the second; then d'Artagnan split open the third with a knife. When Planchet heard the intoxicating sound of the gold and silver coins, saw tumbling out of the bags the shining crowns glittering like fish from the net; when he plunged his arms to the elbow in that tide of yellow and silver pieces, giddiness seized him, and he sank down on to the huge heap. Planchet, overcome with joy, had lost his senses. D'Artagnan threw a glass of wine over his face, bringing him back to life.

'Ah! good heavens! good heavens!' said Planchet, wiping his moustache and beard.

'*Mordioux!*' said the Musketeer. 'There are a hundred thousand livres for you, partner. Draw your share, and I will draw mine.'

'Oh, the lovely sum, M. d'Artagnan, the lovely sum!'

'Now, let us close our account; for as they say, short reckonings make long friends.'

'Oh rather, to begin with, tell me the whole story. That must be even better than the money.'

'*Ma foi!*' said d'Artagnan, stroking his moustache, 'I can't say no to that! And if ever the historian turns to me for information he will be able to say he hasn't dipped his bucket into a dry well. Listen then, Planchet, and I will tell you all about it.'

'And I will build piles of crowns, dear master.'

'Well, this is it,' said d'Artagnan, drawing breath.

'And this is it,' said Planchet, picking up the first handful of crowns.

* * *

With the chapter 'Mazarin's Card Party' we make a return to the Parisian scene and the penultimate solo appearance of Athos. As I have already stated, Dumas is always at his best when bringing Mazarin on the scene. This is set in the cardinal's bed-chamber where he was giving a card party for the king, queen, queen-mother and the more nearly allied members of the court. Now in the last year of his life, and ill, the cardinal, 'very weary, reclined his attenuated form on his bed, his cards being held for him by the Comtesse de Soissons, and he watched them with an incessant look of eagerness and cupidity'. General conversation began to turn on the rumours that Prince Charles had left Holland, landed at Dover and been hailed as King of England. In the midst of the play and talk Bernouin, Mazarin's secretary, entered and whispered in his ear ' "An envoi from His Majesty the King of England, Monseigneur." ' Mazarin excused himself and followed Bernouin into his cabinet adjoining the bedroom, where he found the Comte de la Fère standing and awaiting him. But his normal diplomatic greeting was changed to exasperation when, after holding out his hand for the despatch, the icy figure in black with a simple lacing of silver and wearing the orders of the Holy Ghost, Garter, and Golden Fleece, refused saying 'Your pardon, Monseigneur, but my despatch is for the king.'

'Since you say you are a Frenchman, Monsieur, you ought to know what the position of Prime Minister is at the court of France.'

'There was a time,' replied Athos, 'when I bothered myself about the importance of Prime Ministers; but long ago I decided to treat with no one but the king.'

'Then, Monsieur,' said Mazarin who began to be irritated, 'you will see neither the minister nor the king.' Saying which he rose. Athos put the despatch back in the bag, bowed gravely and took several steps towards the door. This coolness exasperated Mazarin.

'What strange diplomatic proceedings are these?' he cried. 'Are we back in the times when Cromwell sent us bullies in the guise of *chargés d'affaires?* You want nothing, Monsieur, but a steel cap on your head and a Bible at your girdle.'

'Monsieur,' riposted Athos dryly, 'I have never had, as you have, the pleasure of treating with M. Cromwell, and I have only met his *chargés d'affaires* sword in hand. I am therefore ignorant as to how he treated with Prime Ministers. As for the King of England, I know that when he writes to King Louis XIV he does not write to his Eminence the Cardinal Mazarin. I see no diplomacy in that distinction.'

'Ah!' exclaimed Mazarin, striking his head with his attenuated hand. 'I remember you now!'

Athos looked at him in astonishment. 'Yes, that is it,' the cardinal went on looking piercingly at his interlocutor. 'I know you now, Monsieur. *Diavolo!* I am no longer astonished.'

'In fact I was surprised that with the memory your Eminence has,' Athos replied smiling, 'you did not recognize me before.'

'Always refractory and grumbling, Monsieur — Monsieur — what do they call you? The name of a river — Potamos. No — the name of an island — Naxos. No *Per Giove!* — the name of a mountain — Athos! Yes, now I have it! Delighted to see you again, but no longer at Rueil where you and your cursed companions made me pay ransom.* *Fronde!* still *Fronde,* accused *Fronde!* Why, Monsieur, have your hatreds survived my own? If anyone had cause to complain it could not be you, who came out of the affair not only with a sound skin but with the cordon of the Holy Ghost round your neck!'

'Monsieur the Cardinal,' replied Athos, 'permit me to dispense with considerations of such a kind. I have a mission to fulfil. Will you assist me in fulfilling that mission?'

'I am astonished,' Mazarin resumed, delighted at having regained remembrance and bristling with malicious points — 'I am astonished Monsieur Athos, that a *Frondeur* like you should have accepted a mission to that so-and-so Mazarin, as it used to be said in the good old days.' And Mazarin began to laugh in spite of a painful cough which turned his words into sobs.

'I only accepted the mission to the King of France,' retorted Athos, 'because it was requested of me.'

'So be it. But I say again, this negotiation must pass through my hands. Let us lose no time, then. Tell me the terms.'

---

* As narrated in *Twenty Years After*, chapters XCII–XCIII

'I have the honour of repeating to Your Eminence that the letter alone for His Majesty —'

'Pooh! you are being ridiculous with your obstinacy, M. Athos,' the cardinal interrupted. 'It is obvious you have been keeping company with those Puritans over there. As for your secret, I know it better than you do, and you have done wrong in not showing respect due to an old and suffering man who has striven during his life to keep the field bravely for his ideas as you have for yours. You will not give the letter to me? Very well. Come with me, and you shall speak to the king.'

He led the way back into his bedroom, and after dismissing the company with the exception of the queen-mother and family with a wave of his hand and the words 'An affair of state,' he introduced Athos to the king, ending with 'This gentleman is the bearer of a letter in which Charles II, restored to his throne, demands an alliance between Monsieur and Mademoiselle Henrietta. Now will you hand your credentials to His Majesty, Monsieur le Comte?'

For a moment Athos remained stupefied. How could the cardinal possibly know the matter of the letter which had never left his keeping? Nevertheless, always master of himself, he held out the despatch to the young king, who took it with a self-conscious blush. A silence reigned in the chamber, broken only by the dull sound of the gold which Mazarin, with his dry yellow hand, piled up in a box while the king was reading.

In reply to the king's request for details of Charles II's restoration Athos then related the sequence of events, and finally, when pressed, confessed himself as being the one who had known the secret of the million and kept it.

'Is it also true,' Louis continued, 'that one man penetrated into General Monk's camp and carried him off?'

'That man had ten aides.'

'Nothing but that?'

'Only that, Sire.'

'And his name?'

'D'Artagnan, formerly lieutenant of the Musketeers of Your Majesty.' Anne of Austria blushed; Mazarin grew yellow with shame; Louis was deeply thoughtful. 'What men!' he exclaimed under his breath, and darted a glance at his minister which would have terrified him if he had not hidden his head in his pillow.

'Monsieur,' said the young Duc d'Anjou placing his hand, delicate and white as a woman's, on the arm of Athos, 'tell that brave man, I beg you, that Monsieur, the king's brother, tomorrow will drink his health along with a hundred of the first gentlemen of France.' On concluding these words the young man, perceiving that in his enthusiasm he had inadvertently deranged one of his ruffles, began putting it to rights with the greatest care imaginable.

'Let us resume business, Sire,' said Mazarin, who was never enthusiastic and did not wear ruffles.

There follows the final illness and death of Mazarin along with the introduction of Colbert,* destined to be the arch-rival of Fouquet, superintendent of the realm's finances.**

* * *

With the death of Mazarin, at once his mentor and soi-disant father, a new era dawns for the young Louis XIV, and, unsuspected by him, for d'Artagnan. The young king, for the first time his own master, and unexpectedly enriched by thirteen millions from a secret source of the late cardinal via the scrupulous Colbert, and equally unexpectedly made aware that Belle-Ile, belonging to Fouquet, is being secretly fortified, sends for Colbert, but adds

'Oh! but I cannot place all my dependence on that man. He is only the head. I must have an arm.' Then he uttered a cry. 'I had,' he said to a waiting *valet de chambre*, 'a Lieutenant of Musketeers.'
'Yes, Sire: M. d'Artagnan.'
'But he left service for a time.'
'Yes, Sire.'
'Let him be found, and let him be here tomorrow at my levee.'
The valet bowed and went out.
'Thirteen millions in my coffers!' said Louis, 'Colbert bearing my purse, and d'Artagnan carrying my sword! At last I am really king!'

While he is thus being sought for, the ex-Musketeer, for the first time rich and with his time his own, is seen in the dress of a citizen, his nose in the air, his hands behind him, examining a house he has bought. He is shortly joined by Raoul. His conversation with Athos's son, like that with Planchet while telling him of his plan to restore Prince Charles, is among the highlights of the novel. He begins by advising the young man to keep well in with M. Fouquet, the brightest star of the political scene now that Mazarin is dead, ' "if you do not wish to moulder away as I have done almost all my life" '; and he contrasts the French king and France with Charles II and England.

'There is a king, — God speed him!'
'Ah!' cried Raoul, with the artless curiosity of well-born young people while listening to experience and worth.
'Yes; a king who amuses himself, it is true, but who has had a sword in his hand, and can appreciate useful men. Athos is on good terms with Charles II. Take service there, and leave these scoundrels of contractors and farmers-general, who steal as well with French hands as others have stolen with Italian hands; leave the little snivelling king, who is going to give us another reign of Francis II. Do you know anything of history, Raoul?'
'Yes, Monsieur the Chevalier.'

* Facsimile — see p.vii.　　　　　　　　　　　　** See Brief Biographies.

'Do you know, then, that Francis II, always had the earache?'
'No, I did not know that.'
'That Charles IV always had the headache?'
'No.'
'And Henry III the belly-ache?'
Raoul began to laugh.
'Well, *mon cher ami*, Louis XIV always has the heart-ache. It is deplorable to see a king sighing from morning till night without saying once in the course of a day *Ventre-saint-gris! Corboeuf!* or anything to rouse one. What a reign, my poor Raoul, what a reign!'
'You are very hard upon the king, my dear M. d'Artagnan; and yet you scarcely know him.'
'Scarcely know him? Listen, Raoul. Day by day, hour by hour — take note of my words — I will tell you what he will do. He will put on mourning for the dead cardinal, the least silly thing he will do, since he won't shed a tear. Then he will get M. Fouquet to grant him a pension, then go and write verses to some Mancini whose eyes the queen will scratch out. Then, after having torn the silver tags from the uniform of his Swiss because they are too expensive, he will dismount the Musketeers because oats and hay cost five sous a day.'
'Oh, surely not.'
'Of what consequence is it to me? I am no longer a Musketeer. Let them be on horseback; let them be on foot; let them carry a larding pin, a spit, sword, or nothing. What is it to me?'
'My dear M. d'Artagnan, please say no more ill to me of the king. I am almost in his service. And besides, my father would be very angry at having heard words offensive to His Majesty even from you.'
'Oh, your father! He is a knight in every bad cause. A brave man. A Caesar, in fact, but without perception.'
'Now, my dear Chevalier,' said Raoul with a laugh, 'you, speaking ill of him you call the great Athos! You are in a sour mood today. Wealth is making you as peevish as poverty makes other people.'
'*Pardieu!* you are right, Raoul. I am a scoundrel in my dotage; a sorry wretch grown old; a boot without a sole; a spur without a rowel. But do me the pleasure of saying one thing for me. Say: "Mazarin was a sorry wretch." '
'Mazarin was a sorry wretch,' Raoul obliged him, smiling as the other roared with laughter as in his youthful days.

It is with such down to earth drollery as this that Dumas makes us realize that in the course of creating him he has become the Musketeer's *alter ego*, and that you could take him by the arm and chat with him.

But while in this verbal act of *lèse-majesté*, a letter to the Musketeer from Athos is brought which ran: 'Someone has just been here to ask me to find you by the wish of the king. Make haste. His Majesty is anxious to speak to you at the Louvre.'

'Speak to me at the Louvre!' exclaimed d'Artagnan letting the paper fall onto the table. Raoul began laughing immoderately.

'Oh, oh!' said d'Artagnan. 'What the devil can this mean?' The first feeling of surprise over, he reperused Athos's note.

'It is strange,' said he, 'that the king should send for me.'

'Why so?' said Raoul; 'do you not think, Monsieur, that the king must wish such a servant as you back again?'

'Oh!' exclaimed the officer laughing, 'you are flattering me, Master Raoul. If the king had wanted me he would not have let me leave him. No, no; I see in it something better, or worse, if you like. We must part, Raoul.'

'With what a serious face you say that!'

'Ah! but the occasion is worthy of it. Listen to me! I have a very good recommendation to make you.'

'I am all attention, M. d'Artagnan.'

'You will go and inform your father of my departure.'

'Your departure?'

'*Pardieu*! You will tell him that I have gone to England, and that I am living in my little country house.'

'To England, you! — And the king's orders?'

'You get more and more silly; do you imagine I am going in that way to the Louvre to place myself at the mercy of that little crowned wolf-cub?'

'The king a wolf-cub? Why, Monsieur Chevalier, you are mad!'

'On the contrary, I was never so much otherwise. You do not know what he wants to do with me, this worthy son of Louis the Just. But, *mordioux*! that is policy. He wishes to ensconce me snugly in the Bastille, purely and simply, don't you see?'

'What for?' cried Raoul, terrified at what he heard.

'On account of what I told him one day at Blois. I was heated; he remembers it.'

'You told him what?'

'That he was mean, cowardly, and silly.'

'Good God!' cried Raoul, 'is it possible you used such words as those?'

'Perhaps I don't give the letter of my discourse, but I give the sense of it.'

'But did not the king have you arrested immediately?'

'Who by? It was I who commanded the Musketeers; he must have commanded me to convey myself to prison. I would never have consented; I would have resisted myself. And then I went into England — no more d'Artagnan. Now, the cardinal is dead, or nearly so; they learn that I am in Paris, and they lay their hands on me. Go, then, and find your father; relate the fact to him, — and *adieu*!'

'My dear M. d'Artagnan,' said Raoul, very much agitated after having looked out of the window, 'you cannot escape!'

'Why not?'

Because there is below an officer of the Swiss Guards waiting for you.'

'Well!'

'Well, he will arrest you.'

D'Artagnan broke into an Homeric laugh.

'Oh! I know very well that you will resist, that you will fight even; I know very well that you would come off victor. But that amounts to rebellion; and you are an officer yourself, knowing what discipline is.'

'Devil of a boy! how noble, how logical that is!' grumbled d'Artagnan. You agree with me, don't you?'

Yes. Instead of passing into the street, where that oaf is waiting for me, I will slip quietly out at the back. I have a horse in the stable, and a good one. I will ride him to death — my means allow me to do so — and by killing one horse after another I shall arrive at Boulogne in eleven hours. I know the road well, you see. But tell your father one thing.'

'What is that?'

'This: that what he knows about is with Planchet, except a fifth.'

'But my dear M. d'Artagnan, if you run away two things will be said of you.'

'And what are they, *mon cher ami?*'

'The first, that you are afraid.'

'Ah! And who will dare to say that?'

'The king, first of all.'

'Well, he will be telling the truth. I am afraid.'

'The second, that you felt yourself guilty.'

'True again. So then, you advise me to get myself put in the Bastille?'

'I am sure my father would advise you the same as I do.'

'*Pardieu!* I'm sure he would' said d'Artagnan pensively. 'But if they put me in the Bastille?'

'We will get you out again,' said Raoul.

'*Mordioux!* Bravely said, Raoul. That savours of Athos.'

Finally d'Artagnan gives way, accosts the Swiss Guard and follows him to the Louvre where the king was impatiently awaiting him. So follows the second of his four important and outstanding interviews with Louis XIV.

The Musketeer assumed his parade carriage and entered, his eyes wide open, his brow calm, his moustache stiff. The king was seated at a table writing, and did not disturb himself when the Musketeer's step resounded on the floor. D'Artagnan advanced as far as the middle of the room, then seeing that the king paid no attention to him, and suspecting that this was nothing but affectation, a sort of tormenting preamble to what was coming, he turned his back on Louis and began to examine the frescos on the cornices of the ceiling — a manoeuvre accompanied by this silent little monologue: 'Ah! you want to humble me, do you? — you, whom I have seen so young — you, whom I have saved as I would my own child — and all for what? — nothing. Wait awhile, wait awhile! You shall see what a man who has snuffed the fire of the Huguenots under the beard of the great cardinal can do!'

Just then Louis turned in his chair, 'Ah! there you are, M. d'Artagnan,' he said.

D'Artagnan imitated the movement. 'Yes, Sire,' he replied.

'Good! Have the goodness to wait till I have cast this up.'

D'Artagnan bowed. 'That is polite enough,' he said to himself. Louis made a violent dash with his pen and threw it angrily away.

'Go on! Work yourself up!' thought the Musketeer. 'You will put me at my ease that way. You will find I did not empty the bag the other day at Blois.'

But he found a very different Louis now confronting him. After reminding him of his reasons for quitting, quoting his own words at him, and excusing himself on account of his youth and his debt to the late cardinal, the king tells him that everything is changed and that he is now master in his own kingdom, and after congratulating him on his ' "brilliant deed in England" ' and being told that he, d'Artagnan, had earned a fortune by it and had no intention or need of increasing it:

'What!' exclaimed the king. 'Do you contemplate remaining idle?'
'Yes, Sire.'
'To relinquish the sword?'
'I have already done that.'
'Impossible, M. d'Artagnan!' said Louis firmly.
'Why not, Sire?'
'Because I will that you shall not!' said the young prince in a voice so imperious that d'Artagnan evinced surprise and even uneasiness.
'Will Your Majesty allow me one word of reply?' he asked.
'Speak.'
'I formed that resolution when I was poor and destitute.'
'So be it! Go on.'
'Now, when by my industry I have acquired a comfortable means of subsistence, would Your Majesty despoil me of my liberty? Condemn me to the least when I have gained the most?'
'Who gave you permission, Monsieur, to fathom my designs, or to reckon with me?' replied Louis in a voice almost angry. 'Who told you what I shall do, or what you will yourself do?'
'Sire,' said the Musketeer quietly, 'so far as I see, freedom is not the order in this conversation as I believe it was on the day that we came to an explanation at Blois.'
'No, Monsieur; everything is changed.'
'I render Your Majesty my sincere congratulations, but — '
'But you don't believe it?'
'I am not a great statesman, and yet I have my eye upon affairs; it seldom fails. Now, I do not see exactly as Your Majesty does. The reign of Mazarin is over, but that of the financiers has begun. They have the money. Your Majesty will not often see much of it. To live under the paw of those hungry wolves is hard for a man who reckoned upon independence.'

At this point Colbert entered with a report and orders for the king to sign for the execution of some financiers who had been robbing the state. No sooner had Colbert left than M. de Lyonne entered with a letter for the king to sign for his consent to the marriage of his brother with the Princess Henrietta Stuart.

' "He is drubbing me, it seems," murmured d'Artagnan while the king signed the letter and dismissed M. de Lyonne, "but, *ma foi!* I confess the more he drubs me the better I like it." '

Louis then proceeded to offer him all sorts of emoluments: twenty thousand livres a year fixed income, his commission as captain of the Musketeers on his return from a certain expedition, resume his functions, reorganize his company, keep open house and table as a person of importance.

'And I,' said d'Artagnan bluntly, 'I do not like easily gotten money. Your Majesty gives me a sinecure which the first comer would perform for four thousand livres.'
The king began to laugh. 'You are a true Gascon, M. d'Artagnan. You will draw my heart's secret from me.'
'Your Majesty has a secret, then?'

'Yes, Monsieur.'
'Then I accept, for I will keep that secret, and discretion is above all price in these times.'

* * *

D'Artagnan then finds that the expedition referred to by the king consists of his going around Brittany, and in particular Belle-Ile, accoutred as a simple citizen to ascertain what is going on there; for Louis had learned in a letter from Charles II that the place was being secretly fortified, and Belle-Ile belonged to Fouquet. Unknown to the Musketeer the king-Colbert-Fouquet/Aramis-d'Artagnan conflict has been set in motion.

D'Artagnan takes leave of Louis saying to himself ' "The English shower continues. Let us remain under the spout!" '

But before narrating the Musketeer's journey to Belle-Ile and the surprise awaiting him there, Dumas interpolates no fewer than eleven chapters devoted to the sayings, doings and amours of Fouquet and his Epicureans, as they were called, all men of wit and talent, and at the same time libertines and spongers, not least among them being Lafontaine, remembered today for his *Contes* and *Fables*. For the women, those named are all some man's mistress, and intrigantes; the whole culminating in their combined plot to prevent the execution of the two ministers accused, as we have seen, by Colbert for embezzlement: a plot foiled thanks to d'Artagnan and Raoul and the king's Musketeers.

While these episodes reveal Dumas's amazingly acute historical knowledge,[*] and may well be of peculiar interest to French readers (reputedly more literate than their British counterparts), English readers may be forgiven for siding here with Mr Polly, and for classing them among the 'dark corners' of R.L.S.

In fact one has to admit that the whole story of the downfall of Fouquet, along with his character, is never really dug into by Dumas. We are given glimpses of the gorgeous splendours of the finance minister, his spendthrift feasts and entertainments which arouse the jealous hatred of Louis XIV and the malicious envy of Colbert, along with examples of his high sense of personal honour and casual generosity (as witness his payment of salary and emotional gift of a valuable ring to d'Artagnan), but he does not come alive, as Colbert does, and his love affairs seem far-fetched and puzzling. As Stevenson commented, Dumas shows a tendency to enlist the reader's sympathy for the volatile quixotic superintendent rather than the strict-minded competent intendant of finance, probably because 'Dumas saw something of himself there, and drew the figure more tenderly' — always a pitfall for a novelist who should remain purely objective. It is never made clear to us what Fouquet's objectives really are, and why Aramis should hitch his wagon of ambition to such a star. What did

---

[*] A knowledge in part accounted for by his earlier purely historical study *Louis XIV et Son Siècle* (1844–45)

Fouquet aim to become by his conspiracies? Was it merely jealousy — a refusal to tolerate any other sun but himself in his realm which made Louis XIV have Fouquet arrested and thrown into prison for the rest of his life?

Hurrying over these chapters, then, we return thankfully to d'Artagnan and his Belle-Ile expedition. The chapter 'Philosophy of the heart and mind' shows us the Musketeer not only leaving Planchet's and setting out on the journey which was to end so momentously for himself and others, but trying to sum up for himself the political and moral perspective *vis-à-vis* the superintendent and intendant, with both of whom he had just had characteristic interviews.

> He had done right in not thinking over, the evening before, all the political and diplomatic affairs which solicited his attention; for in the morning, in the freshness of the mild twilight, his ideas developed themselves with clearness and fluency.
>
> 'Now,' said he to himself, 'let us inhale freely the morning air; let us invite freedom from care, and abundant health; let us allow my horse Zephyr, whose flanks swell as if he had to snuff in a hemisphere, to breathe; and let us be very ingenious in our little calculations. It is time,' pursued d'Artagnan, 'to form a plan of the campaign, and draw a portrait of the generals to whom we are to be opposed. What is M. Fouquet? M. Fouquet,' replied d'Artagnan to himself, 'is a handsome man, very much beloved by the women; a generous man, very much beloved by the poets; a man of wit, much execrated by the polloi. Not being woman, nor polloi, I neither love nor hate Monsieur the Superintendent. Now, what does the king wish? That does not concern me. Now, what does M. Colbert wish? Oh, that's another thing. M. Colbert wishes all that M. Fouquet does not wish. Then what does M. Fouquet wish? Oh, that is serious! M. Fouquet wishes precisely all that the king wishes.'
>
> This monologue ended, d'Artagnan began to laugh, while making his whip whistle in the air. He was already on the highroad, frightening the birds in the hedges, listening to the louis dancing in his leather pocket at every step.
>
> 'Come,' said he, 'the expedition is not a very dangerous one; and it will fall out with my voyage as with that play M. Monk took me to see in London, which was called, I think, "Much Ado about Nothing".'

* * *

The next chapter, 'The Journey', is prefaced by — a rare interpolation in Dumas — a psychological interpretation of the character of his hero in the form of a monologue on that character's part endeavouring to assess his attitude to the complex situation wherein he finds himself placed — a method adopted by Dumas in preference to the more common one of novelists and perforce all playwrights. But then Dumas was a playwright long before he became a novelist.

> It was perhaps the fiftieth time since the day on which we opened this history, that this man, with a heart of bronze and muscles of steel, had left house and friends — everything, in short — to go in search of fortune and death. The one — that is to say, Death — had constantly retreated before him, as if afraid of him; the other — that is to say, Fortune — only for a month past had really made an alliance with him. Although he was not a great philosopher. after the fashion of either Epicurus

or Socrates, his was a powerful mind, having knowledge of life and endowed with thought. No one is as brave, as adventurous, or as skilful as d'Artagnan, without being at the same time inclined to be a dreamer. He had picked up here and there some scraps of M. de la Rochefoucauld, worthy of being translated into Latin by the gentlemen of Port Royal; and he had made a collection, while passing the time in the society of Athos and Aramis, of many morsels of Seneca and Cicero, translated by them and applied to the uses of common life. That contempt of riches which our Gascon had observed as an article of faith during the first thirty-five years of his life had for a long time been considered by him as the first article of the code of bravery. 'Article first,' said he: 'A man is brave because he has nothing; a man has nothing because he despises riches.' Therefore, with these principles, which, as we have said, he had regulated the first thirty-five years of his life, d'Artagnan was no sooner possessed of riches than he felt it necessary to ask himself if in spite of his riches he were still brave. To this, for any other than d'Artagnan, the episode of the Place de Grève might have served as an answer. Many consciences would have been satisfied with it, but d'Artagnan was unflinching enough to ask himself sincerely and conscientiously if he were brave. Therefore to his, 'But it appears to me that I drew promptly enough and cut and thrust shrewdly enough on the Place de Grève to be satisfied of my bravery,' d'Artagnan had himself replied:-

'Gently, Captain; that is not an answer. I was brave that day because they were burning my house; and there are a hundred, and even a thousand, odds against one, that if those gentlemen of the riots had not formed that unlucky idea, their plan of attack would have succeeded, or at least it would not have been I who opposed myself to it. Now, what will be brought against me? I have no house to be burned in Bretagne; I have no treasure there that can be taken from me. No; but I have my skin, — that precious skin of M. d'Artagnan, which to him is worth more than all the houses and all the treasures of the world; that skin to which I cling above everything, because it is, everything considered, the binding of a body which encloses a heart very warm and very well satisfied to beat and consequently to live. Then, I do desire to live; and in reality I live much better, more completely since I have become rich. Who the devil ever said that money spoiled life? Upon my soul, it does no such thing; on the contrary, it seems as if I absorb a double quantity of air and sunlight. *Mordioux!* what will it be, then, if I double that fortune, and if instead of the switch I now hold in my hand I should ever carry the baton of a marshal? Then I really don't know if there will be enough air and sunlight for me. In fact, this is not a dream; who the devil would oppose it if the king made me a duke and a marshal, as his father, King Louis XIII, made a duke and constable of Albert de Luynes? Am I not as brave as that imbecile de Vitry, and much more intelligent? Ah! that's exactly what will prevent my advancement; I have too much wit. Luckily, if there is any justice in this world, Fortune owes me many compensations. She owes me, certainly, a recompense for all I did for Anne of Austria, and an indemnification for all she has not done for me. Then at the present I am very well with a king, and with a king who has the appearance of determining to reign. May God keep him in that illustrious road! For if he is resolved to reign, he will want me; and if he wants me, he will give me what he has promised me, — warmth and light; so that I march, comparatively, today, as I marched formerly — from nothing to everything. Only, the nothing of today is the all of former days; there has only this little change taken place in my life. And now let us see! let us take into consideration the heart, as I just now was speaking of it. But, in truth, I only spoke of it from memory;' and the Gascon applied his hand to his breast, as if he were actually seeking the place where his heart was.

'Ah, wretch!' he murmured, smiling with bitterness. 'You hoped for an instant that you had not a heart, and now you find you have one — bad courtier as you are — and even one of the most seditious. You have a heart which speaks to you in favour of M. Fouquet. And what is M. Fouquet when the king is in question? A conspirator, a real conspirator, who does not even give himself the trouble to conceal his being a conspirator; therefore, what a weapon would you not have against him if his good grace and his intelligence had not made a scabbard for that weapon! An armed revolt! — for, in fact, M. Fouquet has been guilty of an armed revolt. Thus, while the king vaguely suspects M. Fouquet of rebellion, I know it, — I could prove that M. Fouquet had caused the shedding of the blood of His Majesty's subjects. Now, then, let us see! Knowing all that, and holding my tongue, what further would this pitiful heart wish in return for a kind action of M. Fouquet's, for an advance of fifteen thousand livres, for a diamond worth a thousand pistoles, for a smile in which there was as much bitterness as kindness? — I save his life.

'Now, I hope.' continued the Musketeer, 'that this imbecile of a heart is going to preserve silence, and so be fairly quits with M. Fouquet. Now that the king has become my sun, let him beware who places himself between me and my sun! Forward, for His Majesty Louis XIV! Forward!'

After a couple of days delay he is landed by a fisherman's boat on the shore of Belle-Ile after learning from innocent conversations with various ordinary inhabitants that their seigneur Fouquet, souzerain of the island, was their revered overlord, even before the king, and from the fisherman who disembarked with him that ' "there are seventeen hundred men in Belle-Ile, Monsieur," ' and (added proudly) ' "Do you know that the smallest garrison has twenty companies of infantry."

"*Mordieux!*" cried d'Artagnan to himself, stamping with his foot; "His Majesty was right enough!" ' But why Fouquet was fortifying and arming his island we never really learn, unless we accept his own apologetic confession to the king (quoted later) at its face value.

Then, as d'Artagnan slowly advanced inland, came the great surprise. He observed a group of workmen trying to lift a stone slab and to slip a roller under it. 'A giant of a man wearing a hat covered with plumes and gesticulating in the most majestic manner, and who seemed to be the engineer in charge' was urging the men on, but without success.

'Come now!' said he, 'what is all this about? Have I to do with men of straw? *Corboeuf*! stand on one side, and you shall see how this is to be done.'

'Peste!' said d'Artagnan, 'will he try to raise that rock? That would be a sight worth looking at.'

The workmen, as commanded by the engineer, drew back crestfallen and shaking their heads, with the exception of the one who held the joist and who prepared to perform his office. The man with the plumes went up to the stone, stooped, slipped his hands under the face lying upon the ground, stiffened his Herculean muscles, and without a jerk, but with a slow motion like that of a machine, lifted the end of the rock a foot from the ground. The workman who held the joist profited by the space thus given him, and slipped the roller under the stone.

'There, that's it!' said the giant, not letting the rock fall again, but placing it upon its support.

'*Mordioux!*' cried d'Artagnan, 'I know but one man capable of such a feat!'

'Hey!' said the colossus, turning round.

'Porthos!' murmured d'Artagnan, seized with amazement; 'Porthos at Belle-Ile!'

On his part, the man with the plumes fixed his eyes upon the pretended steward, and, in spite of his disguise, recognized him. 'D'Artagnan!' he exclaimed; and the colour mounted to his face. 'Hush!' he said to d'Artagnan.

'Hush!' in his turn said the Musketeer.

In fact, if Porthos had just been discovered by d'Artagnan, d'Artagnan had just been discovered by Porthos. Their share in each other's particular secret struck them both at the same time. Nevertheless, the first move of the two men was to throw their arms round each other. What they wished to conceal from the bystanders was not their friendship, but their names. But after the embrace came reflection.

'Why the devil is Porthos at Belle-Ile lifting stones?' said d'Artagnan; only, d'Artagnan uttered that question to himself in a low voice.

Less strong in diplomacy than his friend, Porthos thought aloud. 'How the devil did you come to Belle-Ile?' he asked of d'Artagnan, 'and what do you come to do here?'

It was necessary to reply without hesitation. To hesitate in his answer to Porthos would have been a check for which d'Artagnan self-love could never have consoled itself. '*Pardieu! mon ami*, I am at Belle-Ile because you are here.'

By crafty circumlocution d'Artagnan managed to convince Porthos that he had traced him via Bazin, and learned from him that Aramis was in residence as Bishop of Vannes, and didn't mean to stop there in his climb upwards for social position and influence. To which the Musketeer, half jesting, replied

'What! do you think he will not be contented with violet stockings and a red hat?'

'Hush! That is promised him.'

'Bah! By the king?'

'By somebody more powerful than the king.'

'Oh, the devil! Porthos, what incredible things you tell me, *mon ami*!'

'Why incredible? Is there not always somebody in France more powerful than the king?'

'Oh, yes! in the time of King Louis XIII it was the Duc de Richelieu; in the time of the regency it was Cardinal Mazarin; in the time of Louis XIV; it is M. —'

'Go on.'

'It is M. Fouquet.'

'You've hit it first time.'

'So it is M. Fouquet who has promised Aramis the hat?'

Porthos assumed an air of reserve. '*Cher ami*,' said he, 'heaven preserve me from meddling with the affairs of others, above all from revealing secrets it may be to their interests to keep. When you see Aramis, he will tell you what he thinks fit to tell you.'

'You are right, Porthos; and you are a vertable padlock for safety.'

By such light-hearted dialogue Dumas gives the reader hints in advance of the power of Fouquet and the ambitions of Aramis.

Changing the subject, d'Artagnan then congratulated the unsuspecting Porthos on the efficacy of the fortifications being engineered, using all the most modern methods and designs. In return Porthos, swelling with pride, showed his friend a large plan giving detailed instructions as to the fortifications, all written in Porthos's 'formidable writing'.

> But however short the time he had the plan in his hands, d'Artagnan had been able to distinguish, under the enormous writing of Porthos, a much more delicate hand, which reminded him of certain letters to Marie Michon,* with which he had been acquainted in his youth. Only, the India-rubber had passed and repassed over this writing, so that it might have escaped a less practised eye than that of our Musketeer.
>
> 'Bravo! my friend, bravo!' said d'Artagnan.

Finally Porthos took d'Artagnan to Vannes to meet with Aramis. But in the town the Musketeer's hope of taking the other by surprise was frustrated by the occurrence of a religious procession. As they stood by, held up and impatiently watching.

> a magnificent dais approached, preceded by a hundred Jesuits and a hundred Dominicans, and escorted by two archdeacons, a treasurer, a penitentiary, and twelve canons. Under the dais appeared a pale and noble countenance, with black eyes, black hair streaked with threads of silver, a delicate, compressed mouth, a prominent and angular chin. This head, full of graceful majesty, was covered with the episcopal mitre — a head-dress which gave it, in addition to the character of sovereignty, that of asceticism and evangelic meditation.
>
> 'Aramis!' cried the Musketeer involuntarily, as this lofty countenance passed before him.
>
> The prelate started at the sound of the voice. He raised his large black eyes with their long lashes, and turned them without hesitation towards the spot whence the exclamation proceeded. At a glance he saw Porthos and d'Artagnan close to him. On his part, d'Artagnan, thanks to the keenness of his sight, had seen all, grasped all. The full portrait of the prelate had entered his memory, never to leave it. One thing had particularly struck d'Artagnan. On perceiving him, Aramis had coloured; then he had concentrated under his eyelids the fiery look of the master and the affectionate look of the friend. It was evident that Aramis addressed this question to himself: 'Why is d'Artagnan there with Porthos, and what does he want at Vannes?' Aramis comprehended all that was passing in the mind of d'Artagnan, on turning his look upon him again, and seeing that he had not lowered his eyes. He knew the acuteness and intelligence of his friend; he feared to let him divine the secret of his blush and his astonishment. He was still the same Aramis, always having a secret to conceal. Therefore, to put an end to this searching examination, which it was necessary to get rid of at all events, as at any price a general silences

---

* v. *The Three Musketeers*.

the fire of a battery which annoys him, Aramis stretched forth his fine white hand, upon which sparkled the amethyst of the pastoral ring, cut the air with the sign of the cross, and poured out his benediction upon his two friends. Perhaps, thoughtful and absent, d'Artagnan, impious in spite of himself, might not have bent beneath this holy benediction; but Porthos saw his distraction, and laying his friendly hand upon the back of his companion, crushed him down towards the earth. D'Artagnan was forced to give way; indeed, he was little short of being flat on the ground. In the meantime Aramis had passed. D'Artagnan, like Antaeus, had only touched the ground, and he turned towards Porthos, quite ready to quarrel with him. But there was no mistaking the intention of the honest Hercules; it was a feeling of religious propriety that had influenced him. Besides, speech with Porthos, instead of disguising his thought, always revealed it.

'It is very kind of him,' said he, 'to have given his benediction to us alone. Decidedly, he is a holy man and a brave one.'

Less convinced than Porthos, d'Artagnan made no reply.

'Observe, my friend,' continued Porthos, 'he has seen us; and instead of continuing to walk on at the simple pace of the procession, as he did just now, — see what a hurry he is in! Do you see how the cortege is increasing its speed? He is eager to come to us and to embrace us, is that dear Aramis!'

'That is true,' replied d'Artagnan, aloud. Then to himself: 'It is equally true that he has seen me, the fox, and will have time to prepare himself to receive me.'

* * *

Their meeting at last in the bishop's palatial residence (the first time three of the Four are together) is genuinely warm enough, but their dialogue, each having a secret to conceal, becomes a skirmish of thrusts and feints. The Musketeer grows more and more suspicious of the other's protestations of ignorance concerning the outside world and its ways, of the rivalry between Fouquet and Colbert, and of taking any interest in current politics; and in his turn Aramis is secretly dubious about his friend's seeming break with the king and service, and his proposed intention of buying some salt mines in the district and becoming a neighbour.

So that, after supping and chatting until one o'clock in the morning, then showing d'Artagnan to his splendid room, waiting until he saw his light put out, Aramis tiptoed to Porthos's room, woke him, and told him he must dress, get on horseback and ride like the devil to Fouquet in Paris with a letter, explaining that it is a matter of life or death, and that his (Porthos's) prospects of becoming ' "a duke and peer" ' depended on it. Thus next morning d'Artagnan found his friend missing, and on enquiring from Aramis was fobbed off with vague suggestions that he might have gone fishing or shooting somewhere on the island. After a day spent vainly looking for him d'Artagnan, more and more suspicious, returned, only to be confronted by the bishop's *valet de chambre*, who smirkingly presented him with a note from His Greatness informing him that he would be away for some days on an affair of the most urgent nature in a distant parish.

'*Mordioux!*' cried d'Artagnan, 'I am tricked! Ah! blockhead, brute, triple fool that I am! But let them laugh best who laugh last. Oh, duped, like a monkey cheated with an empty nutshell!' And with a hearty blow bestowed upon the nose of the still grinning *valet de chambre*, he made all haste out of the episcopal palace. Furet, however good a trotter, was not equal to present circumstances. D'Artagnan therefore took the post, and chose a horse which he made to understand, with good spurs and a light hand, that stags are not the most agile coursers in creation.

The climax to all this is narrated in the next three chapters. In the first of these, headed 'In which d'Artagnan makes all speed, Porthos snores, and Aramis counsels', and wherein we move to Fouquet's residence at St Mandé, we find its owner surprised by the unexpected arrival of Aramis in 'a carriage drawn by four horses streaming with sweat and entering the court at full gallop' — an Aramis bruised and battered and exhausted, who tells the superintendent that he has followed his letter via Porthos with all possible speed to warn him of impending disaster. He questions Fouquet as to d'Artagnan's part in the execution of his two financier friends, learns that the Musketeer had come to him for his salary payment authorized by the king.

'Signed by His Majesty.'
'There, then! Well, d'Artagnan has been to Belle-Ile; he was disguised passing himself for some sort of a steward charged by his master to purchase salt mines. Now, d'Artagnan has no other master than the king.'
'And you think that the king sent him there?' said Fouquet thoughtfully.
'I am certain.'
'And d'Artagnan, in the hands of the king, is a dangerous instrument?'
'The most dangerous imaginable.'
'Then I formed a correct opinion of him at the first glance.'
'How so?'
'I wished to attach him to myself.'
'If you judged him to be the bravest, the most acute, and the most adroit man in France, you have judged correctly.'
'He must be ours, then, at any price.'
'D'Artagnan?'
'Is not that your opinion?'
'It may be my opinion, but you will never have him.'
'Why?'
'Because we have allowed the time to go by. He was dissatisfied with the court; we should have profited by that. Since that, he has been over to England; there he powerfully assisted in the restoration, and gained a fortune; since then he has returned to the service of the king. Well, the reason of his return to the service of the king is that he has been well paid for the service.'
'We will pay him still better, that is all.'
'Oh, Monsieur, excuse me; d'Artagnan has a high sense of his word, and where that word is once engaged, it remains inviolable.'
'What do you conclude, then?' said Fouquet, with great uneasiness.
'That for the present the principal thing is to parry a dangerous blow.'

'And how is it to be parried?'
'Go to the Louvre, and see the king before he sees d'Artagnan.'
'What shall I say to the king?'
'Nothing; give him Belle-Ile.'
'Oh, M. d'Herblay! M. d'Herblay!' cried Fouquet, 'What projects crushed all at once!'
'After one project has failed, there is always another which may lead to good; we should never despair. Go, Monsieur, and go quickly.'
'But that garrison, so carefully chosen, the king will change it directly.'
'That garrison, Monsieur was the king's when it entered Belle-Ile; it is yours today. It will be the same with all garrisons after a fortnight's occupation. Let things go on, Monsieur. Do you see any inconvenience in having an army at the end of a year instead of one or two regiments? Do you not see that your garrison of today will make you partisans at La Rochelle, Nantes, Bordeaux, Toulouse, — everywhere they may be placed? Go to the king, Monsieur; go! Time flies; and d'Artagnan, while we are losing our time, is flying like an arrow along the highroad.'

On his hurried arrival at the Louvre Fouquet finds his enemy Colbert in conference with the king. Following the attempted coup to save the two finance ministers from the execution, Louis had been questioning the intendant as to his opinion on Fouquet and his purposes. The latter's reply sums it all up, and I quote for the reason that his answer brings us the nearest we ever get to the truth.

'I think, Sire, that M. Fouquet, not satisfied with keeping all the money for himself, as M. de Mazarin did, and by that means depriving Your Majesty of a part of your power, still wishes to attract to himself all the friends of easy life and pleasures — of what idlers call poetry, and politicians corruption. I think that, by holding the subjects of Your Majesty in pay, he trespasses upon the royal prerogative, and cannot, if this continues so, be long in relegating Your Majesty among the weak and obscure.'
'How would you designate all these projects, M. Colbert?'
'The projects of M. Fouquet, Sire?'
'Yes.'
'They are called crimes of high treason.'
'And what is done to criminals guilty of high treason?'
'They are arrested, tried, and punished.'
'You are quite sure that M. Fouquet has conceived the idea of the crime you impute to him?'
'I can say more, Sire.'
'And what is that?'
'I have just learned that M. Fouquet is fortifying Belle-Ile-en-Mer.'
'Ah, indeed!'
'Yes, Sire.'
'Are you sure?'
'Perfectly. Do you know, Sire, what soldiers there are at Belle-Ile?'
'No, upon my word. Do you?'
'I am ignorant likewise, Sire; I should therefore propose to Your Majesty to send somebody to Belle-Ile.'
'Who?'

'Me, for instance.'

'And what would you do at Belle-Ile?'

'Inform myself whether it is true that, after the example of the ancient feudal lords, M. Fouquet is fortifying his walls.'

'And with what purpose would he do that?'

'With the purpose of defending himself some day against his king.'

'But if it be thus, M. Colbert,' said Louis, 'we must immediately do as you say; M. Fouquet must be arrested.'

'That is impossible.'

'I thought I had already told you, Monsieur, that I suppressed that word in my service.'

'The service of Your Majesty cannot prevent M. Fouquet from being superintendent-general.'

'Well?'

'And in consequence of holding that post he has for him all the Parliament, as he has all the army, by his largess, all literature by his favours, and all the nobility by his presents.'

'That is to say, then, that I can do nothing against M. Fouquet?'

'Absolutely nothing — at least at present, Sire.'

'Come, then, where shall we begin to undermine this colossus? Let us see;' and His Majesty began to laugh with bitterness.

'He has grown great by money; kill him by money, Sire.'

'If I were to deprive him of his position?'

'A bad means, Sire.'

'The good — the good, then?'

'Ruin him, Sire, I tell you.'

'But how?'

'Occasions will not be wanting; take advantage of all occasions.'

'Point them out to me.'

'Here is one, first of all. His Royal Highness Monsieur is about to be married; his nuptials must be magnificent. That is a good occasion for Your Majesty to demand a million of M. Fouquet. M. Fouquet, who pays twenty thousand livres down when he need not pay more than five thousand, will easily find that million whenever Your Majesty shall demand it.'

'Very well; I will demand it,' said Louis.

'If Your Majesty will sign the order, I will have the money drawn myself,' and Colbert pushed a paper before the king, and handed him a pen.

They were precisely at this point when Fouquet was announced by an usher and entered with a roll of papers under his arm. Carrying out Aramis's advice he showed Louis a plan of the fortifications at Belle-Ile, explaining that he was fortifying the island against possible attacks by the English or the Dutch.

> Louis began to waver, undermined between the hatred which this so powerful man inspired him with, and the pity he felt for that other man, so cast down, who seemed to him the counterfeit of the former. But the consciousness of his kingly duty prevailed over the feelings of the man, and he stretched out his finger to the paper.
>
> 'It must have cost you a great deal of money to carry these plans into execution,' said he.

'I believe I had the honour of telling Your Majesty the amount?'
'Repeat it, if you please; I have forgotten it.'
'Sixteen hundred thousand livres.'
'Sixteen hundred thousand livres? You are enormously rich, Monsieur.'
'It is Your Majesty who is rich, since Belle-Ile is yours.'
'Yes, thank you; but however rich I may be, M. Fouquet — ' The king stopped.
'Well, Sire?' asked the superintendent.
'I foresee the moment when I shall want money.'
'You, Sire? And at what moment, then?'
'Tomorrow, for example.'
'Will Your Majesty do me the honour to explain yourself?'
'My brother is going to marry the Princess of England.'
'Well, Sire?'
'Well, I ought to give the young princess a reception worthy of the granddaughter of Henry IV.'
'That is but just, Sire.'
'Then I shall want money.'
'No doubt.'
'I shall want — ' Louis hesitated. The sum that he was going to demand was the same that he had been obliged to refuse Charles II. He turned towards Colbert, that he might give the blow.
'I shall want, tomorrow — ' he repeated, looking at Colbert.
'A million,' said the latter bluntly, delighted to take his revenge.
Fouquet turned his back on the intendant to listen to the king. He did not turn round at all, but waited till the king repeated, or rather murmured, 'A million.'
'Oh, Sire,' replied Fouquet disdainfully, 'a million! What will Your Majesty do with a million?'
'It appears to me, nevertheless — ' said Louis.
'That is not more than is spent at the nuptials of one of the most petty princes of Germany. Your Majesty must have two millions at least. The horses alone will run away with five hundred thousand livres. I shall have the honour of sending Your Majesty sixteen hundred thousand livres this evening.'
With these words, bowing respectfully to the king, the superintendent made his exit backward.
Fouquet had not passed the door of the cabinet when an usher, passing by him, called out, 'A courier from Bretagne for His Majesty.'
'M. d'Herblay was right,' murmured Fouquet, pulling out his watch; 'an hour and fifty-five minutes. I was only just in time.'

Fouquet left the king's presence in an apparent triumph over Colbert, but aware that the battle of attrition had begun.

As he passed the superintendent, d'Artagnan, recalling his kind first reception of him, 'in the goodness of his heart' felt an urge to warn him of his perilous position; but realizing that to do so here and now 'would have only been to betray his cause and ruin himself gratuitously without saving anybody, instead contented himself with bowing courteously'.

At that moment the king was fluctuating between the joy the last words of Fouquet had given him and his pleasure at the return of d'Artagnan as the

Musketeer, his clothes dusty, his face inflamed, his hair dripping with sweat, his legs stiff, his spurs bloody, made his entry.

'I love to see one of my servants in this disorder,' said the king, admiring the martial stains upon the clothes of his envoy.

'I thought, Sire, my presence at the Louvre was sufficiently urgent to excuse my coming before you like this.'

'You bring me great news, then, Monsieur?' asked the king, smiling.

'Sire, the thing is this, in two words: Belle-Ile is fortified, admirably fortified. Belle-Isle has a double *enceinte*, a citadel, two detached forts; its port contains three corsairs, and the side batteries only wait for their cannon.'

'I know all that, Monsieur,' replied the king.

'What! Your Majesty knows all that?' replied the Musketeer, stupefied.

'I have the plan of the fortifications of Belle-Ile,' said the king.

'Your Majesty has the plan?'

'Here it is.'

'It is really it, Sire; and I saw a similar one on the spot.' D'Artagnan's brow became clouded. 'Ah! I understand. Your Majesty has not trusted to me alone, but has sent some other person,' said he in a reproachful tone.

'Of what importance is the manner, Monsieur, in which I have learned what I know, so that I know it?'

'Be it so, Sire,' replied the Musketeer without seeking even to conceal his dissatisfaction; 'but I must be permitted to say to Your Majesty that it is not worth while to make me use such speed, to risk twenty times breaking my neck, if you are to salute me with such intelligence on my arrival. Sire, when people are not trusted or are deemed insufficient, they should not be employed;' and d'Artagnan, with a movement quite military, stamped with his foot, leaving upon the floor dust stained with blood.

The king looked at him, inwardly enjoying his first triumph. 'Monsieur,' said he at the expiration of a minute, 'not only is Belle-Ile known to me, but still further, Belle-Ile belongs to me.'

'That is well, that is well, Sire! I ask no more,' replied d'Artagnan. 'My discharge!'

'What! your discharge?'

'Certainly! I am too proud to eat the bread of the king without gaining it, or rather by gaining it badly. My discharge, Sire!'

'Oh, oh!'

'My discharge, or I shall take it.'

'You are angry, Monsieur?'

'I have reason, *mordioux*! I am thirty-two hours in the saddle, I ride night and day, I perform prodigies of speed, I arrive stiff as a corpse, and another arrives before me! I am a fool! My discharge, Sire!'

'M. d'Artagnan,' said Louis, resting his white hand upon the dusty arm of the Musketeer, 'what I have just told you will not at all affect what I promised you. A promise given must be fulfilled;' and the young king, going to his table, opened a drawer and took out a folded paper. 'Here is your commission of Captain of Musketeers; you have won it, M. d'Artagnan.'

* * *

I have quoted the above episodes generously, partly to let the reader enjoy their savour, but also to compensate for the dearth of the same over the next dozen chapters. These, relating long-windedly 'the petty interest of the court' (the phrase is Dumas's own), the doings and misdoings of MM. Malicorne and Manicamp, the appointments of Montalais and La Vallière as the Princess Henrietta's maids of honour, the affairs of de Wardes, the arrival of that princess at Havre, the quarrels between the English and French participants and of de Wardes and Raoul, the mad passion of Buckingham for the princess displayed in an exaggerated and un-English-like way,* the beginning of de Guiche's love for her — all this tends to make the English reader at least impatient and feel some sympathy with Mr Polly.

Nevertheless, they contain fragments for the future, events casting shadows before. Two of the most important incidents exemplifying this are (1) the hatred towards Raoul professed openly by the vindictive de Wardes and for the newly appointed Captain of Musketeers on account of his long-ago affair with his father* — a hatred overspilled on to Raoul, and which leads to the later 'lesson' meted to de Wardes by d'Artagnan. (2) During the celebrations at the French court in honour of the wedding of the royal couple, seen as a gesture of peace and goodwill between England and France, Raoul unexpectedly meets Louise and Montalais, and finds to his distaste that they are now maids of honour, thanks to the efforts of MM. Malicorne and Manicamp, and expresses his wonder at discovering the fact only now after having written four letters to Louise, all unanswered. The 'giddy' but perceptive Montalais explains how she had intercepted the letters to prevent them falling into the hands of Louise's antagonistic mother, and in reply to her friend's ' "Did you not inform M. Raoul, as I begged you to do?" ' replied tartly ' "Why should I? — to give him an opportunity of making some of his severe remarks and moral reflections, and undo what we had so much trouble in obtaining? Oh, certainly not!" ' Montalais had Louise's lover taped! Clearly his creator here confesses to his creation's character. But then, after answering Montalais's criticism of him with the query ' "Am I so severe, then?" ', the vicomte for once comes to life by taking Louise aside and pouring his heart out to her, in his love for her blind to her hesitancies and protestations which to anyone but a lover would reveal her true feelings. The climax comes when in answer to his demand ' "Without falsehood or subterfuge, Louise, am I to believe Montalais's words? Did you come to Paris because I was no longer at Blois?" ' For her only answer the girl 'blushed and hid her face in her hands'. He takes that for confession, offers her marriage and tells her he will get his father's consent. And the scene ends subtly and equivocally:

* Son of the Buckingham of *The Three Musketeers*, assassinated by Felton and legendary lover of Anne of Austria. Described by one historian as 'the wildest and wickedest of all the Restoration roués', and as the 'Zimri' of Dryden's *Absalom and Achitophel*, perhaps Dumas's portrayal is not so exaggerated after all.
** This of course is a reference to d'Artagnan's affair with Milady and his duel with her lover de Wardes, father of the present so-named, found in *The Three Musketeers*.

'Oh, M. Raoul, reflect, wait!'

'Wait? Impossible! Reflect, where you are concerned, Louise? It would be an insult to you. Give me your hand, dear Louise. I am my own master. My father will give his consent, I know. Give me one word in answer — just one word. If you can't, I shall begin to think that to change you from me nothing more was needed than a single breath of favour, a smile from the queen, a single look from the king.'

Raoul had no sooner pronounced the last word than Louise became pale as death. With a movement as rapid as thought she placed both her hands in those of Raoul, then fled without a word, without casting a look behind her. Raoul felt his whole frame tremble at the touch of her hands, and received her gesture as a solemn promise wrung by love from the modesty of innocence.

* * *

In the meantime and elsewhere passions are running high. The princess's marriage to Monsieur, as the king's younger brother was termed, has made no difference either to her own conduct or that of her two would-be lovers, Buckingham and de Guiche; so much so that her husband began to complain, choosing as his comforter his mother, Anne of Austria. Writing in the 19th century, even the French (let alone the British) dare not overtly describe a character as homosexual, but there can be little doubt that Philippe d'Orléans was a 'gay', to use the current word, and his 'favourite' the Chevalier de Lorraine, who treats him contumaciously as an equal or less, his 'lover'. Dumas's revealing him as 'rougeing his face' and continually 'looking at himself and in the mirror like a woman', and later, during the Fontainebleau fête, 'dressing himself as a woman, which he delighted to do', enforce the supposition. And the fact that he chooses his mother as his confidante underlines it. In Dumas's own words —

> the queen-mother was extremely attached to her son, for he was handsome and amiable, and more affectionate, more effeminate than the king.

The *effeminate* is significant.

The outcome of his complaint to his mother is that she tells him she will deal with the duke in her own way. Her way, in a private interview with him, is by recalling her own love for his father (according to history-cum-legend) touchingly related in the chapter 'Forever!' Talking to him like a mother to a recalcitrant son, she tenderly upbraids him for his thoughtless passion which is endangering French-English relationship, and appeals to him to resist it, to forgo his intention to stay in France, and to return to his own country and king. He finally yields to her entreaties, but only after a fleeting reference to his father.

> 'Silence!' said the queen, kissing the duke upon the forehead with an affection which she could not restrain. 'Go, go! spare me, and forget yourself no longer. I am the queen. You are the subject of the King of England; King Charles awaits your return. *Adieu*, Villiers, — farewell!'

'Forever!' replied the young man; and he fled, endeavouring to master his emotion.

Anne leaned her head upon her hands, and then looking at herself in the glass, murmured, 'It has been truly said that a woman is always young, and that the age of twenty years always lies concealed in some secret corner of her heart.'

The episode ends, as its chapter heading proclaims, with a superb example of dramatic irony: viz 'King Louis XIV does not think Mademoiselle de la Vallière rich enough or beautiful enough for a gentleman of the rank of the Vicomte de Bragelonne.' Following Raoul's insistence on his love for Louise, and moved by his obvious unhappiness, Athos reluctantly gives way, and, since 'belonging to the king' his permission to marry is needed, tells him he will go to Paris and beseech the king himself.

The interview is yet another example of dramatic irony, prefiguring what is to come. Louis, after listening to Athos and considering all the pros and cons, remarks:

'The young lady does not seem to me to be very pretty, Count. I have seen her, but she did not strike me as being so.'
'She seems to be a sweet and modest girl, but has little beauty, Sire.'
'Beautiful fair hair, however?'
'I think so.'
'And quite beautiful blue eyes?'
'Yes, Sire.'
'With regard to beauty, then, the match is but an ordinary one. Now for the money side of the question.'

But then, sensing that Athos himself is not partial to the match, and getting that confession from him, Louis asks him why he does not refuse his consent. Athos quotes his son's unhappiness, in reply to which the king says "Tell me, Count, is she in love with him?" Athos replies that he does not think so, and that he believes that "her appointment as maid of honour and delight at being at court counteract in her head whatever affection she may have in her heart". And the interview ends by Louis refusing his consent — for the time being.

* * *

As if to make amends for the prolix narration of (to quote again) 'the petty interests of the court', we are given yet another highlight, viz. d'Artagnan's 'lesson' to De Wardes. At a royal levee at the Palais Royal d'Artagnan, making his 'victorious entry in his new uniform of Captain of the King's Musketeers', after exchanging a few good-humoured words with Fouquet about Belle-Ile and his visit there, seeks out de Wardes, who has just annoyed Raoul by a characteristic jeer at Buckingham's expressed decision to leave for England. Placing a hand on the young man's shoulder, he invites him to go with him to his apartments as he has something to say to him. They go, the captain deliberately collecting several witnesses on the way.

Athos was already there, and behind d'Artagnan came de Wardes, Manicamp, de Guiche, Raoul and Buckingham. D'Artagnan opens the scene by telling de Wardes he has come to hear of the injurious reports he has been spreading about him, and requests him to explain to the company his reasons. Taken aback, and at first protesting, de Wardes finally comes out with:

'Listen, then! My father loved a woman of noble birth, and this woman loved my father.' D'Artagnan and Athos exchanged looks. De Wardes continued: 'M. d'Artagnan intercepted some letters which indicated an assignation, substituted himself under a disguise for the person who was expected, and took advantage of the darkness.'

'That is true,' said d'Artagnan.

A slight murmur was heard from those present. 'Yes, I was guilty of that dishonourable action. You should have added, Monsieur, since you are so impartial, that at the period when the circumstance with which you reproach me happened, I was not one-and-twenty years of age.'

'The action is not the less shameful on that account,' said de Wardes; 'and it is quite sufficient for a gentleman to have attained the age of reason, to avoid committing such an act of indelicacy.'

A renewed murmur was heard, but this time of astonishment and almost of doubt.

'It was a most shameful deception, I admit,' said d'Artagnan, 'and I have not waited for M. de Wardes's accusations to reproach myself for it, and very bitterly too. Age has made me more reasonable, and above all less headstrong, and this injury has been atoned for by lasting regret. But I appeal to you, gentlemen; this affair took place in 1626, at a period happily for yourselves known to you by tradition only at a period when love was not over-scrupulous, when consciences did not distil, as in the present day, poison and bitterness. We were young soldiers, always fighting or being attacked, our swords always out of the scabbard or at least half drawn. Death then always stared us in the face, war hardened us, and the cardinal pressed us sorely. In short, I have repented of it; and more than that, — I still repent it, M. de Wardes.'

'I can well understand that, Monsieur, for the action itself needed repentance; but you were not the less the cause of that lady's disgrace. She of whom you have been speaking, covered with shame, borne down by the affront she had received, fled, quitted France, and no one ever knew what became of her.'

'Stay!' said the Comte de la Fère, stretching his hand towards de Wardes with a sinister smile; 'you are mistaken. She was seen; and there are persons even now present who, having often heard her spoken of, will easily recognize her by the description I am about to give. She was about five-and-twenty years of age, slender in form, of a pale complexion, and fair-haired; she was married in England.'

'Married!' exclaimed de Wardes.

'So you were not aware that she was married? You see we are far better informed than yourself, M. de Wardes. Do you happen to know that she was usually styled "Milady", without the addition of any name to that title?'

'Yes, I know that.'

'Good heavens!' murmured Buckingham.

'Very well, Monsieur. That woman, who came from England, returned to England after having thrice attempted M. d'Artagnan's life. That was but just, you will say, since M. d'Artagnan had insulted her. But that which was not just was that this woman, when in England, by her seductions completely enslaved a young man in the service of Lord Winter by the name of Felton. You change colour, my Lord Buckingham, and your eyes kindle with anger and sorrow. Let Your Grace finish the recital, then, and tell M. de Wardes who that woman was who placed the knife in the hand of your father's murderer.'

A cry escaped from the lips of all present. The young duke passed his handkerchief across his forehead which was covered with perspiration. A dead silence ensued among the spectators. 'You see, M. de Wardes,' said d'Artagnan, whom this recital had impressed more and more as his own recollection revived while Athos was speaking, — 'you see that my crime did not cause the destruction of a soul, and that the soul in question was altogether lost before my offence. It is, however, a matter of conscience on my part. Now that this matter is settled, therefore, it remains for me, M. de Wardes, to ask with the greatest humility your forgiveness for this shameless deed, as most certainly I should have asked it of your father if he were still alive, and if I had met him after my return to France, subsequent to the death of King Charles.'

'That is too much, M. d'Artagnan,' exclaimed many voices with animation.

'No, gentlemen,' said the captain. 'And now, M. de Wardes, I hope that all is finished between us, and that you will have no further occasion to speak ill of me. Do you consider the matter cleared up?'

De Wardes bowed, stammering his excuses.

But d'Artagnan has not finished with de Wardes there. Following up his own apology he forces him to apologize to Raoul for a slanderous sneer as to his parentage with the words ' "You will do this, M. de Wardes as I, an old officer, did to your boy's moustache." ' And the scene ends with 'D'Artagnan courteously saluting those who had witnessed the explanation, and everyone on leaving the room shook hands with him; but not one hand was held out to de Wardes.'

Perhaps more than any other episode this bears out Stevenson's statement in the course of his panegyric of the novel: 'D'Artagnan has mellowed into a man so witty, rough, kind and upright, that he takes the heart by storm.'

The incident over, Dumas then proceeds to show his skill as a narrator by bringing on to the scene the governor of the Bastille, Baisemeaux de Montlezun, and that personage simply and naturally because d'Artagnan had mentioned his name during his threat of imprisonment to de Wardes, but making it coincide with the oncoming plot of Aramis and the Iron Mask. Now the worthy governor has come specially to see d'Artagnan because of complicated embroilment in his financial affairs. Why d'Artagnan? the reader asks. After a long and detailed lament over his sources of income on the one hand and his debts on the other, he leaks the fact that M. d'Herblay had offered himself as a surety of a certain payment, much to the Musketeer's astonishment. Baisemeaux explains that he is earnestly seeking for Aramis and will be ' "stripped of everything" ' unless he can find him before next midday, and he has come to d'Artagnan pretty certain that as his close friend he will know his address. In brief, for his reply the Musketeer tells Baisemeaux that all he has to do is to go and see Fouquet in the morning and he will learn where Aramis is. The worthy governor of the Bastille then takes his leave with profound relief, but leaving the Musketeer soliloquizing.

> ' "This is strange," murmured D'Artagnan as he slowly ascended the staircase. "What possible interest can Aramis have in obliging Baisemeaux in this way? Well, I suppose we shall learn some day or other." '
> He was to do that later in no uncertain manner.

* * *

From now on the novel unfolds its ramifications much along the lines of a sonata: exposition — development — recapitulation. Roughly speaking, we are now at the development. The various themes have been announced, and remain to be manipulated.

The next chapter, 'The King's Card Table', like the previous one already noted (viz. 'Mazarin's Gaming Party') is used by Dumas to further the character of Madame as the newly married Princess Henrietta is now styled, while at the same time bringing into play the king's animosity, encouraged by Colbert, to Fouquet and his determination to ruin him through the very source of his popularity and power, namely money.

Madame first. Now through her marriage becoming one of France's royal family, she gives rein to the effect her youth (she is only eighteen) and dazzling beauty are having on her male courtiers, enhanced as it was by her 'wit and spirit so typically French in its nature and enhanced by English humour'.

> Even the king ... like a child, was captivated by her radiant beauty and wit. The whole court, submissive to her enchanting grace, found for the first time that laughter could be indulged in before the greatest monarch in the world by people worthy to be called the wittiest and most polished in the world. From that evening Madame enjoyed a success capable of dazzling the whole court: from that moment Louis XIV acknowledged Madame as an important personage, Buckingham regarded her as a coquette deserving the cruellest tortures, de Guiche looked upon her as a divinity, and the courtiers as a star whose light might become the focus of all favour and power.

So it was that, the gaming over, in defiance of propriety,

> the king, without looking at Monsieur his brother, offered his hand to Madame and led the young princess to the door of her apartments. It was remarked that at the threshold of the door His Majesty, freed from every restraint, let a deep sigh escape him. The ladies present — for nothing escapes a woman's observation, Mademoiselle de Montalais's for instance — did not fail to say to one another, 'The king sighed;' and 'Madame sighed too.' This had been indeed the case. Madame

had sighed very noiselessly, but with an accompaniment much more dangerous to the king's repose. Madame had sighed, closing her beautiful black eyes; then, opening them, laden as they were with an indescribable melancholy, she had raised them to the king, whose face at that moment had visibly heightened in colour. The consequence of these blushes, of these interchanged sighs, and of this royal agitation was that Montalais committed an indiscretion which certainly affected her companion; for Mademoiselle de la Vallière, less clearsighted perhaps, turned pale when the king blushed, and, her attendance being required upon Madame, she tremblingly followed the princess without thinking to take the gloves which court etiquette required her to do. True it is that this young country girl might allege as an excuse the agitation into which the king threw her; for Mademoiselle de la Vallière, busily engaged in closing the door, had involuntarily fixed her eyes upon the king, who, as he retired backward, had his face towards it.

The episode, slight though it is, does two things: it anticipates Louis's later interview with Madame on behalf of his brother; it nudges the reader's elbow as to Louise's fixation for the king. But then Louis is brought to prosaic earth by Colbert,

who now approached him with great respect but with much urgency, and murmured something in his ear, words which caused the king to call out 'Is M. Fouquet here?'

'Yes, Sire, I am here,' replied the voice of the superintendent, who was engaged with Buckingham; and he approached the king, who advanced a step towards him with a smiling and unceremonious air.

'Forgive me,' said Louis, 'if I interrupt your conversation; but I claim your attention whenever I may require your services.'

'I am always at the king's service,' replied Fouquet.

'And your cash-box too,' said the king with a false smile.

'My cash-box more than anything else,' said Fouquet coldly.

'The fact is, Monsieur, I wish to give a fête at Fontainebleau — to keep open house for a fortnight; and I shall require — ' He stopped, glancing at Colbert.

Fouquet waited without showing discomposure; and the king resumed, answering Colbert's cruel smile — 'four million livres.'

'Four million?' repeated Fouquet, bowing profoundly. The nails of the hand which was thrust in his bosom made bleeding furrows in his flesh, but the tranquil expression of his face remained unaltered.

'When will they be required, Sire?'

'Take your time, — I mean — No, no; as soon as possible.'

'A certain time will be necessary, Sire.'

'Time?' exclaimed Colbert, triumphantly.

'The time, Monsieur,' said the superintendent with the haughtiest disdain, 'simply to count the money; a million cannot be drawn and weighed in a day.'

'Four days, then,' said Colbert.

'My clerks,' replied Fouquet, addressing himself to the king, 'will perform wonders for His Majesty's service, and the sum shall be ready in three days.'

Arrived home with despair in his heart, Fouquet seeks out Aramis (who is there with Porthos) and there follows a meaningful dialogue between them which covers not only the present but the future. Not only does Aramis assure the superintendent that the four million demanded by the king will be found, but he borrows the 50,000 from him necessary for him to take to the governor of the Bastille next day, in this way linking up with d'Artagnan's conversation with Baisemeaux. When Fouquet, forgetful in his multifarious and vast financial dealings of the arrangement made with Baisemeaux, asks Aramis for details and reasons, the latter goes so far as to confess it was a ploy for keeping on the right side of Baisemeaux, and goes on to explain:

> 'Monseigneur, we have our own poets, our own engineers, our own architect, our own painters. One day we might need our own governor of the Bastille. I am certain he will not remain ungrateful for that money.'
> 'What a bedevilled affair — usury in a matter of benevolence!'
> 'Do not mix yourself up with it, Monseigneur. It is I who practise it, and both of us who profit by it, that is all.'
> 'Some intrigue, d'Herblay?'
> 'I do not deny it.'
> 'With Baisemeaux an accomplice?'
> 'Why not?'

Aramis's limited confession to Fouquet preludes the final and fatal one he was to make to his undoing following the *coup* he had so grandly brought off.

* * *

The next chapter shows Aramis on the first stage of that *coup* when, 'dressed as a simple citizen, and on horseback', he makes his way to the Bastille with the money for Baisemeaux. So relieved is the poor governor to receive the money that in a euphoric state he allows his guest to look into the prison register of names in order to prove an argument. In it he sees the name of *Seldon*, followed by that of *Marchiali*, and asks casually whether the latter is Italian.

> 'Hush!' said Baisemeaux.
> 'Why hush?' said Aramis, involuntarily clinching his white hand.
> 'I thought I had already spoken to you about that Marchiali.'
> 'No; this is the first time I ever heard his name pronounced.'
> 'That may be, but I may have spoken to you about him without naming him.'
> 'Is he an old offender?' asked Aramis, attempting to smile.
> 'On the contrary, he is quite young.'
> 'Is his crime, then, very heinous?'
> 'Unpardonable.'
> 'Has he assassinated any one?'
> 'Bah!'
> 'An incendiary, then?'
> 'Bah!'
> 'Has he slandered any one?'

> 'No, no! It is he who — ' and Baisemeaux approached Aramis's ear, making a sort of ear-trumpet of his hands, and whispered, — 'it is he who presumes to resemble the — ' 'Yes, yes,' said Aramis, 'I remember now that you spoke to me about it last year; but the crime appeared to me so slight.'
> 'Slight!'
> 'Or rather, so involuntary.'
> 'My Lord, it is not involuntarily that such a resemblance is detected.'
> 'Well, the fact is, I had forgotten it.'

Invited to breakfast with him, Aramis makes the governor more and more euphoric over the food and wine, manoeuvres the conversation on to the subject of the two prisoners, and pretends to disbelieve Marchiali's suppositional resemblance to the king for which he had been imprisoned, and so pooh-poohs it that he drives Baisemeaux into offering to let him see the prisoner for himself. The governor leads the way to 'the second floor of La Bertaudière', where, always in the presence of Baisemeaux, he sees and talks to both prisoners and learns something of their backgrounds and the 'crime' for which they are imprisoned.

Back in the governor's quarters Aramis, on being questioned by Baisemeaux as to what he thinks about the 'criminal' resemblance of Marchiali to the king, replies that he sees nothing in it at all, dismisses the accusation as being simply imaginary, and takes his leave with

> 'Now, you would not be angry with me, would you, if I were to carry off one of your prisoners?'
> 'What do you mean?'
> 'By obtaining his pardon, of course. Have I not already told you that I took a great interest in poor Seldon?'
> 'Yes, quite true.'
> 'Well?'
> 'That is your affair; do as you think proper. I see you have an open hand, and an arm that can reach a great way.'
> 'And Aramis left, carrying with him the governor's blessings.

The Iron Mask complot is under way.

* * *

The next six chapters lower the temperature of the narrative and may well remind the reader of Mr Polly's negation, consisting as they do of a love scene between Fouquet and Mme de Bellière; the ridiculous duel between de Wardes and Buckingham on the seashore; long-winded conversation and action on the parts of Monsieur, de Lorraine and de Guiche all concerning the last-named's growing and too-obvious passion for Madame, which drives Monsieur to complain about it again to his mother as he had done about Buckingham. However, the purpose of these petty scenes of jealousy becomes apparent with the entry of Louis to see his mother as his brother, on hearing him announced, makes his escape.

On learning from her of his brother's complaints and demands, he takes it on himself to patch up the family quarrel, and to his mother's ' "May you be successful! May you be the family's peacemaker!" ' answers her light-heartedly ' "I do not employ an ambassador — which is as much as to say I shall succeed," and went away laughing, and carefully brushed his dress as he walked.'

In view of what is to come his words are amusingly ironic. And the next chapter, 'The Mediator', was selected by Stevenson, and has been done so by others, as being a masterly example of literary psychology. Who runs may read.

Louis finds his sister-in-law in her boudoir. After the preliminary skirmishes as to her health, and her pretence of not feeling well enough to attend the ballet he had arranged for her, she takes the wind out of his sails by saying

'Sire, I wish to ask Your Majesty's permission to return to England.'

The king started. 'Return to England!' he said; 'do you really say what you mean, Madame?'

'I say it reluctantly, Sire,' replied the granddaughter of Henry IV, firmly, her beautiful black eyes flashing. 'I regret to have to confide such matters to Your Majesty; but I feel myself too unhappy at Your Majesty's court, and I wish to return to my own family.'

'Madame, Madame!' exclaimed the king, approaching her.

Louis denies it was he who had dismissed Buckingham: then the name of de Guiche coming up, Madame protests and weeps.

The king took one of her hands in his, and kissed the tears away. She looked at him so sadly and with so much tenderness that his heart was melted.

'You have no feeling, then, for de Guiche?' he said, more disturbed than became his character of mediator.

'None, absolutely none.'

'Then I can reassure my brother in that respect?'

'Nothing will satisfy him, Sire. Do not believe that he is jealous. Monsieur has been badly advised by someone, and he is of an uneasy disposition.'

'He may well be so when you are concerned,' said the king. Madame cast down her eyes, and was silent; the king did so likewise, holding her hand all the while. His momentary silence seemed to last an age. Madame gently withdrew her hand, and from that moment she felt that her triumph was certain, and that the field of battle was her own.

But when she defends de Guiche and declares she would regret him if he were too to be sent away, he replies lightly ' "As a good brother, I warn you I shall take a dislike to M. de Guiche," ' — a threat which, made half in jest, is soon to eventuate. Finally, on her asking again 'languishingly' for his permission to return to England, Louis rejoins,

> 'Never! never!'
> 'I am a prisoner, then?'
> 'In France, yes.'
> 'What must I do, then?'

His answer is to suggest a pact between her and himself as her ally and protector, and the scenario ends

> 'Our alliance shall date from to-day,' exclaimed the king with a warmth that was not assumed. 'You will not think any more of the past, will you? I myself am resolved that I will not. I shall always remember the present; I have it before my eyes, — look!' and he led the princess before a mirror, in which she saw herself reflected, blushing and beautiful enough to overcome a saint.
> 'It is all the same,' she murmured; 'it will not be a very strong alliance.'
> 'Must I swear?' inquired the king, intoxicated by the voluptuous turn the whole conversation had taken.
> 'Oh, I do not refuse a good oath,' said Madame; 'it has always the semblance of security.'
> The king knelt upon the footstool, and took hold of Madame's hand. She, with a smile which a painter could not render and which a poet only could imagine, gave him both her hands, in which he hid his burning face. Neither of them could utter a syllable. The king felt Madame withdraw her hands, caressing his face as she did so. He rose immediately and left the apartment. The courtiers remarked his heightened colour, and concluded that the scene had been a stormy one. The Chevalier de Lorraine, however, hastened to say, 'Nay, be comforted, Messieurs! His Majesty is always pale when he is angry.'

The scenario is taken a step further in the next chapter. Dumas begins it with a brief but adept further piece of psychological analysis.

> It must not be supposed that Louis proposed to himself any plan of seduction. The tie which united Madame to his brother was, or at least would seem to him, an insuperable barrier; he was even too far removed from that barrier to perceive its existence. But on the downward path of those passions in which the heart rejoices, towards which youth impels us, no one can say where he will stop — not even he who has in advance calculated all the chances of success or failure. As for Madame, her regard for the king may easily be explained; she was young, a coquette and ardently fond of inspiring admiration. Hers was one of those buoyant, impetuous natures which upon a stage would pass through coals of fire to obtain applause from the spectators. It was not surprising, then, that by a sort of progression, after having been adored by Buckingham and by de Guiche, who was superior to Buckingham, — even if it were only from that great merit so much appreciated by women, that is to say, novelty, — it was not surprising, then, we say, that the princess should raise her ambition to being admired by the king, who not only was the first person in the realm, but one of the handsomest and wittiest men in it.

After which Louis informs his brother that ' "everything had been quietly arranged" ', information which Monsieur does not find comforting. Then at a state reception giving out invitations to the forthcoming ballet, the king, intercepting meaningful glances between de Guiche and Madame, who is beginning to find the count more and more pleasing, and to feel 'she had acted unjustly towards one who loved her with such a depth of devotion', 'bit his royal lips' and addressed him with

> 'Count, this is the season for the second sowing of crops; I am sure that your tenants in Normandy will be glad to see you upon your estate.'
>
> The king, after this cruel blow, turned his back on the unhappy man, whose turn it was now to become pale; he advanced a few steps towards the king, forgetting that His Majesty is never spoken to except in reply to questions addressed. 'I have perhaps misunderstood Your Majesty,' he stammered out.
>
> The king turned his head slightly, and with a cold and stern glance, which plunged like a sword relentlessly into the hearts of those under disgrace, repeated, 'I said, retire to your estates,' allowing every syllable to fall slowly one by one.
>
> M. de Guiche was left alone in the king's cabinet, the whole of the company having departed. Shadows danced before his eyes. He suddenly broke through the fixed despair which overwhelmed him, and flew to hide himself in his own rooms, where Raoul still awaited him, confident in his own sad presentiments.
>
> 'Well,' murmured the latter, seeing his friend enter, bareheaded, with a wild gaze and tottering steps.
>
> 'Yes, yes, it is true,' said de Guiche, unable to utter more, and falling exhausted upon the couch.
>
> 'And she?' inquired Raoul.
>
> 'She!' exclaimed his unhappy friend, as he raised his hand, clinched in anger towards heaven. 'She! — '
>
> 'What did she say and do?'
>
> 'She said that her dress suited her admirably, and then she laughed.'

The king in his turn has become jealous of the poor duke!

* * *

We come now to that series of chapters (eleven of them) which describe in detail the follies and 'petty interests' (the phrase is Dumas's own) of royalty and the court, personages of privilege and wealth who with none of the ordinary citizens' work to occupy them invent recreations, emotions and dissipations to combat boredom and fill the long hours of their leisure time.

There are two ways of reacting to these fugitive episodes during which d'Artagnan and his comrades are banished into the wings while the less interesting ones take the centre stage. One is to skip through them with resentment, as no doubt Mr Polly would have done had he bothered to read the book at all; the other is to remain philosophical enough to admire the intuitive faithfulness of the picture drawn by the creator. For as the anonymous writer of the Introductory Note to the 6-volume translation of the novel* rightly observes:

* London. J. M. Dent and Co. 1895.

> The romance ... offers a marvellously faithful picture of the French court from a period immediately preceding the young king's marriage to his cousin, Maria Theresa, the Infanta of Spain, to the downfall of Fouquet... The historical accuracy of the author of 'Bragelonne'... is perhaps more striking in this than in any other of his romances. It is not only in the matter of the events of greater or less importance that one familiar with the history of the period seems to be reading some contemporary chronicle, but the character-sketches of the prominent personages are drawn with such fidelity to life that we seem to see the very men and women themselves as they appeared to their contemporaries.

The chapters in question treat in stages of the passion of the king for his new sister-in-law Princess Henrietta, and played on by her for first stage. For second, their scheme, suggested by her but agreed to by him, to cloak their intrigue from her husband, Monsieur, and the world in general, by his feigning an attachment to another. For third, that other turns out to be Louise de la Vallière, generally regarded as Raoul's intended; and lastly, that choice made in cold blood becoming transformed by an unexpected incident into a sincere love for the maid of honour on the part of the king.

The whole scenario, while perhaps over-stretched in its detailed telling, nevertheless, with the future and historical facts in view, is full of dramatic irony and contains many passages well worth quoting.

The action begins with the fête in the countryside of Fontainebleau arranged by Louis especially for Henrietta — a lavish affair with the king and his court entertaining themselves with 'bathing, riding, banquets, balls, concerts, mythological ballets, dancing and promenades'. Louis and Henrietta make opportunities to be together and enjoy their amorous flirtation by furtive hand clasps and inflaming whispered conversations; and it is because of their frustration and lack of privacy that Madame devises her scheme of a false relationship. Her answer to his question as to which of her maids of honour is to be honoured with his suppositional choice comes first in the approach to them of Mlle de Tonnay-Charente, surrounded by a group of admiring gentlemen.

> 'What do you think of Mademoiselle de Tonnay-Charente, Henrietta?' inquired the king.
> 'I think that she is rather fair in complexion,' replied Madame.
> 'Rather fair, yes; but beautiful, I think, in spite of that.'
> 'Is that your opinion, Sire?'
> 'Yes, really.'
> 'Well, then, it is mine too.'
> 'And she seems to be much sought after.'
> 'Oh! that is a matter of course; lovers flutter from one to another. If we had hunted for lovers instead of butterflies, you can see from those who surround her what successful sport we should have had.'

But the lovers finally decide that the young lady in question is rather too beautiful, and might come to inspire an undesired jealousy. To which Louis exclaims ' "Yes, yes, you are right. Mlle de Tonnay-Charente is too beautiful to serve as a cloak." '

To appreciate to the full the dramatic irony of the episode the English reader needs to know his French history. Mlle de Tonnay-Charente was to become the Mme de Montespan destined to supplant La Vallière in their royal master's favour, and to bear him eight children.

But then Louise herself appears in their sights.

> While the king was speaking, Madame had risen from her seat and looked around the greensward; and after a careful and silent examination she called the king to her side, and said, 'See, Sire, upon the slope of that little hill, near that clump of gelder-roses, that beautiful girl walking alone behind the others, her head down, her arms hanging by her side, with her eyes fixed upon the flowers which she crushes beneath her feet like one who is lost in thought.'
> 'Mademoiselle de la Vallière, do you mean?' remarked the king.
> 'Yes.'
> 'Oh!'
> 'Will she not suit you, Sire?'
> 'Why, look how thin the poor child is! She has hardly any flesh on her bones.'
> 'Nay; am I so plump, then?'
> 'She is so melancholy.'
> 'The greater contrast to myself, who am accused of being too lively.'
> 'She is lame.'
> 'Do you think so?'
> 'No doubt of it; look, she has allowed every one to pass by her lest her defect should be remarked.'
> 'Well, she will not run so fast as Daphne, and will not be able to escape Apollo.'
> 'Henrietta,' said the king, out of temper, 'of all your maids of honour you have really selected for me the one most full of defects.'
> 'Still, she is one of my maids of honour; take note of that!'
> 'Who never opens her lips.'
> 'But who, when she does open them, displays a beautiful set of teeth.'
> 'Who may serve as a model for an osteologist.'
> 'You favour will ripen her charms.'
> 'Henrietta!'
> 'At all events, you have allowed me to be the mistress.'
> 'Alas! yes.'
> 'Well, my choice is made; I impose her upon you, and you must submit.'
> 'Oh! I would accept one of the Furies if you were to insist upon it.'
> 'La Vallière is as gentle as a lamb; do not fear that she will ever contradict you when you tell her you love her,' said Madame, laughing.
> 'You are not afraid, are you, that I shall say too much to her?'
> 'It would be for my sake.'
> 'Very well.'
> 'The treaty is agreed to, then?'
> 'And signed.'
> 'You will continue to show me the friendship of a brother, the attention of a

brother, the gallantry of a monarch, will you not?'

'I will preserve for you a heart which can no longer beat except at your command.'

'Very well. Do you not see that we have secured the future by this means?'

* * *

But both Louis and Henrietta were to get more than they bargained for. Later that evening, under the 'royal oak,' he and his 'favourite' Saint-Aignan, taking a moonlight stroll in the park, happened to overhear the trio of La Vallière, Montalais and Tonnay-Charente chatting, as young women do, on the various aspects of love and their lovers, actual or would-be. Their triologue is worthy of Trollope. As against the cynical nature of the other two, Louise's simplicity and sincerity shine out. On being asked which of the men whom they danced with earlier she preferred, she rashly declared that none of them could stand comparison beside the king, and, her emotion breaking through her long-held control, in reply to their assertion ' "Alas! the king is not one upon whom our poor eyes have a right to be fixed," ' replies ' "That is too true. It is not the privilege of all eyes to gaze upon the sun; but I will look upon him even if I were to be blinded." '

From then on the king's feigned love for La Vallière becomes a genuine one. The transformation is yet another example of Dumas's astute psychology. A man has only to learn of a woman's love for him for him to convince himself that he must respond. Louis was caught more surely by overhearing Louise's secret passion than if she had brazenly exposed it to him. Dumas knew his young men.

The change in Louis's feelings is of course realized by Henrietta, who proceeds to exemplify the truth of Congreve's dictum 'Hell hath no fury like a woman scorned.' After overhearing de Guiche declare his passion for her to his friend Raoul, she begins her revenge by at last succumbing to his passionate pleading with the abrupt heart-shattering ' "Love me, then, since you will have it so." '

There follow a couple of chapters devoted to our old friends Malicorne, Manicamp, Montalais and Saint-Aignan, all determined to profit from the latest state of the royal amours. After which the Rev. the Bishop of Vannes enters the scene again. In the hotel the Beau Paon from which Malicorne complains he has been ousted by a dying Franciscan friar, the reader is informed that a 'Jesuit of the eleventh year' is awaiting to interview several possible successors, of which Aramis is one, in the hope of finding an outstanding one who will ensure the power of the Order. Aramis is the sixth. After handing the Franciscan a letter in a secret code originated by himself, and disclosing the mystery of the resemblance of the Bastille prisoner and his plot, he is adjudged the successful candidate. The power invested in such a position at that time was immense, and for Aramis brought Marchiali, Baisemeaux, 'the second Bartaudière' a vital step nearer.

* * *

The chapter 'The Mission' reveals the king's subtle perfidy. In discussing La Vallière with Saint-Aignan it had suddenly come into his memory that she had a 'betrothed'; more, that he had been besought by the Comte de la Fère for his permission to marry her; that this betrothed was the Vicomte de Bragelonne; and finally that he had refused that permission, considering the girl neither rich nor beautiful enough. These remembrances caused him a moment's remorse; but, now in love with her himself, and over and above that, knowing she loved him, he saw in the vicomte a rival.

So it was that in the midst of a conversation between Louise and Montalais, Raoul suddenly appeared before them booted and spurred and obviously about to travel. He explained that he had just been designated by the king as his messenger to King Charles II of England, and was about to set off. The deluded lover took the appointment as an honour on the part of the king, but was at the same time full of misgivings over their unavoidable separation for an unknown length of time. In heart-moving despair he again avowed his constant love for her. At which Louise 'threw herself into Montalais's arms and burst into tears, and even that giddy young lady felt deeply moved'. They were interrupted by the arrival of Tonnay-Charente, who came not only to inform Raoul that the princess was awaiting him with a letter for her brother, but had delivered an ultimatum to the maids of honour. Raoul left abruptly, and as the three asked one another what Madame's order could consist of, 'they heard the sound of a horse galloping along the road outside the gates of the château'.

* * *

As already related, Madame's first retaliation for the king's desertion of her for La Vallière had been her ' "*Allons, aimez-moi, donc*" ' to de Guiche. The second was to regale the king and others at one of her receptions with a fanciful account, disguised as a pastoral tale of shepherds and shepherdesses, naiads and dryads, in which one of them is deliberately deluded into believing he is beloved by overhearing a confession of love for him. The object of the fable is so obviously meant that Louis leaves early and angrily. Madame's blow had struck home. The next chapter, 'Royal Psychology', depicting his reaction, like that earlier one 'The Mediator' is one of the outstanding episodes of the novel, and its very title a confutation of those pedagogues and academic critics who tell us that Dumas is lacking in psychology.

> Back in his apartments with Saint-Aignan Louis was utterly bewildered by the whole affair. For the first time since he had escaped from the trammels of Mazarin he found himself treated as a man. Such treatment from any of his subjects would normally have been repulsed by him. But to attack women, to be imposed on by country girls ... it was the depths of dishonour for a sovereign... There was nothing he could do. To show anger towards women — what humiliation, especially when they had ridicule on their side as a means of vengeance!
>
> There was nothing he could do then but swallow the affront in silence, to go

on treating Madame as a friend. After all, who was it who had sought her affection in the first instance, whispered words of love in her ear, who had dared to seduce her into the thought of committing a crime against the marriage vow — a crime the more deplorable because of the relationship between them? And she had listened to the royal voice, had been influenced by his seductive tones. And now, after morally sacrificing her honour in listening to him, she saw herself repaid for her sacrifice by an infidelity all the more humiliating in its being occasioned by a woman far beneath her own station.

All these various reasonings were like so many stings to the king's pride; for when he had in his mind gone over all his causes for grievance, he was forced to acknowledge that there was another one which he hardly dare to confess even to himself, namely, that the hurt from which he was suffering had its seat in his heart. For the truth was, he had found his heart gratified by Louise's innocent confession of her love, answering his dream of a pure affection — an affection for himself as a man and not a king — of an affection free from all self-interest; and his heart, simpler and more youthful than he had imagined, had leapt to meet that other heart which had so lately revealed itself to him.

The commonest aspect in the complex history of love is the duple inoculation of it to which any two hearts are subjected: the one almost always loves before the other, and that other almost always loves in turn. In this way the mysterious current is established in proportion to the intensity of the passion so kindled. The more Louise had revealed her love, the more Louis's feelings had increased. And it was precisely this which had surprised the king in that there had been no expression of love in the first place, since such an expression would have been an outrage towards both the man and the king; and finally because — and the thought of it burned like a hot iron all the more as it seemed to be nothing but a hoax after all — a hoax on him, a king who had but to bestow a glance, to indicate with a finger, to drop a handkerchief. Yet since the previous evening his mind had been so absorbed with this girl, his imagination so occupied in clothing her image with charms to which she could lay no claim, that he could think and dream of nothing but her. In very truth, he whom such vast interest summoned, and on whom so many women smiled invitingly, since the previous evening consecrated every moment of his time, every throb of his heart, to this sole dream.

It was indeed either too much or too little.

Let those classical scholars and fastidious academics who see in Dumas only a facile historical romancer read that passage (itself only one of many) and then ponder.

But then, just as Louis is passing from anger to enforced philosophical acceptance of the situation and telling Saint-Aignan nothing can be done about it, a valet brings him a letter from Louise begging for an interview so that she can 'tell the truth to my king'. Being only a man and a young one, the king could not hold out against such a despairing appeal; with the result that in the course of the next chapter suggestively headed 'What neither the Naiad nor the Dryad had foreseen', we are shown the king, first giving vent to the hurt rankling in his heart, then becoming overwhelmed by the truthful simplicity of the stricken girl as, falling on her knees before him, her hands in his, she makes confession of her love.

Carried away by her desire for revenge, Madame had certainly never anticipated this finale!

But their now confessed love affair proceeds only slowly, consisting of furtive too-brief moments as and when opportunity occurs; so that it is only after a longish interval of time and frustration that, thanks to the drawn-out complicated plotting of Messrs Malicorne and Manicamp, aided and abetted by Saint-Aignan, and the construction of screens, trapdoors and staircases that the lovers are at last are able to meet in secret.

* * *

And it is here that Dumas prefers to abandon the court and its affairs to make return to Aramis and d'Artagnan. First the former.

Now General of the Jesuit Order and armed with the power that such a state accorded him, Aramis knew that a vast stride had been taken towards the fulfilment of his fantastic secret ambition, and now, from being Fouquet's servitor could become his saviour: to such an extent indeed that on the superintendent's lamenting that the king had invited himself to a fête at his Vaux palace with the purpose of ruining him financially, and in despair asking where the money is to come from, he tells him that he, Aramis, will find it, and even gives a hint that not only can he do this now, but he can arrange things so that he, Fouquet, will be returned to the king's favour.

> 'Upon my word, my dear d'Herblay,' said Fouquet, 'your confidence alarms me more than the king's displeasure. Who can you possibly be, after all?'
> 'You know me well enough, I should think.'
> 'Of course; but what is it you are aiming at?'
> 'I wish to see upon the throne of France a king devoted to M. Fouquet, and I wish M. Fouquet to be devoted to me.'
> 'Oh!' exclaimed Fouquet, pressing his hand, 'as for belonging to you, I am yours entirely; but believe me, my dear d'Herblay, you are deceiving yourself.'
> 'In what respect?'
> 'The king will never become devoted to me.'
> 'I do not remember to have said that the king would be devoted to you.'
> 'Why, on the contrary, you have this moment said so.'
> 'I did not say *the* king; I said *a* king.'
> 'Is it not all the same?'
> 'No, on the contrary, it is quite different.'
> 'I do not understand you.'
> 'You will shortly. Suppose, for instance, the king in question were to be a very different person from Louis XIV.'
> 'Another person?'
> 'Yes, who is indebted for everything to you.'
> 'Impossible?'
> 'His very throne even.'
> 'Oh, you are mad! There is no other man but Louis XIV who can sit on the

throne of France. I see none, not one.'

'But I see one.'

'Unless it be Monsieur,' said Fouquet, looking at Aramis uneasily. 'Yet Monsieur — '

'It is not Monsieur.'

'But how can it be that a prince not of the royal line, that a prince without any right — '

'My king, or rather your king, will be everything that is necessary, be assured of that.'

'Be careful, M. d'Herblay; you make my blood run cold, and my head swim.'

Aramis smiled. 'There is but little occasion for that,' he replied.

'Again, I repeat, you terrify me!' said Fouquet.

Aramis smiled.

'You laugh,' said Fouquet.

'The day will come when you will laugh too; only, at the present moment I must laugh alone.'

'One word more,' said Fouquet. 'You have never yet spoken to me in this manner; you have never yet shown yourself so confident — I should rather say so daring.'

'Because it is necessary, in order to speak confidently, to have the lips unfettered.'

'And that is now your case?'

'Yes.'

'Since a very short time, then?'

'Since yesterday only.'

'Oh, M. d'Herblay, take care! Your confidence is becoming audacity.'

'One can well be audacious when one is powerful.'

'And you are powerful?'

'I have offered you ten millions; I offer them again to you.'

Fouquet rose, much agitated and disturbed. 'Come, come,' he said; 'you spoke of overthrowing kings and replacing them by others. God forgive me! but if I am not really out of my senses, is or is not that what you said just now?'

'You are not out of your senses, for it is perfectly true that I did say that just now.'

'And why did you say so?'

'Because one may speak in this manner of thrones being cast down and kings being raised up when one is one's self far above all kings and thrones, of this world at least.'

'Your power is infinite, then?' cried Fouquet.

'I have told you so already, and I repeat it,' replied Aramis, with glistening eyes and trembling lips.

* * *

It is in this way that Dumas subtly makes the reader aware that Aramis's scheme is ripening. Then at last, self-confessionary, he felt compelled to follow this with:

> During this long and violent contention between the ambitions of the court and the affections of the heart, one of our characters, the least deserving of neglect, in fact, was, however, very much neglected, forgotten and unhappy. In fact d'Artagnan

— we must recall him by his name to remind our readers of his existence — had absolutely nothing to do amid this brilliant world of fashion. Assailed by persons asking him what he thought about their costume, or saying 'M. d'Artagnan, how do you intend to dress yourself this evening?' he replied 'I shall undress myself,' at which the ladies laughed. But after a couple of days passed in this manner, the Musketeer, perceiving that nothing serious was likely to arise which could concern him, and that the king had completely — or at least appeared to have completely — forgotten Paris, St Mandé, and Belle-Ile; that M. Colbert's mind was occupied with illuminations and fireworks; that for the next month, at least, the ladies had glances to bestow and receive, — asked the king for leave of absence for a matter of private business.

We shall not look for d'Artagnan, therefore, at Fontainebleau, for this would be quite useless; but with the permission of our readers we shall find him in the Rue des Lombards, at the sign of the Pilon d'Or, in the house of our old friend Planchet.

D'Artagnan, reclining upon an immense flat-backed chair, with his legs placed upon a stool, formed the most obtuse angle that was ever seen....

Once in Planchet's shop we are also in a sense enjoying a repeat of the scene of the Musketeer's proposal to restore Charles II, the whole chapter 'Malaga' consisting of nothing but a beguiling but seemingly purposeless dialogue between friends — dialogue which, learned early in his career as a playwright, was Dumas's birthright, it being part of his genius that he could make something out of nothing and anything interesting and in which he has no superior in fiction. The reader feels himself transported into the imagined scene of its creator and literally overhearing the conversation. Planchet, despite the Musketeer's denial, contends that the Musketeer is bored and becoming thinner and even worse, troubled, and goes on to assert that if he continues in that state he will take his sword and have it out with the man who is the cause of his companion's preoccupation, namely M. d'Herblay. In response to the other's startled ' "What's that you say, Planchet? What has M. d'Herblay's name to do with your groceries?" ' the worthy grocer tells him he has heard him call out in his sleep ' "Aramis! Sly Aramis!" ' On which d'Artagnan, startled, promises he will get fatter and not dream of Aramis any more. The point being that the reference to Aramis comes as much a shock to the reader as it did to Planchet, and brings closer the growing division between the two former comrades-in-arms: the one loyal to the king, the other to Fouquet.

To ensure the ratification of the Musketeer's promise, Planchet then, with sly winks, innuendos and philosophical comments about making the best of life and its pleasures, proposes to take him away from the shop to Fontainebleau where, he divulges with a meaningful smile, he has ' "a little bit of a house" '. D'Artagnan, 'quite fidgety with curiosity', agrees. Planchet then leaves him, and the chapter ends:

> D'Artagnan resumed his original position upon his chair; and his brow, which had been unruffled for a moment, became more thoughtful than ever. He had already forgotten the whims and fancies of Planchet. 'Yes,' said he, taking up again the

thread of his thoughts which had been broken by the agreeable conversation in which we have just permitted our readers to participate, — 'Yes, yes, those three points include everything: First, to ascertain what Baisemeaux wanted with Aramis; secondly, to learn why Aramis does not let me hear from him; and thirdly, to ascertain where Porthos is. The whole mystery lies in these three points. Since, therefore,' continued d'Artagnan, 'our friends tell us nothing, we must have recourse to our own poor intelligence. I must do what I can, *mordioux*! or rather *Malaga*! as Planchet says.'

The whole scene is a superb delineation of action in character as opposed to character in action.

* * *

The following chapters relate the Musketeer's carrying out his three-point plan. He finds the governor of the Bastille suspiciously reserved and noncommittal. By means of a trick played on a messenger bearing a message to Porthos, he learns that he is at Fouquet's residence St Mandé, and decides to pay his old friend a surprise visit.

With the re-entry of Porthos the narrative changes character. The good-hearted, simple-minded Porthos brings a breath of light-heartedness and humour into play, a humour unique in French literature which, while rich in *esprit*, is singularly lacking in that quality at least as we British understand it — not one of the side-splitting examples perhaps, but rather of the quiet chuckle variety, and adds enormously to the variety of mood in the novel and eases its length.

Porthos is both surprised and embarrassed by his friend's unexpected visit, not having seen him since his desperate flight from Vannes. With his usual tact and acumen the Musketeer convinces him that Aramis is keeping him sequestered here in Fouquet's palatial residence while taking all the merit for the fortification of Belle-Ile to himself, and taking the plunge, tells him that he, d'Artagnan, will present him to the king. So that, after laughing heartily at Porthos's naïve account of the damage he had inflicted on one of the rooms by accidentally 'cannonading' his foot through a partition, and of uprooting trees in the park in a search for birds' eggs for an enormous salad, a delighted Porthos, against the promise he had made to Fouquet not to leave his house without informing him, follows the advice of his old friend as he had done so often in the early days of their careers together, at the risk of upsetting Aramis.

But first of all, engaged as he is to go along with Planchet, d'Artagnan takes Porthos to the worthy grocer's, where the great man's size, strength and voracious appetite cause mayhem in the shop and delight to the reader. After which the three ride out together to Planchet's 'country house'.

The description of the room as seen through the open window by the three travellers is redolent of rural contentment and a vignette of sheer delight.

The room, softly lighted by a lamp on the table, seemed like a smiling picture of repose, comfort, and happiness... The table, covered by a table-cloth as white as snow, was laid for two... Near the table, in a high-backed armchair reclined, fast asleep, a woman of about thirty, her face the picture of health and freshness. Curled up on her lap lay a large yellow cat... The two friends paused before the window in amazement, while Planchet, perceiving their astonishment, was filled with delight.

'Ah, Planchet, you rascal!' said d'Artagnan, 'I understand now your absences from your shop.'

'Oh, there is some white linen!' exclaimed Porthos in a voice of thunder.

At the sound of his voice the cat took flight, the housekeeper woke up suddenly, and Planchet, assuming a gracious air, introduced his two companions into the room.'

Aided by Trüchen's cooking, Planchet's ten wine bottles and Porthos 'twirling his moustache and looking at Trüchen in his most killing manner', the evening was a hilarious one. Further bottles were added to the ten.

'The sparkling Anjou wine very soon produced a remarkable effect upon the three companions. Planchet was singing loudly. D'Artagnan had hardly balance enough to take a candlestick to light Planchet up his own staircase, who was pulling Porthos along, who was following Trüchen, herself in a state of rare jolliment. It was d'Artagnan who found out the rooms and the beds. Porthos threw himself into the one destined for him after his friend had undressed him. D'Artagnan got into his own bed, saying to himself, 'Mordioux! I had made up my mind never to touch that light-coloured wine which brings my early camp-days back again. Fie! fie! if my Musketeers were only to see their captain in such a state!' And drawing the curtains of his bed he added, 'Fortunately though, they will not see me.' Planchet was taken in charge by Trüchen, who undressed him and closed the doors and curtains.

'The country is very amusing,' said Porthos stretching out his legs, which passed through the wooden foot-board making a tremendous noise, of which, however, no one was capable of taking the slightest notice. By two o'clock in the morning every one was fast asleep.

But this visit to Planchet's country house is not introduced merely for the sake of variety, a bucolic change of scene, a fresh look at characters, a relief from the historical personages and their intrigues. True to form, Dumas adds a cunning thread to what is becoming the salient plot.

One of the windows of Planchet's house overlooked a cemetery, and the sight of it occasioned philosophical comments from the now sober inmates. While Porthos and d'Artagnan tended to dislike the view, Planchet declared that living most of his time in the heart of Paris, and forced to put up with the endless noise of vehicles and people, he felt it did him good to feel the quiet of a cemetery, explaining

'I once met with a maxim somewhere which I have remembered, that as we must all die one day or another, the thought of death is one that will do us all good.'

'Upon my word, Planchet,' said d'Artagnan, 'You are quite a philosopher as well as a grocer.'

> 'Monsieur,' said Planchet, 'I am one of those good-humoured men that heaven has created who consider all things good they meet with during their stay on earth.'

Stevenson, noting the passage, observed that in Planchet's words Dumas was probably expressing his own philosophy of life. While that may well be true, the present writer perceives another aspect to it, namely, a further vindication of his previous contention as to the more literary-minded, more educated outlook of the average Frenchman and reader as compared with his British counterpart. Can one imagine a British grocer speaking so, even to a friend? Yet the words come from Planchet in the most natural way. As George Orwell observed in his searching study on Dickens* (and I unashamedly make use of his analogy), 'You cannot hold an imaginary conversation with a Dickens character as you can with, say, Pierre Bezukhov ... or even Wells's Mr Polly. It is because they have no mental life. They say perfectly the things that they have to say, but they cannot be conceived as talking about anything else. They never learn, never speculate.' Now as I have stressed and endeavoured to show earlier, such a charge can never be laid against the characters of Dumas. In fact the boot might be put on the other foot in that they talk too much and speculate about anything! But if that is a criticism, it is surely a plus rather than a minus. And so — to conclude my deviation — it is that Planchet's philosophizing causes no surprise, no sense of being far-fetched, no charge that Dumas has fallen into the trap of speaking for himself via his character.

But to return to the narrative. As the three were looking out and conversing, a funeral procession came into view. Only a single man, apart from the priest, beadle and chorister, followed the coffin. Porthos, finding the scene dull, left, followed by Planchet, but d'Artagnan chose to remain, having observed something which interested him. The solitary 'mourner' proved to be none other than Aramis. In addition, after the internment he was joined at the grave side by a woman.

> 'Ah! who would have thought it?' said d'Artagnan to himself. 'The Bishop of Vannes at a rendezvous! Still the same Aramis as when he played the gallant at Noisy-le-Sec! Yes, but as it is in a cemetery, the rendezvous is sacred:' and he began to laugh.

The conversation between Aramis and the woman lasted a good half-hour, after which they left together, Aramis to return to the Beau Paon, the lady making for a waiting equipage further down the road. Intrigued, and determined to find out who she was, d'Artagnan followed her. Hearing him behind her, she turned to look.

> D'Artagnan started as if he had received a charge of small shot in his legs, and then turning suddenly round, as if he were going back the same way he had come, murmured, 'Madame de Chevreuse!' D'Artagnan would not go home until he had learned everything. He asked Daddy Celestin to inquire of the gravedigger whose body it was they had buried that morning.

* *The Penguin Essays of George Orwell.*

'A poor Franciscan mendicant friar,' replied the latter, 'who had not even a dog to love him in this world and to accompany him to his last resting-place.'

'If that were really the case,' thought d'Artagnan, 'Aramis would not have been present at his funeral. The Bishop of Vannes is not precisely a dog so far as devotion goes; his scent, however, is quite as keen, I admit.'

The Aramis mystery, which Planchet had declared was giving the Musketeer nightmares and making him thin, has moved yet another step nearer.

* * *

The next two chapters swing the atmosphere from bucolic innocence to court chicanery. Waiting at the king's audience along with others, d'Artagnan and Porthos see Aramis being presented to Louis by Fouquet with a request for a cardinal's hat. Whereupon the Musketeer, using his privileged relationship with the king, joins them, leading Porthos and in turn presenting him as ' "M. le Baron du Vallon, one of the bravest gentlemen of France." ' Three of the Four are together for the second time, but in very different circumstances. Aramis and Fouquet are taken aback. But once again, thanks to d'Artagnan's ready wit, an embarrassing contretemps is avoided, and the scene ends with a pleasantly surprised king not only promising Aramis his cardinal's hat "at the first promotion", but rewarding Porthos by inviting him to sup with him that same evening — always considered a great honour.

But still Aramis, uneasy, decides that explanations are due, and decides to have it out with his old friend. Which he does, and between them they clear the air. Aramis complains that by informing the king of the state of affairs at Belle-Ile he might have been rendering Porthos and himself ' "a very bad turn" '; to which the other turns the table on him by asking him why, instead of his subterfuge, he hadn't told him simply that they were fortifying the place not for the benefit of Fouquet but for the king, if in fact that was the case, and so putting him (d'Artagnan) ' "in a false position" ', instead of acting as they did (a question, incidentally, which not a few readers may also well have asked at the time). For answer Aramis had the decency to 'hang his head'. But recovering, he proceeds to interrogate his friend as to his relationships with Colbert and the king, and tries to tempt him to join forces with him and ' "belong to Fouquet" ' with the prospects of making a dazzling career for himself, becoming ' "a marshal of France, peer, duke, with a million of revenue" '. The Captain of the Musketeer's response is,

'But, *cher ami*, the king can give me all that. Is not the king master?'
'There are many stumbling-blocks round the king,' said Aramis.
'Not for the king.'
'Very likely not; still —'
'One moment, Aramis. I observe that everyone thinks of himself and never of this poor young prince; I will maintain myself in maintaining him.'

'And if you meet with ingratitude?'
'The weak alone are afraid of that.'
'You are quite certain of yourself?'
'I think so.'
'Still, the king may have no further need of you.'
'On the contrary, I think his need of me will be greater than ever; and hearken, my dear fellow; if it became necessary to arrest a new Condé, what would do it? — this — this alone in all France!' and d'Artagnan struck his sword.

'You are right,' said Aramis, turning very pale; and then he rose and pressed d'Artagnan's hand.

'There is the last summons for supper,' said the Captain of the Musketeers; 'will you excuse me?'

Aramis threw his arm round the Musketeer's neck and said, 'A friend like you is the brightest jewel in the royal crown.' Then they separated.

'I was right,' thought d'Artagnan; 'there is something afoot.'

'We must make haste to fire the train,' said Aramis, 'for d'Artagnan has discovered the match.'

Again the sheer loyalty and uprightness of d'Artagnan comes over, making the reader take him to his heart as he had already taken Stevenson's and Thackeray's.

* * *

The narrative then goes on to portray the growing love between Madame and de Guiche, the return of de Wardes, the sneers of the last-named at the hapless situation of Raoul *vis-à-vis* La Vallière and the king, all leading to the somewhat long-winded challenge of de Guiche, as Raoul's friend, to de Wardes, and their unusual duel. Learning of this, and doubly angry on account of the violation of his edict against duelling and suspicion as to the reason for it, and refusing to be fobbed off by Manicamp's tale of a boar hunt, Louis sends his Captain of Musketeers to investigate and make a report. D'Artagnan's deductions form the finest piece of detective work between Poe and Conan Doyle, Dupin and Sherlock Holmes.* In the dusk and with only a lantern to see by, after examining the terrain, the Musketeer, from imprints of the hoofs of the two horses on the damp ground, the black hairs from the tail of one of them caught in some brambles, the pistol bullet in the head of the dead horse left there, a hat with a hole in it made by a pistol ball, the spilt wadding of a pistol, two small pools of blood from the wounded man, presents the king with a *de facto* account of what had occurred so accurate as to make him 'clap his hands together in sign of admiration and exclaim "M. d'Artagnan, you are positively the cleverest man in all my kingdom!" To which the Musketeer's reply comes "The very thing M. de Richelieu thought and M. de Mazarin said, Sire."

* The true Dumasian, who will have read his author's *Mohicans de Paris*, that later novel (1854–59) of mystery and deduction, may well reflect that the duel between de Guiche and de Wardes could be cited as one more example furnished by Monsieur Jackal, chief of the Paris police, of his famous oft-quoted dictum *Cherchez la femme!*

The duel and its results expounded, Dumas returns us to the La Vallière-Louis axis, now about to move into crisis. Madame, still incensed against her supplanter in the king's affection, and spurred into further stirring of her cauldron of hate and vengeance, takes her venom to the queen-mother, where she finds the king's shadow of a wife, Maria Theresa, also complaining of his infidelity and neglect because of his growing passion for La Vallière. The chapter is well-named 'Triumfeminate', and is a forceful specimen of female savagery. At the end of it Anne of Austria tells her two daughters-in-law that she will deal with the mischief-making maid of honour herself, and sends for her there and then. Her crushing of the timid girl before Madame, her icy demeanour, her threats, annihilate Louise to such an extent that when, later that same evening, Louis pays her a visit, she is beyond greeting him as he had so longingly anticipated, and in response to his agitated questioning as to the reason for her tears and unresponsive languor finds only denials and more tears. Dumas understands and expresses perfectly the feminine mind in such a situation. La Vallière could not give her lover an explanation without confessing to everything, which would be to accuse the queen, and Madame also; the consequence then being that she would have to enter upon an open warfare with those two great and powerful princesses. She thought within herself that as she made no attempt to conceal from the king what was passing in her own mind, the king ought to be able to read her heart, in spite of her silence; and that if he really loved her, he would have understood, and guessed everything. What was sympathy, then, if it were not that divine flame which should enlighten the heart, and save true lovers the necessity of words? She maintained her silence, therefore, satisfying herself with sighing, weeping, and concealing her face in her hands.

Then, after showing his perceptiveness in feminine psychology, Dumas shows his equal perceptiveness in the male equivalent.

> These sighs and tears, which had at first distressed and then alarmed Louis XIV, now irritated him. He could not bear any opposition — not the opposition which tears and sighs exhibited, any more than opposition of any other kind. His remarks, therefore, became bitter, urgent, and aggressive. This was a fresh cause of distress for the poor girl. From that very circumstance which she regarded as an injustice on her lover's part, she drew sufficient courage to bear, not only her other troubles, but even this one also.

The scene ends with Louis leaving the room in a rage, believing that Louise loves Bragelonne, since de Guiche had fought on her behalf, and declaring to his confident who had been with him.

> 'I vow to you, Saint-Aignan, that if three days hence I feel an atom of affection for her in my heart, I should die from very shame.' And the king resumed his way to his own apartments.

But poor Louise had yet to drink her cup of grief to the lees. No sooner had the king left her than Madame, who had seen him go, appeared. Finding Louise prostrate before her prie-dieu, she accused her of religious hypocrisy and then, putting the final stab to the girl's wounds, informed her she had come to give her notice to leave the court and return to her mother at Blois.

There follows a lengthy passage which superbly portrays Louise's reactions. Prostrate before her prie-dieu she lies physically and mentally stunned. Then gradually remembrances of her lover's words of love earlier that same day during the drive to Fontainebleau come back to her.

> Her mind reverted to the journey from Fontainebleau; she saw the king at the door of her carriage, telling her that he loved her, asking for her love in return, requiring her to swear, and himself swearing too, that never should an evening pass by, if ever a misunderstanding were to arise between them, without a visit, a letter, a sign of some kind, being sent, to replace the troubled anxiety of the evening by the calm repose of the night. It was the king who had suggested that, who had imposed a promise upon her, who had himself sworn it also. It was impossible, therefore, she reasoned, that the king should fail to keep the promise which he had himself exacted, unless, indeed, the king were a despot who enforced love as he enforced obedience; unless, too, the king were so indifferent that the first obstacle in his way was sufficient to forfeit his love. The king, that kind protector, who by a word, by a single word, could relieve her distress of mind, — the king even joined her persecutors. Oh, his anger could not possibly last! Now that he was alone, he would be suffering all that she herself was a prey to. But he was not tied hand and foot as she was: he could act, could move, could come to her; while she — could do nothing but wait. And the poor girl waited and waited with breathless anxiety, for she could not believe it possible that the king would not come.
>
> It was now nearly half-past ten.
>
> Everything with La Vallière — heart and look, body and mind — was concentrated in eager expectation. She said to herself that there still remained an hour of hope; that until midnight had struck the king might come or write or send; that by midnight only would every expectation be useless, every hope disappointed. Whenever there was any noise in the palace, the poor girl fancied she was the occasion of it; whenever she heard any one pass in the courtyard below, she imagined that they were messengers of the king coming to her. Eleven o'clock struck; then a quarter-past eleven; then half-past. The minutes dragged slowly on in this anxiety, and yet they seemed to pass far too quickly. And now it struck a quarter to twelve. Midnight, midnight — the last, the final hope, — came in its turn. With the last stroke of the clock the last light was extinguished; with the last light, the last hope. And so the king himself had deceived her; he had been the first to prove false to the oath which he had sworn that very day. Twelve hours only between his oath and his perjury; it was not long, certainly, to have preserved the illusion. And so only did the king not love her, but still more, he despised her, whom every one overwhelmed, — he despised her to the extent even of abandoning her to the shame of an expulsion which was equivalent to having an ignominious sentence passed upon her; and yet it was he, the king himself, who was the first cause of this ignominy. Then, as her knees were no longer able to support her, she gradually sank down upon the prie-dieu, and with her head pressed against the

wooden cross, her eyes fixed, and her respiration short and quick, she watched for the earliest rays of approaching daylight.

At two o'clock in the morning she was still in the same bewilderment of mind, or rather the same ecstasy of feeling. Her thoughts had almost ceased to hold any communion with the things of this world. And when she saw the violet tints of early dawn descend upon the roofs of the palace and vaguely reveal the outlines of the ivory crucifix which she embraced, she rose from the ground with a new-born strength, kissed the feet of the divine martyr, and descended the staircase leading from the room, wrapping herself from head to foot in a mantle as she went along. She reached the wicket at the very moment when the guard of Musketeers opened the gate to admit the first relief-guard belonging to one of the Swiss regiments; and then, gliding behind the soldiers, she reached the street before the officer in command of the patrol had even thought of asking who the young girl was who was making her escape from the palace at so early an hour.

But fortunately for future events, on her way to the convent of the Carmelites, not knowing Paris, she lost her way, and was rescued from the vinous antics of three drunken revellers by no less than the Captain of the Musketeers on his way to the palace to begin the day's duties. After much questioning he gets out of her that she had abandoned the court and had decided to become a nun, but extorted from him an unwilling promise to say nothing to the king. After seeing her safely to the convent door he made all haste to the palace.

The next morning was to be a fateful one for several persons. To begin with, Louis, his anger declining after debating with himself about going back to Louise to make it up with her, had finally not done so, and now, repenting his harshness, made early way to her rooms followed by the invariable Saint-Aignan, only to find her bed unslept in, and Montalais equally unknowing as to why, or where she might be. So it was with an uneasy mind that he only half listened to the speeches of the Dutch and Spanish ambassadors. And it was as this was happening that d'Artagnan, adroitly side-stepping his promise to Louise, began to tell Saint-Aignan, loudly enough for the king to overhear, of his meeting with her, and the reasons for it. Within minutes Louis had abruptly dismissed the ambassadors and was riding towards Chaillot followed by d'Artagnan.

The scene in the convent with Louise is superbly narrated. It took all Louis's passion, power and self-humiliation to break down her resistance and persuade her to renounce her decision to take the veil, admit to her treatment from his mother and sister-in-law, and to return with him to the palace. As a final and subtle touch of dramatic irony, Dumas concludes the scene:

> As she was on the point of leaving the room, she tore herself from the king's grasp, and returned to the stone crucifix, which she kissed, saying 'O Heaven! it was you who drew me hither, you who have rejected me; but your grace is infinite. If ever I return, forget that I have ever separated myself from you; for when I return, it will be — never to leave you again.'*

* See Brief Biographies.

The king could not restrain his emotion, and d'Artagnan, even, could not restrain a tear. Louis bore the young girl away, lifted her into the carriage, and directed d'Artagnan to seat himself beside her; while he, mounting his horse, spurred violently towards the Palais-Royal, where immediately on his arrival he sent to request an audience of Madame.

If the king's task in persuading Louise to believe in his love and to return with him was difficult, an equally formidable one lay on his next, so essential, of inducing Madame to relent and reinstate the girl as one of her maids of honour. The next chapter, entitled simply and aptly 'Madame', describes just that. Louis so humbles himself in his attempt to persuade Henrietta to forgive Louise and take her back, begs so impassionately, as to make her exclaim ' "How passionately you love, Sire, when you do love!" ' But when, against her will, she half relents and tells him she will ' "maintain her in her household" ', and when Louis in gratitude 'seized her hand and covered it with kisses and asked "For my sake will you treat her kindly, Henrietta?" ' she made the mistaken self-condemnatory reply

'I will treat her as your mistress.'
The king rose suddenly to his feet. By this word which had so fatally escaped her lips, Madame had destroyed all the merit of her sacrifice. The king felt freed from all obligation. Exasperated beyond measure, and bitterly offended, he replied, 'I thank you, Madame; I shall never forget the service you have rendered me;' and saluting her with an affectation of ceremony, he took his leave of her.

Dumas sums up the situation between them pithily with,

Madame was not bad-hearted; she was only hasty and impetuous. The king was not imprudent; he was only in love.

But from now on it was a war of attrition between them. Louis, now more than ever in love, was desperate to see Louise; knowing this, Madame maliciously went out of her way to make it impossible for the girl ever to be alone — a situation leading inevitably, as Dumas knew well enough, to the vindication of the lovers' *vade mecum* — love will find out the way, in this instance achieved by means of changed apartments for Saint-Aignan, a trapdoor made in the floor of Louise's room, a staircase leading down into the favourite's rooms, secret love sessions, a portrait painted — all created and guided by M. Malicorne and his vivacious willing partner in such affairs, Montalais. So for a while the king wins the duel, and content reigns in the royal household.

* * *

But not for long. Dumas shifts the scene to England and the court of Charles II to bring on 'the principal hero of our tale, now a poor knight rove-about at the king's caprice'. A strangely long description of Hampton Court is given (one wonders where Dumas got it) along with the emotions of Bragelonne himself, who is unhappy and pining to return to France and Louise, and of Mary Grafton, who is in love with him and wants him to stay. Into this mélange a *camisade* comes in the form of a letter to Charles II from his sister Henrietta — brief but a bombshell, running

> For your own sake, for mine, for the honour and safety of everyone, send M. de Bragelonne back to France immediately.
> Your devoted sister,
> HENRIETTA

with the result that Charles, comprehending, gives Raoul *carte blanche* to leave. An explosion of action follows, and we are shown — the two lovers in their secret hide-out, deliberately left alone by their conspirators, exchanging their first passionate kisses — the warning voice of Montalais from the room above — Louise reluctantly breaking from her lover's caresses, 'beautiful in her disorder', hurrying up the secret staircase to find Montalais waiting for her.

> Montalais was, in fact, waiting for her, very pale and agitated.
> 'Quick, quick! he is coming!' she said.
> 'Who? — who is coming?'
> 'He! I warned you of it.'
> 'But who? You are killing me.'
> 'Raoul,' murmured Montalais.
> 'It is I, — I,' said a joyous voice upon the last steps of the grand staircase.
> La Vallière uttered a terrible cry and threw herself back.
> 'Here I am, dear Louise,' said Raoul, running forward. 'Oh, I was sure you had not ceased to love me!'
> La Vallière, with a gesture partly of extreme terror and partly as if invoking a curse, attempted to speak, but could articulate only a single word. 'No, no!' she said; and she fell into Montalais's arms, murmuring, 'Do not come near us.'
> Montalais made a sign to Raoul, who stood petrified at the door, and did not even attempt to advance another step into the room. Then, looking towards the side of the room where the screen was, she exclaimed, 'Imprudent girl! she has not even closed the trapdoor.' Montalais advanced towards the corner of the room to close, first, the screen, and then, behind the screen, the trapdoor. But suddenly the king, who had heard La Vallière's cry, darted through the opening, and hurried forward to her assistance. He threw himself on his knees before her as he overwhelmed Montalais with questions, who hardly knew where she was or what she was doing.
> At the moment, however, that the king fell on his knees, a cry of utter despair rang through the corridor, accompanied by the sound of retreating footsteps. The king wished to run and see who had uttered the cry, and whose were the footsteps he had heard. It was in vain that Montalais sought to retain him, for the king, leaving La Vallière, rushed towards the door, — too late, however, for Raoul was already at a distance, and the king saw only a kind of shadow turning the angle of the corridor.

'Only a kind of shadow.' Dumas's phrase is an inspired one, describing as it does not only the present but the future. Raoul, already no more than a shadow in character, from now to the end was to become an even paler shadow as a lover.

* * *

The narrative now returns the reader to the Aramis trail by means of a long and complex imbroglio which has for its purpose the downfall of Fouquet machinated by the king and Colbert. As with the earlier example, the chit-chat among Fouquet's Epicurians will be of more interest to French than to British readers, and I propose to reduce the complex web to a single-thread outline.

This began with a meeting between Aramis and his old flame Mme de Chevreuse,* resuscitated by Dumas after being supposedly dead** — a meeting which, ironically entitled 'Two Old Friends'. consists of nothing but suspicious probings of each other. Needing money, the impoverished duchesse tries to sell her former lover some secret letters and accounts of the late Cardinal Mazarin detailing the loan of thirteen millions to Fouquet which, it seems, he has never returned and appropriated to himself. In other words sheer blackmail. Aramis, now the all-powerful General of the Jesuits, having no need of money good or bad, and after a lot of ill-natured banter, finally sees her off cavalierly.*** Undeterred, she next tries Colbert, knowing his enmity for the superintendent and his ambition to take his place. After long debate Colbert agrees to buy the letters from her. But then (wheels within wheels) the intendant summons Vanel, a counsellor of the Parliament and a protégé, and suggests that he should become the purchaser of Fouquet's offer to sell his position of Procureur-général — offer made under the duress of financial need. Vanel succeeds in doing this at the price of fourteen hundred thousand livres. Between the handshake of the agreement and payment Aramis arrives, and is shaken to learn from Fouquet of the sale of his post with its power to prevent his being at the mercy of any adversary or litigant, and so laying himself open to accusation of embezzlement, which is sure to follow, Colbert having the damning letters and, so Aramis informs him, Vanel's wife being Colbert's mistress. From all this Aramis perceives that it is all part of Colbert's machinations to ruin Fouquet, and

* The Marie Michon of *The Three Musketeers*.

** Spoken of as 'dead' by Aramis to the dying General of the Jesuits during his session with him at the Beau Paon. This may well have been a ploy on the part of Aramis rather than a lapse on that of Dumas; for later, during the duchess's interview with her old friend Anne of Austria, the queen-mother tells her she had received 'reports of her death.'

*** It should be said here, I feel, that the whole chapter is one of the weakest of the novel, being in the first place scarcely necessary to the plot at all; in the second too wordy by half and as such an example of Dumas's dubious ability to vie with Henry James in making two characters talk endlessly without getting anywhere; and in the third, its conclusion strikes one as being egregiously cruel and improbable from a man of Aramis's age and a former lover.

therefore that no time must be lost to bring his plot to its conclusion and make his next move. This, to Fouquet's surprise and failure to understand, is to hasten the fête he has promised to give in the king's honour, for which he (Aramis) will meet the enormous expense it will cost, only asking that he should have the general superintendence of it. The reader only understands the reason for the request after the fête itself.

In the meantime Mme de Chevreuse, interlinking unconsciously with Aramis and his plot, pursues her enigmatic way by means of an interview with Anne of Austria. Masked, and under the pretence of being a Béguine with a cure for the queen's cancer of the breast from which she is suffering and which was to kill her, she begins by speaking of Anne's physical condition, but proceeds to move on to express dark hints as to her mental state, and to prove her knowledge of her secret past, recounts in detail the birth not only of the present king but that of a twin later — a birth deliberately concealed from all public knowledge by Richelieu and Louis XIII as being a possible threat of future civil war and anarchy. Incensed and horrified at such knowledge shown by a stranger, the queen threatens her arrest and orders her to take off her mask. This she does.

> 'Madame de Chevreuse!' exclaimed the queen.
> 'With Your Majesty the sole living confidante of the secret.'
> 'Ah,' murmured Anne of Austria, 'come and embrace me, Duchess! Alas! you kill your friend in trifling with her terrible distress.'
> The queen, leaning her head upon the shoulder of the old duchess, burst into a flood of bitter tears. 'How young you are still!' said the latter in a hollow voice; 'you can weep!'

After which Anne throws aside her royalty and once again, though with the lesser candour of age, and renews friendship with her former companion and confidante. This apparently *ad hoc* chat touches the core of the Iron Mask mystery as Dumas chose to use it and as first suggested by Voltaire,* using Aramis as the synthesis as he had used d'Artagnan and Athos in the historical engima of Monk.

* * *

Meanwhile poor Bragelonne, 'left without reason, without will, without purpose', desperately seeking information on what has been happening in Paris during his enforced stay in London, bethought him first of his friend de Guiche who had written to him to put him on his guard. But he, now deeply in love with Madame, refused to inform him further, while advising him to see to his own affairs now he is on the spot. Raoul then tried d'Artagnan, but got nothing out of him either, the Captain of the Musketeers adopting a man to man offhand

---

* See Brief Biographies.

attitude and declaring his young friend of being ' "not in love" ' but merely having his head turned and unable to think straight, a state he had himself been in ' "a hundred times in my life" '; and when Raoul, hiding his face in his hands murmured despairingly ' "I haven't a single friend in the world," ' riposted ' "What, young man! Do you wish me to disgust you with the girl and teach you to execrate women, who are the honour and happiness of our life?" ' Instead, he advised him to see Montalais if he insisted on knowing the true state of affairs. Hardly had he advised this when

> suddenly the door opened, and one of the Musketeers, approaching d'Artagnan, said, 'Captain, Mademoiselle de Montalais is here, and wishes to speak to you.'
> 'To me?' murmured d'Artagnan. 'Ask her to come in. I shall soon see,' he said to himself, 'whether she wishes to speak to me or not.'
> The cunning captain was quite right in his suspicions; for as soon as Montalais entered she exclaimed, 'Oh, Monsieur! Monsieur! — I beg your pardon, M. d'Artagnan.'
> 'Oh, I forgive you, Mademoiselle,' said d'Artagnan; 'I know that at my age those who look for me must have great need of me.'
> 'I was looking for M. de Bragelonne,' replied Montalais.
> 'How very fortunate that is! He was looking for you too. Raoul, will you accompany Mademoiselle Montalais?'
> 'Oh, certainly!'
> 'Go along, then,' he said, as he gently pushed Raoul out of the room; and then taking hold of Montalais's hand he said in a low voice, 'Be kind towards him; spare him, and spare her too, if you can.'
> 'Ah!' she said in the same tone of voice, 'it is not I who will speak to him.'
> 'Who, then?'
> 'It is Madame who has sent for him.'
> 'Very good!' cried d'Artagnan; 'it is Madame, is it? In an hour's time, then, the poor fellow will be cured.'
> 'Or else dead,' said Montalais, in a voice full of compassion.
> 'Adieu, M. d'Artagnan!' she said; and she ran to join Raoul, who was waiting for her at a little distance from the door, very much puzzled and uneasy at the dialogue, which promised no good to him.

Left alone, d'Artagnan, to make up for his somewhat hard-hearted treatment of the young man, wrote a brief letter to Athos, touching on Raoul's visit and the court tittle-tattle, and leaving it to him, as Raoul's father, to act as he thought best. With dramatic results, as the reader is soon to learn.

Madame, taking over Raoul from Montalais, was pitiless. After regaling him with what all the court knew — 'the scene in the storm, the tête-à-tête in the forest, the flight to Chaillot' — to give proof to his as yet scarce-believing mind of his betrothed's falseness, took him to Louise's rooms, showed him the trapdoor, the staircase and the portrait — this last 'a final pang, dredging from him the words "Ah, Louise!... You never looked at me like that!" ' The scene ended with Raoul promising Madame never to divulge who it was who showed him the truth, and by writing and signing there and then a note challenging St-Aignan with the thought ' "Oh, perfidious king! I cannot challenge you, but your panderer, who represents you, shall pay for your crime. Then afterwards we will think of Louise." ' Thereafter events move. Returning to his apartments from riding out with the king, finding Bragelonne's note, Saint-Aignan showed it to Louis, and between them they soon worked out that it must have been Madame, with keys to all her maids of honours' rooms, who had let him in. Enraged, Louis naturally forbade his favourite to accept the challenge — one for which in the meantime Raoul had asked Porthos to act as his second. As Saint-Aignan was telling Louis about the challenge an usher announced that M. le Comte de la Fère was there, requesting an interview with the king. King and courtier, realizing only too well what the reason must be for the requested audition, exchanged a meaningful glance. Then, after sending his minion away with love messages for Louise, bracing himself, Louis directed the usher to introduce the count.

* * *

As this is the last and only time Athos makes his appearance alone, and it is a superb one, embodying at least something of the Athos of old, I give the interview (abridged) in his creator's own version, any other of necessity being weak in comparison.

> The king endeavoured to recover his self-possession as quickly as possible in order to meet M. de la Fère with an undisturbed countenance. He clearly saw that it was not mere chance which had induced the count's visit. He had a vague impression of the serious import of that visit; but he felt that to a man of Athos's tone of mind, to a person so distinguished, nothing disagreeable or disordered should be presented. As soon as the king had satisfied himself that so far as appearances were concerned he was perfectly calm again, he gave directions to the ushers to introduce the count.
>
> A few minutes afterwards Athos, in full court dress and with his breast covered with the orders that he alone had the right to wear at the court of France, presented himself with so grave and solemn an air that the king perceived at the first glance that he had not been mistaken in his anticipations. Louis advanced a step towards the count, and with a smile held out his hand to him, over which Athos bowed with the air of the deepest respect.
>
> 'M. le Comte de la Fère,' said the king rapidly, 'you are so seldom here that it is a very great happiness to see you.'
>
> Athos bowed and replied, 'I should wish always to enjoy the happiness of being near Your Majesty... Your Majesty will remember that at the period of the Duke of Buckingham's departure I had the honour of an interview with you with regard to a demand which I addressed to you respecting a marriage which M. de Bragelonne wished to contract with Mademoiselle de la Vallière.'
>
> 'Ah!' thought the king, 'we have come to it now. Yes, I remember,' he said aloud.
>
> 'At that period,' pursued Athos, 'Your Majesty was so kind and generous

towards M. de Bragelonne and myself that not a single word which then fell from your lips has escaped my memory; and when I asked Your Majesty to accord me Mademoiselle de la Vallière's hand for M. de Bragelonne, you refused.'

'Quite true,' said Louis dryly.

'Alleging,' Athos hastened to say, 'that the young lady had no position in society.'

Louis could hardly force himself to listen patiently.

'That,' added Athos, 'she had but little fortune.'

The king threw himself back in his armchair.

'That her extraction was indifferent.'

Renewed impatience on the part of the king.

'And little beauty,' added Athos, pitilessly.

This last bolt buried itself deep in the king's heart, and made him almost bound from his seat.

'You have a good memory, Monsieur,' he said.

'I invariably have on all occasions when I have had the distinguished honour of an interview with Your Majesty,' retorted the count, without being in the least disconcerted.

'Very good; it is admitted I said all that.'

'And I thanked Your Majesty, because those words testified an interest in M. de Bragelonne which did him much honour.'

'And you may possibly remember,' said the king very deliberately, 'that you had the greatest repugnance to this marriage?'

'Quite true, Sire.'

'And that you solicited my permission against your own inclination?'

'Yes, Sire.'

'And, finally, I remember also, — for I have a memory nearly as good as your own, — I remember, I say, that you observed at the time: "I do not believe that Mademoiselle de la Vallière loves M. de Bragelonne." Is that true?' The blow told, but Athos did not shrink.

'M. de Bragelonne is now so exceedingly unhappy that he cannot any longer defer asking Your Majesty for a solution of the matter.'

The king turned pale; Athos looked at him with fixed attention.

'And what,' said the king, with considerable hesitation, 'does M. de Bragelonne request?'

'Precisely the very thing that I came to ask Your Majesty for at my last audience; namely, Your Majesty's consent to his marriage.'

The king pressed his hands impatiently together.

'Does Your Majesty hesitate?' inquired the count without losing a particle either of his firmness or his politeness.

'I do not hesitate, — I refuse,' replied the kings.

Athos paused a moment as if to collect himself. 'I have had the honour,' he said in a mild tone, 'to observe to Your Majesty that no obstacle now interferes with M. de Bragelonne's affections, and that his determination seems unalterable.'

'There is my will, — and that is an obstacle, I should imagine!'

'That is the most serious of all,' Athos replied quickly.

'Ah!'

'And may we therefore be permitted to ask Your Majesty, with the greatest humility, for your reason for this refusal?'

'The reason! A question to me!' exclaimed the king.

'A demand, Sire!'

The king, leaning with both his hands upon the table, said in a deep tone of concentrated passion: 'You have lost all recollection of what is usual at court. At court no one questions the king.'

'Very true, Sire; but if men do not question, they conjecture.'

'Conjecture! What may that mean, Monsieur?'

'Almost always the conjecture of the subject impugns the frankness of the king.'

'Monsieur!'

'And a want of confidence on the part of the subject,' pursued Athos intrepidly.

'You are forgetting yourself,' said the king, hurried away by his anger in spite of his control over himself.

'Sire, I am obliged to seek elsewhere for what I thought I should find in Your Majesty. Instead of obtaining a reply from you, I am compelled to make one for myself.'

The king rose. 'Monsieur the Count,' he said, 'I have now given you all the time I had at my disposal.'

This was a dismissal.

'Sire,' replied the count, 'I have not yet had time to tell Your Majesty what I came with the express object of saying, and I so rarely see Your Majesty that I ought to avail myself of the opportunity.'

'Just now you spoke of conjectures; you are now becoming offensive, Monsieur.'

'Oh, Sire, offend Your Majesty! I? Never! All my life have I maintained that kings are above all other men, not only in rank and power, but in nobleness of heart and dignity of mind. I can never bring myself to believe that my sovereign — he who passed his word to me — did so with a mental reservation.'

'What do you mean? What mental reservation?'

'I will explain my meaning,' said Athos, coldly. 'If in refusing Mademoiselle de la Vallière to M. de Bragelonne Your Majesty had some other object in view than the happiness and fortune of the viscount.'

'You perceive, Monsieur, that you are offending me.'

'If in requiring the viscount to delay his marriage Your Majesty's only object was to remove the gentleman to whom Mademoiselle de la Vallière was engaged —'

'Monsieur! Monsieur!'

'I have heard it said so in every direction, Sire. Your Majesty's love for Mademoiselle de la Vallière is spoken of on all sides.'

The king tore his gloves which he had been biting for some time. 'Woe to those,' he cried, 'who interfere in my affairs! I have chosen my course; I will crush all obstacles.'

'What obstacles?' said Athos.

The king stopped short, like a runaway horse whose bit being turned in his mouth bruises his mouth. 'I love Mademoiselle de la Vallière,' he said suddenly with nobleness and with passion.

'But,' interrupted Athos, 'that does not preclude Your Majesty from allowing M. de Bragelonne to marry Mademoiselle de la Vallière. The sacrifice is worthy of so great a monarch; it is fully merited by M. de Bragelonne, who has already rendered great service to Your Majesty, and who may well be regarded as a brave and worthy man. Your Majesty, therefore, in renouncing the affection you entertain, offers a proof at once of generosity, gratitude, and good policy.'

'Mademoiselle de la Vallière does not love M. de Bragelonne,' said the king hoarsely.

'Does Your Majesty know that to be the case?' remarked Athos, with a searching look.

'I do know it.'

'Within a short time, then; for doubtless had Your Majesty known it when I first preferred my request, you would have taken the trouble to inform me of it.'

'Within a short time.'

Athos remained silent for a moment, and then resumed: 'In that case I do not understand why Your Majesty should have sent M. de Bragelonne to London. That exile, and with good reason, is a matter of astonishment to all who love the honour of the king.'

'Who presumes to speak of my honour, M. de la Fère?'

'The king's honour, Sire, is made up of the honour of his whole nobility. Whenever the king offends one of his gentlemen, — that is, whenever he deprives him of the smallest particle of his honour, — it is from him, from the king himself, that that portion of honour is stolen.'

'M. de la Fère!' exclaimed the king haughtily.

'Sire, you sent M. de Bragelonne to London either before you were Mademoiselle de la Vallière's lover or since you have become so.'

The king, irritated beyond measure, especially because he felt that he was mastered, endeavoured to dismiss Athos by a gesture.

'Oh, you will listen to me, Sire! I am old now, and I am attached to everything that is really great and true in your kingdom. I am a gentleman who shed my blood for your father and for yourself without ever having asked a single favour either from yourself or from your father. I have never inflicted the slightest wrong or injury on anyone in this world, and have put kings under obligations to me. You will listen to me. I have come to ask you for an account of the honour of one of your servants whom you have deceived by a falsehood or betrayed through weakness. I know that these words irritate Your Majesty; but on the other hand, the facts are killing us. I know you are inquiring what penalty you will inflict for my frankness; but I know what punishment I will implore God to inflict upon you when I set before him your perjury and my son's unhappiness.'

The king during these remarks was pacing to and fro, his hand thrust into the breast of his coat, his head haughtily raised, his eyes blazing with wrath. 'Monsieur,' he cried suddenly, 'if I acted towards you as the king, you would be already punished; but I am only a man, and I have the right to love in this world every one who loves me, — a happiness which is so rarely found.'

'You cannot pretend to such a right as a man any more than as a king, Sire; or if you intended to exercise that right in a loyal manner, you should have told M. de Bragelonne so, and not have exiled him.'

'I think I am condescending to dispute with you, Monsieur!' interrupted Louis XIV with that majesty of air and manner which he alone was able to give to his look and his voice.

'I was hoping that you would reply to me,' said the count.

'You shall know my reply, Monsieur, very soon.'

'You already know my thoughts on the subject,' was the Comte de la Fère's answer.

'You have forgotten you are speaking to the king, Monsieur. It is a crime.'

'You have forgotten you are destroying the lives of two men, Sire. It is a mortal sin.'

'Go! — at once!'

'Not until I have said to you: Son of Louis XIII, you begin your reign badly, for you begin it by seduction and disloyalty! My race — myself, too — are now freed from all that affection and respect towards you to which I bound my son by oath in the vaults of St Denis, in the presence of the relics of your noble forefathers.* You are now become our enemy, Sire; and henceforth we have nothing to do save with heaven alone, our sole master. Be warned!'

'Do you threaten?'

'Oh, no!' said Athos, sadly; 'I have as little bravado as fear in my soul. The God of whom I spoke to you is now listening to me. He knows that for the safety and honour of your crown I would even yet shed every drop of blood which twenty years of civil and foreign warfare have left in my veins. I can well say, then, that I threaten the king as little as I threaten the man; but I tell you, Sire, you lose two servants, — for you have destroyed faith in the heart of the father, and love in the heart of the son: the one ceases to believe in the royal word, the other no longer believes in the loyalty of man or the purity of woman; the one is dead to every feeling of respect, the other to obedience. *Adieu!*'

As he spoke, Athos broke his sword across his knee, slowly placed the two pieces upon the floor, and saluting the king, who was almost choking from rage and shame, quitted the cabinet.

Louis, who sat near the table, completely overwhelmed, spent several minutes in recovering himself, then suddenly rose and rang the bell violently. 'Tell M. d'Artagnan to come here,' he said to the terrified ushers.

* * *

Bragelonne, meanwhile, after writing his challenge to Saint-Aignan, had muttered vague words about seeing to Louise after the intended duel. He was to have that lacerating problem thrust on him sooner than he had bargained for by Louise herself; for on leaving his father immediately after the latter's blistering scene with the king and returning forlornly to his rooms, he found Louise there waiting for him. Followed a long tortuous dialogue between them, she excusing herself by confessing her cause was a bad one; that she loved the king beyond everything in life; that she had not dared to tell Raoul as much partly because she shrank from inflicting the hurt she knew it would cause him; and finally begging his forgiveness and even accepting death at his hand if in his heart he believed she deserved death; he, after much reproaching and condemnation, in turn begging *her* forgiveness in that he, older than herself, ought to have understood their different situations and have demanded a final answer from her. And he ended by telling her ' "I loved you so much, Louise, that my heart is dead, my faith extinguished... I love you still, and to tell you at this moment is to pronounce my own sentence of death." ' Whereupon she

---

* v. *Twenty Years After* ch. XXIV.

faints, and is carried out to her carriage by Olivain. All of which today's reader must feel to be very romantic and unrealistic, and made to hold little sympathy for either of them.

While all this was going on, d'Artagnan, ordered by the guiltily enraged king to arrest Athos, had gone to his friend's house, where he found him alone except for his ever-faithful Grimaud. After relating with his Gascon semi-humorous bluffness the king's state of fury (' "My dear Athos, the king was not just red in the face, he was positively purple." ') he took his friend away ' "to take a walk in my carriage" ' as he lied to the uneasy Grimaud. Arrived at 'the quays', in answer to Athos's ' "You are taking me to the Bastille, I presume," ' d'Artagnan's reply came ' "I am taking you wherever you would like to go," ' following this by suggesting he should make his way to Havre and on to England, and so enabling him (d'Artagnan) to return to the king and tell him that his intended prisoner had disappeared. And he ended with ' "Well, what do you say to my idea?" ' — only to get for reply ' "Take me to the Bastille," ' said Athos, smiling, adding...

> 'I wish to prove to this young man, who is dazzled by the power and splendour of his crown, that he can be regarded as the first among men only by proving himself to be the most generous and the wisest among them. He may punish, imprison, or torture me, — it does not matter. He abuses his opportunities, and I wish him to learn the bitterness of remorse, while heaven teaches him what chastisement is.'
>
> 'Well, well,' replied d'Artagnan, 'I know only too well that when you have once said "No". you mean "No". I do not insist any longer. You wish to go to the Bastille?'
>
> 'I do,'
>
> 'Let us go, then! To the Bastille!' cried d'Artagnan to the coachman; and throwing himself back in the carriage he gnawed the ends of his moustache with a fury which to Athos, who knew him well, signified a resolution either already taken or in course of formation. A profound silence ensued in the carriage, which continued to roll on neither faster nor slower than before.
>
> Athos took the Musketeer by the hand. 'You are not angry with me, d'Artagnan?' he said.
>
> 'I? Oh, no! of course not! What you do from heroism I should have done from sheer obstinacy.'
>
> 'But you are quite of opinion, are you not, that heaven will avenge me?'
>
> 'And I know some persons on earth who will lend a helping hand,' said the captain.

But inside the Bastille a surprise awaited them with the sight of Aramis 'seated beside Baisemeaux at table in expectation of a good meal'. This fact, the Dumasian will say to himself, is the third occasion in the novel when the Three are together. Here it is d'Artagnan, Athos and Aramis, with Porthos missing. In addition, the circumstance is the occasion of the first meeting between Athos and Aramis since their parting ten years back.* But Dumas somewhat disappointingly gives no hint

---

* 'The four friends embraced one another with moist eyes, then separated without knowing whether they would ever meet again.' (*Twenty Years After*)

of any likely emotion felt by the two ex-Musketeers and friends other than surprise at this strange and unexpected meeting. All we are given is that after d'Artagnan had left them,

> Aramis, with many friendly protestations of delight, sat down by Athos, determined to make him speak; but Athos possessed all the virtues in their highest excellence. If necessity had required it he would have been the finest orator in the world; but when there was need of silence he would die rather than utter a syllable.
> He sounded all the depths of the mind of Aramis, who lived in the midst of subterfuge, evasion, and intrigue; he studied his man well and thoroughly, and felt convinced that he was engaged upon some important project. And then he too began to think of his own personal affair, and to lose himself in conjectures as to d'Artagnan's reasons for having left the Bastille so abruptly, and for leaving behind him a prisoner so badly introduced and so badly looked after by the prison authorities.
> But we shall not pause to probe into the thoughts and feelings of these personages; we will leave them to themselves, surrounded by the remains of poultry, game, and fish, mutilated by the generous knife of Baisemeaux, and follow d'Artagnan instead, who, getting into the carriage which had brought him, cried out to the coachman, 'To the king! and burn the pavement!'

* * *

That last sentence of the chapter burns into the reader's mind as well as the pavement, as Dumas obviously intended. The next chapter 'What took place at the Louvre during the supper at the Bastille' was to prove one of the supreme moments of the novel.

But before introducing it to the reader it would be as well to remind him of the Captain of the Musketeer's relationship with the young king. Recalling his previous audiences at Blois and in the Louvre, and especially the important slipped-in sentence when, ordered by Louis to investigate and report to him on the duel between de Guiche and de Wardes, he hazards a joke 'at which the king laughed at the liberty he tolerated in no one but his Captain of Musketeers', the reader is aware, as in fact d'Artagnan himself is, that thanks to his age, position and above all, character, he had made himself a sort of major-domo, a servitor, but a uniquely honoured one. All this must surely have passed through his mind as the driver, taking him at his word to ' "burn the pavement," ' bore him from the Bastille to the Louvre; for he must have known that by facing the king with the words that were in his mind he was dicing with his future.

But just prior to the captain's return, and immediately following Athos's interview, Dumas has skilfully related a brief scene between the king and Saint-Aignan in which the latter had made consoling and quasi humorous references to Bragelonne and his relationship with Louise.

> De Saint-Aignan thought he should have made the king laugh; but on the contrary, from a mere smile Louis passed to the greatest seriousness of manner. He already

began to experience that remorse which the count had told d'Artagnan would be inflicted on him. He reflected that, in fact, these young persons had loved and sworn fidelity to each other; that one of the two had kept his word, and that the other was too conscientious not to feel her perjury most bitterly; and with remorse, jealousy sharply pricked the king's heart.

And this served to act as a break in the king's natural reaction of anger at d'Artagnan's bravado and also against possible criticism of his final capitulation to his Captain of Musketeers.

The comments I made on Athos's interview apply even more meaningfully to this of d'Artagnan; for fine as were the former's words of rebellion, they are outmatched by those of the latter, which can be described without exaggeration as the finest outside Shakespeare. So with this interview too I give it verbatim, but similarly abridged.

De Saint-Aignan was just beginning to feel that his position was becoming awkward, when the curtain before the door was raised. The king turned hastily round. His first idea was that a letter from Louise had arrived; but instead of a letter of love, he saw only his Captain of Musketeers standing upright and silent in the doorway. 'M. d'Artagnan!' he said. 'Ah! well, Monsieur?'

D'Artagnan looked at de Saint-Aignan; Louis's eyes took the same direction as those of his captain. These looks would have been clear to anyone, and they were especially so to de Saint-Aignan. The courtier bowed and quitted the room, leaving the king and d'Artagnan alone.

'Is it done?' inquired the king.

'Yes, Sire,' replied the Captain of the Musketeers, in a grave voice, 'it is done!'

The king was unable to say another word. Pride, however, obliged him not to pause there. Whenever a sovereign has adopted a decisive course, even though it be unjust, he is compelled to prove to all witnesses, and particularly to himself, that he was right in so adopting it. A good means for effecting that — an almost infallible means, indeed — is to try to prove his victim to be in the wrong. Louis, brought up by Mazarin and Anne of Austria, knew better than anyone else his vocation as a monarch; he therefore endeavoured to prove it on the present occasion. After a few moments' pause, which he had employed in making silently to himself the same reflections which we have just expressed aloud, he said in an indifferent tone, 'What did the count say?'

'Nothing at all, Sire.'

'Surely he did not allow himself to be arrested without saying something?'

'He said he expected to be arrested, Sire.'

The king raised his head haughtily. 'I presume,' he said, 'that M. le Comte de la Fère has not continued to play his obstinate and rebellious part?'

'In the first place, Sire, what do you term rebellious?' quietly asked the Musketeer. 'Is that man a rebel, in the eyes of the king, who not only allows himself to be shut up in the Bastille, but who even opposes those who do not wish to take him there?'

'Who do not wish to take him there!' exclaimed the king. 'What do you say, Captain? Are you mad?'

'I believe not, Sire.'

'You speak of persons who did not wish to arrest M. de la Fère?'

'Yes, Sire.'

'And who are they?'

'Those whom Your Majesty entrusted with that duty, apparently.'

'But it is you whom I entrusted with it,' exclaimed the king.

'Yes, Sire; it is I.'

'And you say that, despite my orders, you had the intention of not arresting the man who had insulted me!'

'Yes, Sire, that was really my intention. I even proposed to the count to mount a horse that I had had prepared for him at the Barrière de la Conférence.'

'And what was your object in doing this?'

'Why, Sire, in order that M. le Comte de la Fère might be able to reach Havre, and from that place make his escape to England.'

'You betrayed me then, Monsieur?' cried the king, kindling with a wild pride.

'Exactly so...'

'Ah, M. d'Artagnan, so you set your king at defiance!'

'Sire — '

'M. d'Artagnan, I warn you that you are abusing my patience.'

'On the contrary, Sire.'

'What do you mean by "on the contrary"?'

'I have come to get myself arrested too.'

'To get yourself arrested, — you!'

'Of course. My friend will be lonely down there; and I have come to propose to Your Majesty to permit me to bear him company. If Your Majesty will but give the word, I will arrest myself. I shall not need the Captain of the Guards for that, I assure you.'

The king darted towards the table and seized a pen to write the order for d'Artagnan's imprisonment. 'Pay attention, Monsieur, that this is forever!' cried the king in a tone of stern menace.

'I can quite believe that,' returned the Musketeer; 'for when you have once done such an act as that, you will never be able to look me in the face again.'

The king dashed down his pen violently. 'Leave the room, Monsieur!' he said.

'Sire, I came to speak temperately to Your Majesty. Your Majesty gets into a passion with me: that is a misfortune; but I shall not the less on that account say what I had to say to you.'

'Your resignation, Monsieur, — your resignation!' cried the king.

'Sire, you know whether I care about my resignation or not, since at Blois, on the day when you refused King Charles the million which my friend the Comte de la Fère found for him, I tendered my resignation to Your Majesty.'

'Very well, then, do it at once!'

'No, Sire; for there is no question of my resignation at the present moment. Your Majesty took up your pen just now to send me to the Bastille, why should you change your intention?'

'D'Artagnan! Gascon that you are! who is the king, allow me to ask, — you or myself?'

'You, Sire, unfortunately.'

'What do you mean "unfortunately"?'

'Yes, Sire; for if it were I — '

'If it were you, you would approve of M. d'Artagnan's rebellious conduct, I suppose?'

'Certainly.'

'Really?' said the king, shrugging his shoulders.

'And I should tell my Captain of the Musketeers,' continued d'Artagnan, — 'I should tell him, looking at him all the while with human eyes and not with eyes like coals of fire, "M. d'Artagnan, I have forgotten that I am king; I have descended from my throne to insult a gentleman." '

'Monsieur!' cried the king, 'do you think you can excuse your friend by exceeding him in insolence?'

'Oh, Sire! I shall go much further than he did,' said d'Artagnan; 'and it will be your own fault. I shall tell you what he, a man full of delicacy, did not tell you; I shall say: "Sire, you sacrifice his son, and he defended his son; you sacrificed him; he addressed you in the name of honour, of religion, of virtue, — you repulsed, pursued, imprisoned him." I shall be harder than he was, for I shall say to you: "Sire, choose! Do you wish to have friends or lackeys, soldiers or slaves, great men or puppets? Do you wish men to serve you or to crouch before you? Do you wish men to love you or to fear you? Choose, Sire, and without delay! Whatever remains to you of the grand nobility, guard it with a jealous eye; of courtiers you will always have enough. Delay not — and send me to the Bastille with my friend; for if you have not known how to listen to the Comte de la Fère, if you do not know how to listen to d'Artagnan, that is to say, to the rough voice of sincerity, — you are a bad king, and to-morrow you will be a poor king. Now, bad kings are hated; poor kings are driven away." That is what I had to say to you, Sire; you are wrong to have driven me to it.'

The king threw himself back in his chair, cold and livid. Had a thunderbolt fallen at his feet he could not have been more astonished; he appeared as if his respiration had ceased, and as if he were at the point of death. That rough voice of sincerity, as d'Artagnan had called it, had pierced through his heart like a sword-blade.

D'Artagnan had said all that he had to say. Comprehending the king's anger, he drew his sword, and approaching Louis XIV, respectfully, placed it on the table. But the king, with a furious gesture, thrust aside the sword, which fell on the ground and rolled to d'Artagnan's feet. Notwithstanding his mastery over himself, d'Artagnan too, in his turn, became pale and trembled with indignation. 'A king,' he cried, 'may disgrace a soldier, — he may exile him, and may even condemn him to death; but were he a hundred times a king he has no right to insult him by casting dishonour on his sword! Stained with disgrace as this sword now is, it has henceforth no other sheath than either your heart or my own. I choose my own, Sire; give thanks for it to God, and my patience.' Then snatching up his sword, he cried, 'My blood be upon your head!' and with a rapid gesture he placed the hilt upon the floor and directed the point of the blade towards his breast. The king, however, with a movement still more rapid than that of d'Artagnan, threw his right arm round the Musketeer's neck, and with his left hand seized hold of the blade by the middle and returned it silently to the scabbard. D'Artagnan, upright, pale, and still trembling, suffered the king to do all, without aiding him, to the very end. Then Louis, overcome, returned to the table, took a pen, wrote a few lines, signed them, and offered the paper to d'Artagnan.

'What is this paper, Sire?' inquired the captain.

'An order for M. d'Artagnan to set the Comte de la Fère at liberty.'

D'Artagnan seized the king's hand and kissed it; he then folded the order, placed it in his belt, and quitted the room. Neither the king nor the captain spoke a word.

'Oh, human heart, compass for kings to steer by!' murmured Louis when alone; 'when shall I learn to read you like the pages of a book? No, I am not a bad king, I am not a poor king; but I am still a child.'

* * *

Problem: how to follow such an episode with anything but an anticlimax. Dumas masters it with simple ease. In the company of the Three, plus Baisemeaux, he could hardly fail. D'Artagnan, with both the king's order and counter-order in his belt, arrived in the midst of the conversation, still agitated by his interview; and Athos, perceiving this, and presuming he had made a request which had been refused, felt he was called on to give an explanation of everything.

'The truth is, my friends,' said the Comte de la Fère with a smile, 'that you, Aramis, have been supping with a State criminal, and you, M. de Baisemeaux, with your prisoner.'

Baisemeaux uttered an exclamation of surprise and almost of delight. That worthy man took pride in his fortress. Profit aside, the more prisoners he had, the happier he was; and the higher the prisoners were in rank, the prouder he felt.

Aramis assumed an expression which he thought the situation required, and said: 'Well, dear Athos, forgive me; but I almost suspected what has happened. Some prank of Raoul or La Vallière, is it not?'

'Alas!' said Baisemeaux.

'And,' continued Aramis, 'you, a high and powerful nobleman as you are, forgetful that there are now only courtiers, — you have been to the king, and told him what you thought of his conduct?'

'Yes, you have guessed right.'

'So that,' said Baisemeaux, trembling at having supped so familiarly with a man who had fallen into disgrace with the king, — 'so that, Monsieur the Count — '

'So that, my dear governor,' said Athos, 'my friend d'Artagnan will communicate to you the contents of the paper which I perceive just peeping out of his belt, and which assuredly can be nothing else than the order for my incarceration.'

Baisemeaux held out his hand with his accustomed eagerness. D'Artagnan drew two papers from his belt and presented one of them to the governor, who unfolded it, and then read in a low tone of voice, looking at Athos over the paper as he did so and pausing from time to time: ' "Order to detain in my château of the Bastille M. le Comte de la Fère." Oh, Monsieur! this is indeed a very melancholy honour for me.'

'You will have a patient prisoner, Monsieur,' said Athos, in his calm, soft voice.

'A prisoner, too, who will not remain a month with you, my dear governor,' said Aramis; while Baisemeaux, still holding the order in his hand, transcribed it in the prison register.

'Not a day nor even a night,' said d'Artagnan, displaying the second order of the king; 'for now, dear M. de Baisemeaux, you will have the goodness to transcribe also this order for setting the count immediately at liberty.'

> 'Ah!' said Aramis, 'it is a labour that you have spared me, d'Artagnan;' and he pressed the Musketeer's hand in a significant manner and that of Athos at the same time.

Aramis's interventions, though brief, are full of meaning, and serve to restore him in the reader's opinion as being still at heart one of the Four. His mission achieved, d'Artagnan proceeded to take Athos away with him, leaving Aramis with the governor, the latter 'in a state of admiration for a man who could make the king do as he wished!'

While this scene was being enacted inside the Bastille, another connected with it was taking place outside it. Grimaud and Raoul, each coming at last to the same conclusion viz, that d'Artagnan had come to arrest the count, had found and saddled horses and set off for the Bastille. On their way Raoul suddenly recollected that he had left Porthos still awaiting Saint-Aignan, and they picked him up on their way, arriving just in time to see a carriage bearing Athos and d'Artagnan leaving the prison, and to waylay it.

> Raoul, presenting his pistol, threw himself on the leader, commanding the coachman to stop. Porthos seized the coachman and dragged him from his seat. Grimaud already had hold of the carriage door. Raoul threw open his arms, exclaiming, 'Monsieur the Count! Monsieur the Count!'
> 'Ah! is it you, Raoul?' said Athos, intoxicated with joy.
> 'Not bad, indeed!' added d'Artagnan with a burst of laughter; and they both embraced the young man and Porthos, who had captured them.
> 'My brave Porthos, best of friends!' cried Athos, 'still the same as ever!'
> 'He is still only twenty,' said d'Artagnan. 'Bravo, Porthos!'
> 'Confound it!' answered Porthos, slightly confused, 'we thought that you were arrested.'
> 'While,' rejoined Athos, 'I was, in fact, only taking a drive in M. d'Artagnan's carriage.'

Let the reader note here that for the fourth time the Three were together again, but this time with Aramis missing. Greetings over, they separated, Athos to take his son home with him to Blois, d'Artagnan going with Porthos, to the latter's profound satisfaction.

> Then they embraced, clasped one another's hands, and interchanged a thousand pledges of eternal friendship. Porthos promised to spend a month with Athos at the first opportunity. D'Artagnan engaged to take advantage of his first leave of absence; and then, having embraced Raoul for the last time, 'To you, my boy,' said he, 'I will write.'
> Coming from d'Artagnan, who he knew wrote very seldom, these words expressed everything. Raoul was moved even to tears. He tore himself away from the Musketeer, and departed.

With their retirement from the Parisian scene, both Athos and his son fade out as characters, the son to give himself up spinelessly to thoughts of ending his life, the father to the grief of knowing that.

The chapter in question being headed 'In which Porthos is convinced without having understood anything', Dumas has to make it good, and so concludes it with a typical piece of dialogue:

> D'Artagnan rejoined Porthos in the carriage. 'Well,' said he, '*mon cher ami*, what a day we have had!'
> 'Indeed, we have,' answered Porthos.
> 'You must be quite worn out.'
> 'Not quite; however, I shall retire early to rest, so as to be ready for tomorrow.'
> 'Whatever for?'
> 'Why, to finish what I have begun.'
> 'You make me shudder, *mon ami*; you seem to me quite angry. What the devil have you begun which is not finished?'
> 'Listen! Raoul has not fought; so I must fight instead.'
> 'Who with? The king?'
> 'What do you mean?' exclaimed Porthos, astounded, 'with the king? I assure you it is with M. de Saint-Aignan.'
> 'Look now, this is what I mean; you stupid! You draw your sword against the king in fighting with this gentleman.'
> 'Ah!' said Porthos, staring; 'are you sure of it?'
> 'Indeed, I am.'
> 'How shall we arrange it, then?'
> 'We must try and make a good supper, Porthos. The Captain of the Musketeers keeps a tolerable table. There you will see de Saint-Aignan, and drink his health.'
> 'I!' cried Porthos, horrified.
> 'What!' said d'Artagnan, 'you refuse to drink the king's health?'
> 'But, body alive! I am not talking to you about the king at all; I am speaking of M. de Saint-Aignan.'
> 'But since I repeat that it is the same thing —'
> 'Ah, well, well!' said Porthos, overcome.
> 'You understand, don't you?'
> 'No,' answered Porthos; 'but it's all the same.'
> 'Yes, it is all the same,' replied d'Artagnan; 'let us go to supper, Porthos.'

* * *

The narrative returns us to the Bastille to pick up the scene between Aramis and Baisemeaux where, like a spider murderously weaving its web, the former is about to bring off the penultimate gamble of his plot; and he begins it by making the governor aware that not only is he the new General of the Jesuits but also the Confessor Extraordinary to the prison, and proceeds to crush the poor man by authorizing him to take him to see Marchiali as his confessor. Once alone with the prisoner in his room he extracts from him details of his past life (details which tie with Mme de Chevreuse's account to Anne of Austria). Then by argument, appeal, and finally by showing him a portrait of the king and then a mirror, he brings him round to agreeing to his grandiose scheme.

After Aramis the devious, Porthos the true-hearted: the humour after the high drama. The very title of the next chapter — 'How Mouston had become fatter without giving Porthos notice of it, and of the troubles which befell that worthy gentleman', provokes the anticipatory smile.

D'Artagnan, ever faithful, one morning during an interval of service thought about Porthos, and being uneasy at not having heard anything of him for a fortnight, directed his steps towards his abode, arriving just as he was getting up. The worthy baron had a pensive — nay, more, a melancholy — air. He was sitting on his bed, only half dressed, and with legs dangling over the edge, contemplating a great number of garments, which with their fringes, lace, embroidery, and slashes of ill-assorted hues were scattered all over the floor.

Porthos, sad and reflective as La Fontaine's hare,* did not observe d'Artagnan's entrance, which was moreover screened at this moment by M. Mouston, whose personal corpulence, quite enough at any time to hide one man from another, was for the moment doubled by a scarlet coat which the intendant was holding up by the sleeves for his master's inspection, that he might the better see it all over. D'Artagnan stopped at the threshold and looked at the pensive Porthos; and then, as the sight of the innumerable garments strewing the floor caused mighty sighs to heave from the bosom of that excellent gentleman, d'Artagnan thought it time to put an end to these dismal reflections, and coughed by way of announcing himself.

'Ah!' exclaimed Porthos, whose countenance brightened, 'ah! ah! Here is d'Artagnan. Now we shall have some ideas!'

After a couple of pages of chat and back-chat, the Musketeer is at last made aware of the reason for his old friend's dumps, namely, invited by Aramis to attend Fouquet's grand fête, he finds he has no suitable costume to wear, and explains to the astonished d'Artagnan that among the heap of those littering the floor not one would fit him, or, if one did, it was hopelessly old-fashioned. And all this the fault of poor Mouston. On the amused but perplexed Musketeer failing to see the connection, Porthos explained that, having a horror of letting anyone take his measurements (' "either one is a gentleman or one is not" ') he had the idea of making Mouston stand in for him, and to that end fattening him up to make his measurements the same as his master's, barring height, of course, only to find that Mouston had overdone the process and become too fat, with the result that the last dozen coats were all too large.

As usual, the Gascon had the answer to his friend's dilemma, which was to take him along to M. Percerin, the king's own tailor, and get him to make the elusive garment, but warning,

'Only, you must allow yourself to be measured!'

'Ah!' said Porthos, with a sigh, ' 'tis vexatious, but what would you have me do?'

'Do? As others do, — as the king does.'

* v. La Fontaine, *Fables* — Le Lièvre et les Grenouilles.

'What! Do they measure the king too? Does he put up with it?'

'The king is a beau, my good friend; and so are you, too, whatever you may say about it.'

Porthos smiled triumphantly. 'Let us go to the king's tailor,' he said; 'and since he measures the king, *ma foi*! I think, I may well allow him to measure me!'

After a too-lengthy unnecessary history of the Percerin family and its association with former royalty, the two friends found themselves at the studio of the 80-year-old officious, peevish master-tailor where, after pushing their way through a crowd of waiting customers, the captain's eye came to rest on a man seated on a stool behind a counter, his head barely above it.

This man held up his head too often to be very productively employed with his fingers. D'Artagnan was not deceived, and he saw at once that if this man was working on anything it certainly was not on cloth.

'Eh!' said he, addressing this man, 'and so you have become a tailor's boy, M. Molière?'

'Hush, M. d'Artagnan!' replied the man softly; 'in heaven's name! you will make them recognize me.'

'Well, and what harm is there in that?'

'The fact is, there is no harm; but — '

'You were going to say there is no good in doing it, either, is it not so?'

'Alas! no; I was occupied in looking at some excellent figures.'

'Go on, go on, M. Molière! I quite understand the interest you take in it. I will not disturb your study.'

'Thank you.'

'But on one condition, — that you tell me where M. Percerin really is.'

'Oh, willingly! He is in his own room. Only — '

'Only that one can't enter it?'

'Unapproachable.'

'For everybody?'

'For everybody. He brought me here so that I might be at my ease to make my observations, and then he went away.'

'Well, my dear M. Molière, you can go and tell him I am here.'

'I!' exclaimed Molière, in the tone of a dog from which a bone it has legitimately gained is being snatched. 'I disturb myself? Ah, M. d'Artagnan, how hard you are upon me!'

'If you don't go directly and tell M. Percerin that I am here, my dear Molière' said d'Artagnan, in a low tone, 'I warn you of one thing, — I won't let you examine the friend I have brought with me.'

Molière indicated Porthos by an imperceptible gesture.

'This gentleman, is it not?'

'Yes.'

Molière fixed upon Porthos one of those looks which penetrate the minds and hearts of men. The subject doubtless appeared promising to him, for he immediately rose and led the way into the adjoining chamber.

Once in Percerin's own workshop and sanctum, d'Artagnan introduced Porthos to the harassed and factious old man who, after much pressing, was induced to agree to make a coat for the Baron du Vallon, but failing to persuade him to start on it in time for the Vaux fête. But in the midst of the wrangle Aramis suddenly appeared from behind the tapestry, and after greeting his old comrades addressed Percerin.

'Come come, M. Percerin, make the baron's dress, and I will answer for it you will gratify M. Fouquet;' and he accompanied the words with a sign which seemed to say, 'Agree, and dismiss them.'

It appeared that Aramis had over M. Percerin an influence superior even to d'Artagnan's; for the tailor bowed in assent, and turning round upon Porthos, 'Go and get measured on the other side,' said he, rudely.

Porthos coloured in a formidable manner. D'Artagnan saw the storm coming, and addressing Molière said to him in an undertone, 'You see before you, my dear Monsieur, a man who considers himself disgraced if you measure the flesh and bones that heaven has given him; study this type for me, Aristophanes, and profit by it.'

Molière had no need of encouragement, and his gaze dwelt upon Baron Porthos. 'Monsieur,' he said, 'If you will come with me, I will make them take your measure without the measurer once touching you.'

'Oh!' said Porthos, 'how the devil do you manage that?'

'I say that they shall apply neither line nor rule to the seams of your dress. It is a new method we have invented for measuring people of quality who are too sensitive to allow low-born fellows to touch them. We know some susceptible persons who will not put up with being measured, — a process which, as I think, wounds the natural dignity of man; and if perchance Monsieur should be one of these —'

'*Corboeuf*! I certainly am one of them.'

'Well, that is a capital coincidence, and you will have the benefit of our invention.'

'But how the devil can it be done?' asked Porthos, delighted.

'Monsieur,' said Molière, bowing, 'if you will deign to follow me, you will see.'

But while Porthos went out with Molière, the Musketeer, puzzled and curious at Aramis's visit and obvious authority, remained to see the scene out — a scene ending after verbal manoeuvrings on the part of Aramis by his obtaining from the reluctant Percerin five samples of the various costumes the tailor was making for the king to wear at the fête so that, he declared, ' "M. Fouquet could give the king the surprise of seeing his portrait on his arrival at Vaux ... dressed exactly as he will be on that very day." ' After which Aramis, with the five samples in his pocket, and the Musketeer, the latter half convinced but still 'feeling there was something strange at the bottom of it', repaired into the next room, where they found Porthos.

D'Artagnan found Porthos in the adjoining chamber; but no longer an irritated Porthos, or a disappointed Porthos, but Porthos radiant, blooming, fascinating, and chatting with Molière, who was looking upon him with a species of idolatry, and as a man would who had not only never seen anything better, but not even ever anything so good. Aramis went straight up to Porthos and offered him his delicate white hand, which lost itself in the gigantic hand of his old friend, — an operation which Aramis never hazarded without a certain uneasiness.* But the friendly pressure having been performed not too painfully for him, the Bishop of Vannes passed over to Molière.

'Well, Monsieur,' said he, 'will you come with me to St. Mandé?'

'I will go anywhere you like, Monseigneur,' answered Molière.

'To St. Mandé!' cried Porthos, surprised at seeing the proud Bishop of Vannes fraternizing with a journeyman tailor. 'What! Aramis, are you going to take this gentleman to St Mandé?'

'Yes.' said Aramis, smiling; 'our work is pressing.'

'Besides, my dear Porthos,' continued d'Artagnan, 'M. Molière is not altogether what he seems.'

'In what way?' asked Porthos.

'Why, this gentleman is one of M. Percerin's chief clerks, and he is expected at St. Mandé to try on the costumes which M. Fouquet has ordered for the Epicureans.'

'It is precisely so,' said Molière; 'yes, Monsieur.'

'Come, then, my dear M. Molière,' said Aramis; 'that is, if you have done with M. du Vallon?'

'We have finished,' replied Porthos.

'And you are satisfied?' asked d'Artagnan.

'Completely so,' replied Porthos.

Molière took his leave of Porthos with much ceremony, and grasped the hand which the Captain of the Musketeers offered him.

'Pray, Monsieur,' concluded Porthos mincingly, 'above all, be punctual.'

'You will have your costume after tomorrow, Monsieur the Baron,' answered Molière; and he left with Aramis.

Left alone with Porthos, the Musketeer asked him how it was that M. Molière had managed to make him so satisfied. Porthos's explanation and their dialogue is a vignette of sheer delight. 'The tailor' had taken his measurements without once touching him by placing him before a long mirror on which, after ordering two apprentices to hold his arms in a graceful attitude, he had chalked his outline on the surface of the glass. Added humour comes from the Malapropian mispronunciation and mis-remembering on the part of Porthos of Molière's name as Volière, Coquelin and Poquenard. The little scenario closes with a typical comment by d'Artagnan on the *ci-devant* tailor. In response to Porthos's saying to his friend ' "Congratulate me. It seems I am the first who has had his measure taken in that way. It will be of great use to him in the future, I'm sure," ' the Musketeer remarks ' "You can be sure of that! For you see, of all our known

---

* The fifth occasion of the Three's forgathering.

tailors, friend Molière is the one who is the best fitter of our barons, counts and marquises according to their measure." '*

Let no commentator jump in here to suggest that this is a mistaken aphorism on the part of Dumas. He knew his d'Artagnan inside out; knew that, although primarily a Musketeer and a soldier of fortune, he was a Frenchman and would know his Molière; and in fact the very next chapter describing the preparations of the Epicureans to amuse His Majesty during his visit tells us that one of their items was to be *Les Fâcheux*, a 3-act comedy by Poquelin de Volière, as d'Artagnan called him, or Coquelin de Volière as Porthos had styled him. While conceding that every good Dumasian will know not only his works but those of other classical French writers, this chapter, detailing the whims and fantasies of such as La Fontaine and other of Fouquet's myrmidons, like the similar previous one it will be more of interest to French readers than to English, and could be passed over but for the tailend of it, being a short scene between Aramis and Fouquet, seemingly casual but of vital importance in the former's scheme. After consoling the worried ex-superintendent by assuring him that he has nothing to fear in the future from the king or Colbert, he casually requests from him a letter to a colleague, M. de Lyonne, for a signed *lettre de cachet* for the release of the prisoner Seldon in the Bastille, giving as his reason a feeling of pity for his imprisonment for so slight an offence.

* * *

The reason for the request becomes apparent in the next chapter: 'Another supper at the Bastille' — one of the most vital in the novel, for it means the climactic triumph or failure of Aramis's months of plotting.

> Baisemeaux, seated at table, was rubbing his hands and looking at the Bishop of Vannes, who, booted like a cavalier, dressed in grey, with a sword at his side, kept talking of his hunger and testifying the liveliest impatience. M. de Baisemeaux de Montlezun was not accustomed to the unbending movements of His Greatness My Lord of Vannes; and this evening Aramis, becoming quite sprightly, volunteered confidence on confidence. The prelate had again a little touch of the Musketeer about him. The bishop just trenched on the borders of licence in his style of conversation. As for M. de Baisemeaux, with the facility of vulgar people he gave himself loose rein on this touch of abandon on the part of his guest.
> 'Monsieur,' said he, — 'for indeed tonight I don't like to call you Monseigneur.'
> 'By no means,' said Aramis; 'call me Monsieur, — I am booted.'

But the bonhomie on the part of Aramis is no more than a cover for his design, and the whole scene pursues its planned stages: Baisemeaux, made merry and

---

* The point of d'Artagnan's remark and the reason for Dumas's intercalation of the scene is explained by the heading to the chapter, viz. 'Where in all probability Molière formed his first idea of *Le Bourgeois Gentilhomme.*'

fuddled with good cheer and wine — a courier arriving — brow-beaten by the insistent Aramis the governor reluctantly agreeing to see him — the messenger's missive, marked *urgent*, being for the instant release of the prisoner Seldon. As Baisemeaux, grumbling at being disturbed, turned away from him to ring the bell, Aramis seized the opportunity to change the paper for another looking exactly the same, but for Marchiali instead of Seldon. The crux came when he had to make Baisemeaux misbelieve his own eyes and accept the order of release. This proving difficult, and the governor still evincing doubt as to the viability of the order, little by little Aramis dropped his attitude of equality and friendliness to become more chilly and authoritative, until finally, when the other proposed to have the order checked by its signatories before carrying it out, seeing in this the doom of his plot, he took the ultimate step.

'Well, M. de Baisemeaux,' said Aramis, bending an eagle glance on the governor, 'I adopt so frankly your doubts, and your mode of clearing them up, that I will take a pen, if you will give me one.'

Baisemeaux gave him a pen.

'And a sheet of white paper,' added Aramis.

Baisemeaux handed him some paper.

'Now, I — I, also — I, here present — incontestably, I — am going to write an order to which I am certain you will give credence, incredulous as you are!'

Baisemeaux turned pale at this icy assurance of manner. It seemed to him that that voice of Aramis, but just now so playful and so friendly, had become funereal and sinister; that the wax-lights had changed into the tapers of a mortuary chapel, and the glasses of wine into chalices of blood.

Aramis took a pen and wrote. Baisemeaux, in terror, read over his shoulder.

'A.M.D.G.' wrote the bishop; and he drew a cross under these four letters, signifying *ad maiorem Dei gloriam*, and continued:-

It is our pleasure that the order brought to M. de Baisemeaux de Montlezun, governor, for the king, of the castle of the Bastille, be held by him good and effectual, and be immediately carried into operation.

(signed) D'HERBLAY,

General of the Order, by the grace of God.

Baisemeaux was so profoundly astonished that his features remained contracted, his lips parted, and his eyes fixed. He did not move an inch, nor articulate a sound. Nothing could be heard in that large chamber but that of a moth which was fluttering about one of the candles.

Aramis, without even deigning to look at the man whom he had reduced to so miserable a condition, drew from his pocket a small case of black wax, sealed the letter, and stamped it with a seal suspended at his breast, beneath his doublet; and when the operation was concluded, presented — still in silence — the missive to Baisemeaux. The latter, whose hands trembled in a manner to excite pity, turned a dull and meaningless gaze upon the letter. A last gleam of feeling played over his features, and he fell, as if thunderstruck, on a chair.

'Come, come,' said Aramis, after a long silence, during which the governor of the Bastille had slowly recovered his senses, 'do not lead me to believe, dear Baisemeaux, that the presence of the General of the Order is as terrible as that of the Almighty, and that men die merely from seeing him! Take courage, rouse yourself; give me your hand, and obey!'

Baisemeaux, reassured, if not satisfied, obeyed, kissed Aramis's hand, and rose from his chair. 'Immediately?' he murmured.

'Oh, there is no pressing haste, my dear host; take your place again, and do the honours over this beautiful dessert.'

'Monseigneur, I shall never recover such a shock as this, — I who have laughed, who have jested with you! I who have dared to treat you on a footing of equality!'

'Say nothing about it, old comrade,' replied the bishop, who perceived how strained the cord was and how dangerous it might be to break it; 'say nothing about it. Let us each live in his own way: to you, my protection and my friendship; to me, your obedience. Exactly fulfilling these two requirements, let us live happily.'

Half an hour later:

The horses were in waiting, making the carriage shake with their impatience. Baisemeaux accompanied the bishop to the bottom of the steps. Aramis caused his companion to enter before him, then followed, and without giving the driver any further order, 'Go on!' said he.

The carriage rattled over the pavement of the courtyard. An officer with a torch went before the horses, and gave orders at every post to let them pass. During the time taken in opening all the barriers Aramis barely breathed, and you might have heard his heart beat against his ribs. The prisoner, buried in a corner of the carriage, made no more sign of life than his companion. At length a jolt more severe than the others announced to them that they had cleared the last gutter. Behind the carriage closed the last gate, — that in the Rue St. Antoine. No more walls either on the right or left; heaven everywhere, liberty everywhere, life everywhere!

* * *

The penultimate cast of the die was over, the final one was now to come, was here before him. Stevenson quoted the scene in the forest of Sénart as one of the highlights of the novel. Both as a piece of writing and as the point of no return of the action he was more than justified. Realizing that his plot, his future and that of the impersonating Philippe so necessary for their success were in the balance, Aramis had arranged for the die to be thrown in the darkness and solitude of the forest of Sénart, where no outside interference would mar their final debate on their dual combat with destiny. And in fact, Aramis's final interview with Philippe is a peroration of sheer genius in which he lays before him the pros and cons of their desperate state. Beginning with the pros, and with the purpose of absolving his conscience, he asserts that the present king, as a result of his restricting minority through the crushing parsimony of Mazarin, now that he is his own master, will end by becoming ' "a bad king, devouring the means and substance of his people, and a dictator in all but name," '[*]

---

[*] This incidentally may be seen as a true assessment of Louis XIV, who came to style himself 'Le Roi Soleil' and declare *'L'État c'est moi!'*

following this by stressing his (Philippe's) right as the twin son of Louis XIII and Anne of Austria, to a life of just recognition by his family and country in place of the inhuman cruelty he has received at their hands, thus forcing him to take his rightful place of honour by subterfuge, since it had been denied him by justice and humanity.

So much for the pros. The cons were obvious, being those of discovery with consequent death. If — Aramis goes on — his heart fails him, he (Aramis) will accept his decision and be prepared to take him to a place of safety in the heart of the isolated countryside of Bas-Poitou, where he can spend the rest of his life as a simple countryman in peace and safety, without care or remorse. And he concludes,

> 'If you play the other game, you run the chance of being assassinated on a throne or of being strangled in a prison. Upon my soul, I assure you, now I compare them together, upon my life, I should hesitate.'
>
> 'Monsieur,' replied the young prince, 'before I determine, let me alight from this carriage, walk on the ground, and consult that voice by which God speaks in unsullied Nature. Ten minutes, and I will give you my answer.'
>
> 'As you please, Monseigneur,' said Aramis, bending before him with respect, — so solemn and august in its tone and address had been the voice which had just spoken. It was an anxious time for the Bishop of Vannes, who had never before been in so deadly a dilemma. Was his iron will, accustomed to overcome all obstacles, never finding itself inferior or vanquished, to be foiled in so vast a project from not having foreseen the influence which a few trees and a few cubic feet of free air might have on a human mind? Aramis, overwhelmed by anxiety, contemplated the painful struggle which was taking place in Philippe's mind. This suspense lasted throughout the ten minutes which the young man had requested. During that eternity Philippe continued gazing with an imploring and sorrowful look towards the heavens. Aramis did not remove the piercing glance he had fixed on Philippe. Suddenly the young man bowed his head. His thoughts returned to the earth, his looks perceptibly hardened, his brow contracted, his mouth assumed an expression of fierce courage; and then again his look became fixed, but now it reflected the flame of mundane splendours, — now it was like the face of Satan on the mountain when he brought into view the kingdoms and the powers of earth as temptations to Jesus. Aramis's appearance then became as gentle as it had before been gloomy.
>
> Philippe, seizing his hand in a quick, agitated manner, exclaimed: 'Let us go where the crown of France is to be found!'
>
> 'Is this your decision, Monseigneur?' asked Aramis.
>
> 'It is.'
>
> 'Irrevocably so?'
>
> Philippe did not even deign to reply. He gazed earnestly at the bishop as if to ask him if it were possible for a man to waver after having once made up his mind.
>
> 'Those looks are flashes of fire which portray character,' said Aramis, bowing over Philippe's hand. 'You will be great, Monseigneur; I will answer for that.'

The crowning decision taken, there follows a series of questions on the part of Philippe ending with a searching one as to what Aramis expects in return for his friendship and support, and for reply gets:

'I shall have given you the throne of France; you will confer on me the throne of Saint Peter. Whenever your loyal, firm, and mailed hand shall have for its mate the hand of a pope such as I shall be, neither Charles V, who owned two thirds of the habitable globe, nor Charlemagne, who possessed it entirely, will reach to the height of your waist. I have no alliances; I have no predilections. I will not throw you into persecutions of heretics, nor will I cast you into the troubled waters of family dissension; I will simply say to you: The whole universe is for us two, — for me the minds of men, for you their bodies; and as I shall be the first to die, you will have my inheritance. What do you say of my plan, Monseigneur?'

'I say that you render me happy and proud for no other reason than that of having comprehended you thoroughly. M. d'Herblay, you shall be cardinal, and when cardinal, my prime minister; and then you will point out to me the necessary steps to be taken to secure your election as pope, and I will take them. You can ask what guarantees from me you please.'

'It is useless. I shall never act except in such a manner that you will be the gainer; I shall never mount until I shall have first placed you upon the round of the ladder immediately above me; I shall always hold myself sufficiently aloof from you to escape incurring your jealousy, sufficiently near to sustain your personal advantage and to watch over our friendship. All the contracts in the world are easily violated because the interest included in them inclines more to one side than to another. With us, however, it will never be the case; I have no need of guarantees.'

'And so — my brother — will disappear?'

'Simply. We will remove him from his bed by means of a spring which yields to the pressure of the finger. Having retired to rest as a crowned sovereign, he will awaken in captivity. Alone, you will rule from that moment, and you will have no interest more urgent than that of keeping me near you.'

'I believe it. There is my hand, M. d'Herblay.'

'Allow me to kneel before you, Sire, most respectfully. We will embrace each other on the day when we shall have round our temples — you the crown, and I the tiara.'

'Embrace me this very day; and be more than great, more than skilful, more than sublime in genius, — be good to me, be my father!'

The scene ends with a subtle touch. Most normal men, finding themselves childless in middle age or later, are possessed by a longing for the state of fatherhood. It may be only faint and passing, but it occurs. So Dumas, in response to the young Philippe's emotional appeal, concludes the chapter with

> Aramis was almost overcome as he listened to the voice of the prince. He fancied he detected in his own heart an emotion hitherto unknown to him; but this impression was speedily crushed. 'His father!' he thought; 'yes, his Holy Father.'
> The two resumed their places in the carriage, which sped rapidly along the road to Vaux-le-Vicomte.

* * *

Back at Vaux the conspiracy had moved by devious means remorselessly to its climax. To begin with the very splendour of the fête organized by Fouquet —

the palace itself, 'built by a subject but bearing an even greater resemblance to a royal residence than that presented by Wolsey to his master for fear of making him jealous', with its priceless paintings and statues, its grottos, fountains, park and gardens, the fireworks, the host of liveried servants, the sumptuous meals served from golden dishes on to golden plates, the rare wines and fruits — all this flaunted wealth and power, instead of pleasing Louis only served to make him feel secondary and humiliated and to hate his host the more. Then and there he determined to have the superintendent arrested. But his intention received a check when, walking in the garden accompanied by Colbert, he met with Louise. She, with the intuition of a woman in love, had sensed her lover's mood and was uneasy. On questioning him for the reasons for his ' "sadness" ' she gets as reply

> 'My sadness? You are mistaken, Mademoiselle; no, it is not sadness.'
> 'What is it, then, Sire?'
> 'Humiliation.'
> 'Humiliation? Oh, Sire, what a word for you to use!'
> 'I mean, Mademoiselle, that wherever I may happen to be, no one else ought to be the master. Well, then, look round you on every side, and judge whether I am not eclipsed — I, the King of France — before the king of these wide domains. Oh!' he continued, clinching his hands and teeth, 'when I think that this king — '
> 'Well, Sire?' said Louise, terrified.
> 'That this king is a faithless, unworthy servant, who has become proud with my stolen property — And therefore am I about to change this impudent minister's fête and arrest this haughty Titan, who, true to his motto, threatens to scale my heaven.'
> 'Arrest M. Fouquet, do you say?'
> 'Ah! does that surprise you?'
> 'In his own house?'
> 'Why not? If he be guilty, he is guilty in his own house as anywhere else.'
> 'M. Fouquet, who at this moment is ruining himself for his sovereign!'
> 'I believe, Mademoiselle, you are defending this traitor!'
> Colbert began to chuckle silently. The king turned round at the sound of this suppressed mirth.
> 'Sire,' said La Vallière, 'it is not M. Fouquet I am defending; it is yourself.'
> 'Me! you defend me?'
> 'Sire, you would be dishonouring yourself if you were to give such an order.'
> 'Dishonour myself?' murmured the king, turning pale with anger. 'In truth, Mademoiselle, you put a strange eagerness into what you say.'
> 'I put eagerness not into what I say, but into serving Your Majesty,' replied the noble-hearted girl; 'in that I would lay down my life, were it needed, and with the same eagerness, Sire.'

In the end, succumbing to his mistress's eloquent reasoning and appeal, Louis relented, knelt before her and kissed her hand.

> 'I am lost!' thought Colbert; then suddenly his face brightened again. 'Oh, no, no, not yet!' he said to himself.

> And while the king, protected from observation by the thick covert of an enormous lime, pressed La Vallière to his breast with all the ardour of ineffable affection, Colbert tranquilly looked among the papers in his pocket-book, and drew out of it a paper folded in the form of a letter, slightly yellow, perhaps, but which must have been very precious, since the intendant smiled as he looked at it; he then bent a look full of hatred upon the charming group which the young girl and the king formed together.

This letter was the one Fouquet had misguidedly written to Louise at the instigation of Aramis during the first days of the king's attentions to her, and in which he had compromised himself by offering her his services, the letter being betrayed into Colbert's hands by Aramis's servant, Toby. Now, as the lovers parted, pretending to pick it up from the ground after being unknowingly dropped by La Vallière, he presented it to the king.

The effect was all and more than the venomous intendant could have hoped for, converting Louis into a state of jealous fury. The very defence Louise had made in Fouquet's cause now came home to him, adding fuel to his jealousy and rage. That same evening, the last before his departure from Vaux, he sent for his Captain of Musketeers and gave him the order for Fouquet's immediate arrest. But d'Artagnan baulked. Daringly relying on his age, rank and special relationship with the king, first he insisted on a written order for the arrest ' "because the word of a king when it springs from anger may possibly change when the feeling changes" '; and like La Vallière he argued that to have a man arrested under his own roof would be unworthy of a king. Finally Louis compromised with ' "Guard M. Fouquet until I have made up my mind by tomorrow morning." ' D'Artagnan reluctantly accepted the command and went. Left alone, Louis 'began to walk up and down his apartment at a furious pace, like a wounded bull in the arena who drags after him the coloured streamers and iron darts', until at last, worn out by his emotions, 'he threw himself on his bed dressed as he was… The bed creaked beneath his weight, and apart from the few broken sounds which escaped from his breast, silence reigned in the chamber of Morpheus.'

All this had been seen and heard by Aramis and Philippe through their spy-hole in the Blue Room immediately above.

That same night two momentous events occurred simultaneously: the abduction of the king, and the 'arrest' of Fouquet by d'Artagnan. To take the latter first.

Although forced by the king to carry out his order as regards Fouquet, the Musketeer, who against his will and sense of right and wrong had a soft spot for the superintendent and preferred him to the more righteous intendant, went about performing it in his own original way. Dumas expresses this by giving him a characteristic monologue:

> The Musketeer had scruples. To deliver thus to death (for not a doubt existed that Louis hated Fouquet mortally) the man who had just shown himself so delightful

and charming a host in every way was a real case of conscience. 'It seems to me,' said d'Artagnan to himself, 'that short of being a wretch, I shall let M. Fouquet know the purpose of the king in regard to him. Yet if I betray my master's secret I shall be false-hearted and a traitor, — a crime provided for and punishable by military laws, as proved by the fact that twenty times in the wars I have seen miserable fellows strung up for doing in little degree what my scruples counsel me to do on a larger scale. No, I think that a man of intelligence ought to get out of this difficulty with more skill than that. And now shall we admit that I have intelligence? It is doubtful; having drawn on it for forty years, I shall be lucky if there be a pistole's-worth left.'

D'Artagnan buried his head in his hands, tore his moustache in sheer vexation, and added: 'For what reason is M. Fouquet disgraced? For three reasons: the first, because M. Colbert doesn't like him; the second, because he wished to pay court to Mademoiselle de la Vallière;* and, lastly, because the king likes M. Colbert and loves Mademoiselle de la Vallière. Oh, he is a lost man! But shall I put my foot on his neck, — I, a man, when he is falling a prey to the intrigues of a set of women and clerks? For shame! If he be dangerous I will lay him low enough; if, however, he be only persecuted, I will look on. I have come to such a decisive determination that neither king nor living man shall change my opinion. If Athos were here he would do as I have done. Therefore, instead of going cold-bloodedly up to M. Fouquet and arresting him off-hand and shutting him up, I will try to conduct myself like a man who understands what good manners are.'

He then rounds off the monologue by means of a rare and intimate little touch:

and d'Artagnan, after adjusting his shoulder belt by a gesture peculiar to himself, went straight off to Fouquet.

That a nineteenth century writer who never could have known what it was to wear a sword and baldric should be able, with a stroke of a pen like the flicker of an eyelid, insert such a touch, is proof that he has himself become one with that earlier century and with his own creation.

He found the superintendent on the point of going to bed, worn out partly by the day's activities, but more by his financial situation and his relationship *vis-à-vis* the king. Surprised by d'Artagnan's visit at such a time he naturally questioned him, only to learn by torturing degrees and friendly hints that if he were not yet under arrest he was under duress and the constant if friendly surveillance of the captain and not allowed to leave his apartment. When at last the full realization of it all came home as being the end of the road for him, Fouquet's reaction was pitiable indeed. D'Artagnan tried to comfort him, and his summing up of their two apposite and opposing situations forms the fourth and penultimate example of the Musketeer's Homeric utterances. On Fouquet's anguished cry ' "It is the end for me. I am ruined," ' he tried to console him with

---

* A blunder here. D'Artagnan could not have known this.

'If you are ruined, Monsieur, look at the affair manfully. Stay a moment! Look at me, — I who seem to exercise a kind of superiority over you because I arrest you. Fate, which distributes their different parts to the actors of this world, accorded to me a less agreeable and less advantageous part to fill than yours has been. I am one of those who think that the parts which kings and powerful nobles are called upon to act are of infinitely more worth than those of beggars or lackeys. It is better on the stage, — on the stage, I mean, of another theatre than that of this world — it is better to wear a fine coat and to talk fine language than to walk the boards shod with a pair of old shoes, or to get one's backbone belaboured by sticks well laid on. In one word, you have been a prodigal, have ordered and been obeyed, have been steeped to the lips in enjoyment; while I have dragged my tether after me, have been commanded and have obeyed, and have drudged my life away. Well, although I may seem of such trifling importance beside you, Monseigneur, I do declare to you that the recollection of what I have done serves me as a spur, and prevents me from bowing my old head too soon. I shall remain until the very end a good trooper; and when my turn comes I shall fall perfectly straight, all in a heap, after having selected my place beforehand. Do as I do, M. Fouquet, — you will not find yourself the worse for it; that happens only once in a lifetime to men like yourself, and the chief thing is to do it well when the chance presents itself. There is a Latin proverb — the words have escaped me, but I remember the sense of it very well, for I have thought it over more than once — which says, "The end crowns the work!"'

Fouquet rose from his seat, passed his arm round d'Artagnan's neck and clasped him in a close embrace, while with the other hand he pressed the captain's hand. 'An excellent homily,' he said after a moment's pause.

'A soldier's, Monseigneur.'

It is passages such as the above which make it seem as if Dumas had become so much one with his characters that he lived them without knowing how, and which place him away and beyond all other historical novelists.

When Fouquet asked if he could send for Aramis, d'Artagnan, moved by the other's state, offered to go and look for him himself on condition that his prisoner pledged his word that he would not leave the room during his absence. This Fouquet did, and the Musketeer left, only to return some quarter of an hour later to say that Aramis was not in his room and not to be found. As a last injunction he advised sleep for both of them, Fouquet on his bed, he himself in one of the armchairs. And they passed the night so.

* * *

A reader already knows, Dumas having preceded the above chapter with that which narrates the abduction of the king, why d'Artagnan was unable to find Aramis on Fouquet's behalf. He, along with Porthos, was at that very moment taking Louis XIV at sword- and pistol-point to the Bastille in a carriage. There poor Baisemeaux, summoned at three o'clock in the morning and appearing in his dressing-gown, was informed coolly by Aramis that he was returning

Marchiali for the double reason that he (Baisemeaux) had been right in the first place and that it was Seldon who ought to have been released; and secondly that Marchiali was evidently mad, having made immediate use of his liberty by insisting that he was the real King of France and the present one an imposter. Completely bewildered, but urged on by Aramis, the Bastille governor 'ordered the drums to be beaten and the bells rung as a warning to everyone to retire in order to avoid meeting with a mysterious prisoner'. Once Louis was thrust into his cell with orders that no one was to speak to him, Aramis and Porthos left in the same way as they had come.

The next chapter, 'A Night in the Bastille', is a masterpiece of narration, with Louis's successive emotions so vividly depicted as to make the reader feel he has been incarcerated with him. At first stupefied, unable to believe what had happened to him, he began by wondering by whose machinations he had been betrayed and abducted. Then came thoughts of Louise, and at the idea of being separated from her for ever, leaving her to the antagonistic authority of Madame, he burst into tears. But then his imbued authority of kingship took over. He would summon the governor and demand an explanation on threat of high treason. But there was no bell, no means of communication. After shouting till he was hoarse, in a fury that made his blood boil and his whole body at fever pitch, he fell to battering the door with his chair until it broke.

> With a portion of the broken chair he recommenced his battering against the door. At the end of an hour ... Louis heard the sound of a key in the lock and of the bolts being withdrawn. The king bounded forward to be nearer to the person who was about to enter; but suddenly reflecting that it was a movement unworthy of a sovereign, he paused, assumed a noble and calm expression, which for him was easy enough, and waited with his back turned towards the window in order to some extent to conceal his agitation from the eyes of the person who was entering. It was only a jailer with a basket of provisions. The king looked at the man with anxiety, and waited for him to speak.
> 'Ah!' said the latter, 'you have broken your chair, I see. Why, you must have become quite mad.'
> 'Monsieur,' said the king, 'be careful what you say; it will be very serious for you.'
> The jailer placed the basket on the table, and looked at his prisoner steadily. 'What do you say?' he said with surprise.
> 'Desire the governor to come to me,' added the king with dignity.
> 'Come, my boy,' said the turnkey, 'you have always been very quiet and reasonable; but you are getting violent, it seems, and I wish to give you warning. You have broken your chair, and made a great disturbance; that is an offence punishable by imprisonment in one of the lower dungeons. Promise me not to begin over again, and I will not say a word about it to the governor.'
> 'I wish to see the governor,' replied the king, still controlling his passion.
> 'He will send you off to one of the dungeons, I tell you; so take care!'
> 'I insist upon it! — Do you hear?'
> 'Ah! ah! you are becoming wild again. Very good! I shall take away your knife.'
> The jailer did as he had said, closed the door and departed, leaving the king

more astounded, more wretched, and more alone than ever. In vain he began again to pound the door; in vain he threw the plates and dishes out of the window; not a sound was heard in answer. Two hours later he could not be recognized as a king, a gentleman, a man, a human being; he might rather be called a madman, tearing the door with his nails, trying to tear up the flooring of his cell, and uttering such wild and fearful cries that the old Bastille seemed to tremble to its very foundations for having revolted against its master. As for the governor, the jailer did not even think of disturbing him; the turnkeys and the sentinels had made their report, but what was the good of it? Were not these madmen common enough in the fortress, and were not the walls still stronger than they?

M. de Baisemeaux, thoroughly impressed with what Aramis had told him, and in perfect conformity with the king's order, hoped only that one thing might happen, namely, that the madman Marchiali might be mad enough to hang himself from the canopy of his bed or one of the bars of the window. And the good-natured governor thereupon sat down to his late breakfast.

* * *

Aramis, after overcoming the enormous problems of (1) getting Philippe out of the Bastille (2) persuading him to carry out his plot (3) replacing him for the king, saw himself almost at the end of the road of ambition he had set for himself and at the apogee of his power. He had seen Philippe spend what remained of the night in the royal bed; had stunned d'Artagnan into baffled acceptance of his new familiarity with the king and using it to obtain an order for the release of Fouquet, even going with him to the latter's rooms with the order; and after reminding the Captain of Musketeers about taking the king's orders for his levee — at which d'Artagnan, leaving them, had 'bowed first to Fouquet, and then with an ironical respect to Aramis'. The Captain of Musketeers, it should be said, on leaving Fouquet earlier that same morning to find Aramis for him, had treated the superintendent to a second personal touch even more revelatory of Dumas's affinity with his creation than the one already quoted.

'Stay, I have something of the old Roman in me. This morning, when I got up, I remarked that my sword had not caught in one of the aiguillettes, and that my shoulder-belt had slipped right off. That is an infallible sign.'

'Of prosperity?'

'Yes; be sure of it, — for every time that confounded belt of mine stuck fast to my back, it always signified a punishment from M. de Tréville, or a refusal of money by M. de Mazarin. Every time my sword hung fast to my shoulder-belt, it always predicted some disagreeable commission or other for me to execute; and I have had showers of them all my life through. Every time, too, my sword danced about in its sheath, a duel, fortunate in its result, was sure to follow; whenever it dangled about the calves of my legs, it was a slight wound; every time it fell completely out of the scabbard, I was booked, and made up my mind that I should have to remain on the field of battle, with two or three months under the surgeon's care into the bargain.'

'I never knew your sword kept you so well informed,' said Fouquet, with a faint smile, which showed how he was struggling against his own weaknesses. 'Is your sword bewitched, or under the influence of some charm?'

'Why, you must know that my sword may almost be regarded as part of my own body. I have heard that certain men seem to have warnings given them by feeling something the matter with their legs, or by a throbbing of their temples. With me, it is my sword that warns me. Well, it told me of nothing this morning. But stay a moment; look here, it has just fallen of its own accord into the last hole of the belt. Do you know what that is a warning of?'

'No.'

'Well, that tells me of an arrest that will have to be made this very day.'

'Well,' said the superintendent, more astonished than annoyed by this frankness, 'if there is nothing disagreeable predicted to you by the sword, I am to conclude that it is not disagreeable for you to arrest me.'

'You? arrest you?'

'Of course, The warning —'

'Does not concern you, since you have been arrested ever since yesterday. It is not you I shall have to arrest, be assured of that. That is the reason why I am delighted, and also the reason why I said that my day will be a happy one.'

Little did d'Artagnan know his sword was to prove itself so good a prophet, or the importance of the arrest he was to make.

With d'Artagnan gone, Aramis was left alone with the superintendent. It was to be his great moment, the consummation of his long and secret endeavour both for himself and his friend.

But instead of becoming all that, it was to be the *coup de grâce* of both. Aramis's error consisted in his failure to understand the quixotic sense of honour of the sensual, pleasure-loving, generous superintendent: a failure which was to cause him to see the mole-like subterfuge of years undone in twenty minutes' conversation. If only, he must have told himself in the aftermath, he had said nothing to Fouquet and left him in the dark along with the rest of the world as to what he had achieved! As it was, being at the same time Fouquet's servitor, counsellor and friend, he felt that the superintendent should be the first (and probably the only one) to be told of the *fait accompli*, more especially since it meant the end of his harassment by the king and so ensuring a happy finale to his political life.

Very gradually, hesitantly, step by step Aramis began to unfold the twists and turnings of his discovery of the suppressed state secret and his determination to make use of it for his own ends: the twin birth — the exile of the younger brother, his arrest and inhumane imprisonment — his (Aramis's) determination and plans to set him free. Up to this point Fouquet, avidly listening, expressed nothing but agreement with the other's exposition, jumping ahead to the belief that it was his intention merely to confront the king with his unknown brother and so have him in his power and force him to relent and change his attitude to his superintendent, Fouquet's natural kindness and generous nature saw nothing but a restitution of justice and kindliness in the idea. But the conclusion of Aramis's revelation changed all that. Let Dumas tell it.

'Go to the king's apartment,' continued Aramis, tranquilly; 'and you will know the mystery, I defy even you to perceive that the prisoner of the Bastille is lying in his brother's bed.'

'But the king?' stammered Fouquet, seized with horror at the intelligence.

'What king?' said Aramis, in his gentlest tone; 'the one who hates you, or the one who likes you?'

'The king — of yesterday?'

'The king of yesterday! Be quite easy on that score; he has gone to take the place in the Bastille which his victim has occupied for such a long time past.'

'Great God! And who took him there?'

'I.'

'You?'

'Yes, and in the simplest way. I carried him away last night; and while he was descending into gloom, the other was ascending into light. I do not think there has been any disturbance created in any way. A flash of lightning without thunder never awakens anyone.'

Fouquet uttered a thick, smothered cry, as if he had been struck by some invisible blow and, clasping his head between his clinched hands, he murmured, 'You did that?'

'Cleverly enough, too; what do you think of it?'

'You have dethroned the king; you have imprisoned him?'

'It is done.'

'And such an action was committed here at Vaux?'

'Yes; here at Vaux, in the Chamber of Morpheus. It would almost seem that it had been built in anticipation of such an act.'

'And at what time did it occur?'

'Last night, between twelve and one o'clock.'

Fouquet made a movement as if he were on the point of springing upon Aramis, but he restrained himself. 'At Vaux! under my roof!' he said in a half strangled voice.

'I believe so; for it is still your house, and is likely to continue so, since M. Colbert cannot rob you of it now.'

'It was under my roof, then, Monsieur, that you committed this crime!'

'This crime!' said Aramis, stupefied.

'This abominable crime!' pursued Fouquet, becoming more and more excited; 'this crime more execrable than an assassination; this crime which dishonours my name for ever, and entails upon me the horror of posterity!'

'You are not in your senses, Monsieur,' replied Aramis, in an irresolute tone of voice; 'you are speaking too loudly. Take care!'

'I will call out so loudly that the whole world shall hear me.'

'M. Fouquet, take care!'

Fouquet turned round towards the prelate, whom he looked full in the face. 'You have dishonoured me,' he said, 'in committing so foul an act of treason, so heinous a crime upon my guest, upon one who was peacefully reposing beneath my roof. Oh, woe, woe is me!'

'Woe to the man, rather, who beneath your roof meditated the ruin of your fortune, your life. Do you forget that?'

'He was my guest; he was my king!'

Aramis rose, his eyes literally bloodshot, his mouth trembling convulsively. 'Have I a man out of his senses to deal with?' he said.

'You have an honourable man to deal with.'

'You are mad!'

'A man will prevent you from consummating your crime.'

'You are mad!'

'A man who would sooner die, who would kill you even, rather than allow you to complete his dishonour.'

And Fouquet snatched up his sword, which d'Artagnan had placed at the head of his bed, and clenched it resolutely in his hand. Aramis frowned, and thrust his hand into his breast as if in search of a weapon. This movement did not escape Fouquet, who, noble and grand in his magnanimity, threw his sword from him and approached Aramis so close as to touch his shoulder with his disarmed hand. 'Monsieur,' he said, 'I would sooner die here on the spot than survive my disgrace; and if you have any pity left for me, I entreat you to take my life.'

Aramis remained mute and motionless.

'You do not reply?' said Fouquet.

Aramis raised his head gently, and a glimmer of hope might have been seen to animate his eyes. 'Reflect, Monseigneur,' he said, 'upon everything we have to expect. As the matter now stands, the king is still alive, and his imprisonment saves your life.'

'Yes,' replied Fouquet, 'you may have been acting on my behalf; but I do not accept your service. At the same time, I do not wish your ruin. You will leave this house.'

Aramis stifled the exclamation which escaped his broken heart.

'I am hospitable towards all who are dwellers beneath my roof,' continued Fouquet with an air of inexpressible majesty; 'you will not be more fatally lost than he whose ruin you have consummated.'

'You will be so,' said Aramis, in a hoarse, prophetic voice, — 'you will be so, believe me.'

'I accept the augury, M. d'Herblay; but nothing shall stop me. You will leave Vaux; you must leave France. I give you four hours to place yourself out of the king's reach.'

'Four hours?' said the Bishop of Vannes, scornfully and incredulously.

'Upon the word of Fouquet, no one shall follow you before the expiration of that time. You will therefore have four hours' advance of those whom the king may wish to despatch after you.'

'Four hours!' repeated Aramis, in a thick, smothered voice.

'It is more than you will need to get on board a vessel, and flee to Belle-Ile, which I give you as a place of refuge.'

'Ah!' murmured Aramis.

'Belle-Ile is as much mine for you as Vaux is mine for the king. Go, d'Herblay, go! As long as I live, not a hair of your head shall be injured.'

'Thank you,' said Aramis, with a cold irony of manner.

'Go at once, then, and give me your hand, before we both hasten away, — you to save your life, I to save my honour.'

Aramis withdrew from his breast the hand he had concealed there; it was stained with his blood. He had dug his nails into his flesh as if in punishment for having nursed so many projects, more vain, insensate, and fleeting than the life of man. Fouquet was horror-stricken, and then his heart smote him with pity. He opened his arms to Aramis.

'I had no weapons,' murmured Aramis, as wild and terrible as the shade of Dido.

And then, without touching Fouquet's hand, he turned his head aside, and stepped back a pace or two. His last word was an imprecation, his last gesture a curse, which his bloodstained hand seemed to invoke, as it sprinkled on Fouquet's face a few drops of his blood; and both of them darted out of the room by the secret staircase which led down to the inner courtyard. Fouquet ordered his best horse, while Aramis paused at the foot of the staircase which led to Porthos's apartment. He reflected for some time, while Fouquet's carriage left the stone-paved courtyard at full gallop.

Pausing there, Aramis, after a soliloquy on the fickleness of Fortune, Fate, Destiny, Chance, call it what you will, and the hopelessness of men to change it, asked himself what he should do about Philippe now that the substitution had been discovered and the treason uncloaked and soon to be followed by arrest, renewed imprisonment, possibly death. Rather than face the consequences of saving him with its prospect of civil war, he decided to leave him to his fate. Hurrying to Porthos and rousing him from his beatific slumbers, he helped him to dress under the very eyes of d'Artagnan who stood in the doorway watching them.

'What the devil are you doing there in such an agitated manner?' said the Musketeer.
'Hush!' said Porthos.
'We are going off on a mission,' added the bishop.
'You are very fortunate,' said the Musketeer.
'Oh!' said Porthos, 'I feel so wearied; I would much prefer to sleep. But the service of the king —'
'Have you seen M. Fouquet?' inquired Aramis of d'Artagnan.
'Yes; this very minute, in a carriage.'
'What did he say to you?'
'He bade me *adieu.*'
'Was that all?'
'What else do you think he could say? Am I worth anything now, since you have all got into such high favour?'
'Listen,' said Aramis, embracing the Musketeer; 'your good times are returning again. You will have no more occasion to be jealous of anyone.'
'Ah, bah!'
'I predict that something will happen to you today which will increase your importance.'
'Really?'
'You know that I know all the news?'
'Oh, yes!'
'Come, Porthos, are you ready? Let us go.'
'Let us embrace d'Artagnan first.'
'*Pardieu!*'
'But the horses?'
'Oh! there is no want of them here. Will you have mine?'
'No; Porthos has his own stud. So *adieu, adieu!*'
The two fugitives mounted their horses beneath the eyes of the Captain of the Musketeers, who held Porthos's stirrup for him and gazed after them until they were out of sight.

'On any other occasion,' thought the Gascon, 'I should say that those gentlemen were making their escape; but in these days politics seem so changed that this is called going on a mission. I have no objection. Let me attend to my own affairs;' and he philosophically entered his apartments.

* * *

The narrative now returns to Fouquet and his race to the Bastille to release Louis. Only after threatening to order the army to storm the prison unless he confirms to his order for release does the bewildered Baisemeaux agree to take him to the prisoner, where, after snatching the keys from him and dismissing him, Fouquet unlocks the cell door to be confronted by the king.

> The two men were on the point of darting towards each other, when they suddenly stopped as mutual recognition took place, and each uttered a cry of horror.
> 'Have you come to assassinate me, Monsieur?' said the king, when he recognized Fouquet.
> 'The king in this state!' murmured the minister.
> Nothing could be more terrible, indeed, than the appearance of Louis at the moment Fouquet had surprised him; his clothes were in tatters; his shirt, open and torn to rags, was stained with sweat and with the blood which streamed from his lacerated breast and arms. Haggard, pale, foaming, his hair dishevelled, Louis XIV presented a vivid picture of despair, hunger and fear combined in one figure. Fouquet was so touched, so affected and disturbed, that he ran to the king with his arms stretched out and his eyes filled with tears.

Only after explaining the whole plot does Fouquet succeed in making the king see that he had no hand in it; but even when convinced of his innocence, no amount of his appealing for the forgiveness of the instigators and executioners of the act of treason could persuade Louis to forgive them, or to believe in the existence of an unknown brother; nor unsuspected by Fouquet — a subtle touch here — would he ever forgive him, his liberator. For despite the superintendent's first greeting of him and compassion

> Louis, recalled to himself by the change of situation, looked at himself, and ashamed of his disordered state, ashamed of his conduct, ashamed of the protection he was receiving, drew back. Fouquet did not perceive that the king's pride would never forgive him for having been a witness of so much weakness.

Finally they quit the prison,

> passing before Baisemeaux, who looked completely bewildered as he saw Marchiali once more leave, and in his helplessness tore out the few remaining hairs he had left. It is true that Fouquet wrote and gave him an authority for the prisoner's release, and that the king wrote beneath it, 'Seen and approved, Louis,' — a piece of madness that

Baisemeaux, incapable of putting two ideas together, acknowledged by giving himself a blow with his fist on his own jaw.

* * *

Meanwhile Philippe, unaware of these events and of the Damoclean sword suspended over his head, was beginning his usurped kingship with a levee attended by Anne of Austria, Monsieur, Madame and Saint-Aignan. At this, the first sight of his mother, he found it difficult to hide his emotion. He took her hand and kissed it tenderly; she did not understand that in that kiss, given in spite of repulsions and bitterness of the heart, there was a pardon for eight years of unforgettable suffering. But still all went well for him in that none of the family had shown any suspicion that he was not his brother Louis. His only misgiving was the strange non-appearance of his right-hand counsellor and supporter. At the appearance of the Captain of Musketeers Philippe asked him to find him and bring him to him at once. This request naturally astonished d'Artagnan who, the reader will recall, had just seen him and Porthos leave the place in obvious hurry. It was then that the fatal dénouement struck.

Dumas's own words must be given to describe the scene.

'What is all that noise?' said Philippe, turning round towards the door of the second staircase.

And a voice was heard saying, 'This way! This way! A few steps more, Sire!'

'The voice of M. Fouquet,' said d'Artagnan, who was standing close to the queen-mother.

'Then M. d'Herblay cannot be far off,' added Philippe. But he then saw what he little thought to see. All eyes were turned towards the door at which M. Fouquet was expected to enter; but it was not M. Fouquet who entered. A terrible cry resounded from all corners of the chamber. It is not given to men, even to those whose destiny contains the strangest elements and accidents the most wonderful, to contemplate a spectacle similar to that which presented itself in the royal chambers at the moment. The half-closed shutters admitted the entrance of only an uncertain light, passing through large velvet curtains lined with silk. In this soft shade the eyes were by degrees dilated, and everyone present saw others rather with faith than with positive sight. In these circumstances, however, not one of the surrounding details could escape; and any new object which presented itself appeared as luminous as if it had been enlightened by the sun. So it was with Louis, when he showed himself pale and frowning in the doorway of the secret stairs. The face of Fouquet appeared behind him, impressed with sorrow and sternness. The queen-mother, who perceived Louis, and who held the hand of Philippe, uttered the cry of which we have spoken, as if she had beheld a phantom. Monsieur was bewildered, and kept turning his head in astonishment from one to the other. Madame made a step forward, thinking she saw the form of her brother-in-law reflected in a glass; and, in fact, the illusion was possible.

The two princes, both pale as death, — for we renounce the hope of being able to describe the fearful state of Philippe — both trembling, and clenching their hands convulsively, measured each other with their looks and darted their eyes like poniards into each other. Mute, panting, bending forward, they appeared as if about to spring upon an enemy. The unheard-of resemblance of countenance, gesture, shape, height, even of costume, — produced by chance, for Louis had been to the Louvre and put on a violet coloured suit — the perfect likeness of the two princes completed the consternation of Anne of Austria. And yet she did not at once guess the truth. There are misfortunes in life that no one will accept; people would rather believe in the supernatural and the impossible. Louis had not reckoned upon these obstacles. He expected that he had only to appear and be acknowledged. A living sun, he could not endure the suspicion of parity with anyone. He did not admit that every torch should not become darkness at the instant he shone out with his conquering ray. At the aspect of Philippe, then, he was perhaps more terrified than anyone round him, and his silence, his immobility, were this time a concentration and a calm which precede violent explosions of passion....

D'Artagnan, leaning against the wall in front of Fouquet, with his hand to his brow, asked himself the cause of such a wonderful prodigy. He could not have said at once why he doubted, but he knew assuredly that he had reason to doubt, and that in this meeting of the two Louis lay all the mystery which during late days had rendered the conduct of Aramis so suspicious to the Musketeer. These ideas were, however, enveloped in thick veils. The actors in this assembly seemed to swim in the vapours of a confused waking.

Suddenly Louis, more impatient and more accustomed to command, ran to one of the shutters, which he opened, tearing the curtains in his eagerness. A flood of living light entered the chamber, and made Philippe draw back to the alcove. Louis seized upon this movement with eagerness, and addressing himself to the queen, 'Mother,' said he, 'do you not acknowledge your son, since everyone here has forgotten his king?' Anne of Austria started, and raised her arms towards heaven without being able to articulate a single word.

'Mother,' said Philippe, with a calm voice, 'do you not acknowledge your son?' And this time, in his turn, Louis drew back.

Anne of Austria, struck in both head and heart with remorse, was no longer able to stand. No one aiding her, for all were petrified, she sank back in her *fauteuil*, breathing a weak, trembling sigh. Louis could not endure this spectacle and this affront. He bounded towards d'Artagnan, upon whom the vertigo was beginning to gain, and who staggered as he caught at the door for support. 'A moi, *Mousquetaire!*' said he. 'Look us in the face and say which is the paler, he or I?'

The cry roused d'Artagnan, and stirred in his heart the fibre of obedience. He shook his head, and without more hesitation he walked straight up to Philippe, upon whose shoulder he laid his hand, saying, 'Monsieur, you are my prisoner.' Philippe did not raise his eyes towards heaven, nor stir from the spot, where he seemed nailed to the floor, his eye intently fixed upon the king, his brother. He reproached him by a sublime silence with all his misfortunes past, with all his tortures to come. Against this language of the soul Louis XIV felt he had no power; he cast down his eyes, and led away precipitately his brother and sister, forgetting his mother, sitting motionless within three paces of the son whom she left a second time to be condemned to death. Philippe approached Anne of Austria, and said to her in a soft and nobly agitated voice, 'If I were not your son, I should curse you, mother, for having made me so unhappy.'

D'Artagnan felt a shudder pass through the marrow of his bones. He bowed respectfully to the young prince, and said as he bent, 'Excuse me, Monseigneur; I am but a soldier, and my oaths are his who has just left the chamber.'

'Thank you, M. d'Artagnan; but what is become of M. d'Herblay?'

'M. d'Herblay is in safety, Monseigneur,' said a voice behind them, 'and no one, while I live and am free, shall cause a hair to fall from his head.'

'M. Fouquet!' said the prince, smiling sadly.

'Pardon me, Monseigneur,' said Fouquet, kneeling; 'but he who is just gone out from hence was my guest.'

'Here,' murmured Philippe, with a sigh, 'are brave friends and good hearts. They make me regret the world. On, M. d'Artagnan, I follow you!'

At the moment the Captain of the Musketeers was about to leave the room with his prisoner, Colbert appeared, and after delivering to d'Artagnan an order from the king, retired. D'Artagnan read the paper, and then crushed it in his hand with rage.

'What is it?' asked the prince.

'Read, Monseigneur,' replied the Musketeer.

Philippe read the following words, hastily traced by the hand of the king:-

'M. d'Artagnan will conduct the prisoner to the Ile Ste. Marguerite. He will cover his face with an iron visor, which the prisoner will not raise without peril of his life.'

'It is just,' said Philippe, with resignation; 'I am ready.'

'Aramis was right,' said Fouquet in a low voice to the Musketeer, 'this one is as much of a king as the other.'

'More,' replied d'Artagnan. 'He needs only you and me.'

* * *

After this climax the narrative loses something of its intensity and becomes a succession of brief scenes and, as it were, silhouettes. The first of these is a final meeting of Aramis, Porthos and Athos at the latter's home which the fugitives happened to pass on their desperate flight to safety. They found Athos there with Raoul, living in total isolation after La Vallière's betrayal, Athos endeavouring to console his son, Raoul oblivious to everyone and everything and uttering Wertheresque despondencies. The contrast between the sombre mien of Aramis with the joyous one of Porthos perplexed Athos until Aramis, taking him on one side, confessed his plot and its ruinous failure, and in addition his deception of the simple-minded, loyal-hearted Porthos. At the conclusion of his recital Athos said:

'It was a great idea, but a great error.'
    'For which I am punished, Athos.'
'Therefore I will not tell you my entire thought.'
'Tell it, nevertheless.'
'It is a crime.'
'I know it is, — high treason.'
'Porthos! Poor Porthos!'
'What should I have done? Success, as I have told you, was certain.'

'M. Fouquet is an honourable man.'

'And I am a fool for having so ill judged him,' said Aramis. 'Oh, the wisdom of man! Oh, vast millstone which grinds a world, and which is one day stopped by a grain of sand which has fallen, no one knows how, in its wheels!'

'Say by a diamond, Aramis. But the thing is done. How do you think of acting?'

'I am taking Porthos away. The king will never believe that he has acted innocently. He could never believe that Porthos thought he was serving the king while acting as he has done. His head would pay for my fault. It shall not be so.'

'Where are taking him?'

'To Belle-Ile, first. This is an impregnable place of refuge. There I have the sea, and a vessel to pass over into England, where I have many relatives.'

'You? In England?'

'Yes; or else in Spain, where I have still more.'

'But our excellent Porthos! You ruin him, for the king will confiscate all his property.'

'All is provided for. I know how, when once in Spain, to reconcile myself with Louis XIV, and restore Porthos to favour. Rest assured, Athos, whatever happens to me, Porthos will come out safe and sound.'

After pressing Aramis's hand, Athos turned to embrace Porthos with strong emotion.

'I was born lucky, wasn't I?' the latter murmured as he folded his cloak around him.

'Come, *mon cher ami*,' said Aramis.

Raoul had gone out to give orders to have the horses ready saddled. Athos saw his two comrades on the point of departure, and something like a mist passed over his eyes and a weight oppressed his heart. Just then Porthos came towards his old friend with open arms. This last endearment was as affectionate as in their young days. Porthos mounted his horse as Aramis embraced Athos in farewell, then mounted in his turn. The count watched them as they rode away in their white cloaks. Elongated by the shade, like two phantoms they seemed to grow before they disappeared in the declivity of the road. At the end of the perspective both appeared to have given a spring which made them seem to evaporate into the clouds.

Then Athos with an oppressed heart made his way back to the house saying to Raoul, 'I don't know how it is, but something tells me I have seen them both for the last time.'

'That does not astonish me, Monsieur, for I feel the same about them.'

Their premonitions were to be only too well justified. They were never to meet again.

Almost immediately following their departure the Duc de Beaufort, with noise and torches and a cavalcade of boisterous followers arrived on the scene. He had come to bid Athos farewell, remembering how he owed his escape from his imprisonment in Vincennes prison to him and Grimaud,* being 'commanded by the king to make conquests among the Arabs'. Hearing this, Raoul seized the opportunity to beg the duke to take him with him. To the despair of Athos

---

* As related in *Vingt Ans Après*.

the duke not only agreed to his request but promised to make him his aide-de-camp. Once the duke and his party had left, Athos rounded on his son, accusing him of enlisting only with the aim of getting himself killed in action. Raoul did not deny the accusation.

With the next half a dozen chapters the reader is taken over the last days spent together of Athos and his son — chapters sentimentalized to the point of morbidity, and relieved only by a couple of dramatic events occurring in the course of them, the first being a chance but significant encounter with Montalais during Raoul's brief visit to the Louvre to bid farewell to his friend de Guiche — Montalais, who called back to him the memory of that episode in the turret of Blois castle and his then hopes of being loved by Louise.

'You were looking for M. de Guiche?' she said.

'Yes, Mademoiselle.'

'I will go and tell him you are here presently, after I have spoken to you. Are you angry with me?'

Raoul looked at her for a moment, then looking away 'Yes,' he replied.

'You think I was implicated in the plot which caused your rupture with Louise, I suppose?'

'Rupture!' he cried with bitterness. 'Oh, Mademoiselle, there can be no rupture where there had been no love.'

'You are wrong, Monsieur. Louise did love you.' Raoul started.

'Not perhaps with the sort of love you wanted, I know, but she was fond of you, and you ought to have married her before you set off for England.'

'You say that very easily, Mademoiselle. Do people marry whom they only like? You seem to forget that the king kept her as his mistress.'

'Listen,' said the young woman, pressing Raoul's cold hands in her own; 'you were wrong in every way. A man of your age ought never to leave a woman of hers alone.'

'There is no longer any faith in the world then?'

'No, Vicomte,' she said quietly. 'Nevertheless, let me tell you that if instead of loving Louise coldly and philosophically you had awakened her to love...'

'Enough, I pray you, Mademoiselle,' he interrupted her...

Though he resented her feminine reasoning, unknowingly Raoul had been given the sharp lesson of truth by Montalais, and one which any intelligent reader could have presented him with.

From another brief visit to Planchet in his shop to glean news of d'Artagnan they learned two things: that the worthy grocer was in the midst of selling his business and planning to retire to his country house with Trüchen; and that the Captain of Musketeers had disappeared on a mysterious mission to the *midi*, was all that Planchet knew. This was proved in the course of their journey south to join up with the Duc de Beaufort by accidental contact with d'Artagnan in dramatic and nearly tragic circumstances. Following up what they considered to be a cock and bull story of a fisherman about taking two men and a carriage in his smack to the Ile Ste. Marguerite, one of the men being in ' "a black helmet and a black mask"', they decided to discover the truth for themselves, chartered a boat and sailed for the island. As they casually explored the park with its fortress, and inhabited only by a governor and a garrison of some dozen soldiers, suddenly, from a window of the *donjon*, they heard a shout, and looking up saw a waving hand, followed by the throwing out to them of a silver plate.

The hand which had thrown this plate made a sign to the two gentlemen and then disappeared. Athos and Raoul began an attentive examination of the dusty plate; and they discovered, in characters traced upon the bottom of it with the point of a knife, this inscription:

'I AM THE BROTHER OF THE KING OF FRANCE; A PRISONER TODAY, A MADMAN TOMORROW. FRENCH GENTLEMEN AND CHRISTIANS, PRAY TO GOD FOR THE SOUL AND THE REASON OF THE SON OF YOUR MASTERS.'

The plate fell from the hands of Athos while Raoul was endeavouring to make out the meaning of these dismal words. At the same instant they heard a cry from the top of the *donjon*. As quick as lightning Raoul bent down his head, and forced down that of his father likewise. A musket-barrel glittered from the crest of the wall, a white smoke floated like a plume from the mouth of the musket, and a ball was flattened against a stone within six inches of the two men. Another musket appeared, which was aimed at them.

'*Cordieu!*' cried Athos. 'What! Are people assassinated here? Come down, cowards!'

'Yes, come down!' cried Raoul, furiously shaking his fist at the citadel.

But to their amazement it transpired that their assailants were no other that Saint-Mars, the governor, and d'Artagnan.

'*Mordioux!*' cried the captain. 'I was sure I was not mistaken.'

'What is the meaning of this?' asked Athos. 'What! were we to be shot without warning?'

'It was I who was going to shoot you; and if the governor missed you, I should not have missed you, my dear friends. How fortunate it is that I am accustomed to take a long aim instead of firing at the instant I raise my weapon! I thought I recognized you. Ah, my dear friends, how fortunate!' and d'Artagnan wiped his brow — for he had run fast, and his emotion was far from feigned.

'And is the gentleman who fired at us the governor of the fortress?' said Athos.

'In person.'

'And why did he fire at us? What have we done to him?'

'*Pardieu!* You received what the prisoner threw to you?'

'That is true.'

'That plate, — the prisoner has written something on the bottom of it, has he not?'

'Yes.'

'Good heavens! I was afraid he had.'

And d'Artagnan, with all the marks of mortal alarm, seized the plate to read the inscription. When he had read it, a fearful pallor spread over his countenance.

'Oh, good heavens!' repeated he. 'Silence! here is the governor.'

'And what will he do to us? Is it our fault?' asked Raoul.

'It is true, then?' said Athos, in a subdued voice; 'It is true?'

'Silence, I tell you, silence! If he only believes you can read, if he only suspects you have understood — I love you, my dear friends, I will be killed for you; but...'

'But...' said Athos and Raoul.

'But I could not save you from perpetual imprisonment, if I saved you from death. Silence, then! Silence again!'

The governor came up, having crossed the ditch upon a plank bridge. 'Well,' said he to d'Artagnan, 'what stops us?'

'You are Spaniards; you do not understand a word of French,' said the captain, to his friends in a low voice.

By this piece of typical d'Artagnan quicksilver invention this dangerous immediate hurdle was got over, the governor finally left the three friends together to talk and roam around the environs. D'Artagnan, still agitated and fearful from his continual personal guard of the 'royal' prisoner, began by trying to bluff them and maintaining that the words on the plate were those of a self-deluded madman, to be cut short by Athos's simple

'Tell Aramis that.'

'You have seen Aramis?' cried the Musketeer, quite taken aback.

'Yes, after his flight from Vaux with Porthos. Seen him ruined, pursued, a fugitive. And he told me enough to make me believe in the words this unfortunate young man has written on the silver plate.'

D'Artagnan's head sank upon his breast with confusion. 'This is the way,' said he, 'in which fate turns to nothing that which men call their wisdom! A fine secret must that be of which twelve or fifteen persons hold the tattered fragments! Athos, cursed be the chance which has brought you face to face with me in this affair! for now...'

'Well,' said Athos, with his customary mild severity, 'is your secret lost because I know it? Consult your memory, *mon ami*. Have I not borne secrets as heavy as this?'

'You have never borne one so dangerous,' replied d'Artagnan in a tone of sadness. 'I have something like a sinister idea that all who are concerned with this secret will die, and die unfortunately.'

As with Athos's premonition regarding Aramis and Porthos, this of the Musketeer was to be proved right, at least partially.

* * *

To the captain's intense relief a messenger from the king arrived ordering him to return to Paris. Realizing the time of farewells was at hand for both Raoul and d'Artagnan, Athos unburdens his lacerated heart to his old friend. His words, along with those of d'Artagnan in the following chapter, constitute the most emotive passages in the whole novel. D'Artagnan had just remonstrated with Athos on his refusal to accompany Raoul on the campaign because of his inability to witness the death of his son — remonstrance ending with ' "Why have you this fear, Athos? Man on this earth must face up to everything." ' To which Athos replies

'I am strong against everything, except against the death of those I love. For that only there is no remedy. He who dies, gains; he who sees others die, loses. No; this it is — to know that I should no more meet upon earth him whom I now behold with joy; to know that there would nowhere be a d'Artagnan any more, nowhere again be a Raoul, — oh! I am old, see you, I have no longer courage. I pray God to spare me in my weakness; but if he struck me so plainly and in that fashion, I should curse him. A Christian gentleman ought not to curse his God, d'Artagnan; it is quite enough to have cursed his king!'

'Humph!' said d'Artagnan, a little confused by this violent tempest of grief.

'D'Artagnan, you who love Raoul, look at him,' he added, pointing to his son; 'see that melancholy which never leaves him. Can you imagine anything more dreadful than to witness minute by minute the ceaseless agony of that poor soul?'

'Let me speak to him, Athos. Who knows?'

'Try, if you please, but I am convinced you will not succeed.'

'I will not attempt to console him, I will lecture him.'

'You will?'

'Doubtless. Do you think this would be the first time a woman has repented of an infidelity? I will go to him, I tell you.'

Athos shook his head, and continued his walk alone. D'Artagnan, cutting across the brambles, rejoined Raoul, and held out his hand to him.

'Well, Raoul! you have something to say to me?'

'I have a kindness to ask you,' replied Bragelonne.

'Ask it, then.'

'You will some day return to France?'

'I hope so.'

'Ought I to write to Mademoiselle de la Vallière?'

'No.'

'But I have so many things to say to her.'

'Say them to her, then.'

'Never!'

'Pray, what virtue do you attribute to a letter which your speech might not possess?'

'Perhaps you are right.'

'She loves the king,' said d'Artagnan bluntly; 'and she is an honest girl.'

Raoul started. 'And you, you whom she abandons,' added the captain, 'she perhaps loves better than she does the king, but after another fashion.'

'D'Artagnan, do you believe she loves the king?'

'To idolatry. Her heart is inaccessible to any other feeling. But you might continue to live near her, and be her best friend.'

'Ah!' exclaimed Raoul, with a passionate burst of repugnance for such a painful hope.

'Will you do so?'

'It would be base.'

'That is a very absurd word, which would lead me to think slightly of your understanding. Please understand, Raoul, that it is never base to do that which is imposed by a superior force. If your heart says to you, "Go there, or die," why, go there, Raoul. Was she base or brave, she whom you loved, in preferring the king to you, — the king whom here heart commanded her imperiously to prefer to you? No, she was the bravest of women. Do, then, as she has done. Obey yourself. Do you know one thing of which I am sure, Raoul?'

'What is that?'

'Why, that by seeing her closely with the eyes of a jealous man...'

'Well?'

'Well; you would cease to love her.'

'Then I am decided, my dear d'Artagnan.'

'To set off to see her again?'

'No; to set off that I may never see her again. I wish to love her forever.'

'Frankly,' replied the Musketeer, 'that is a conclusion which I was far from expecting.'

'That is what I wish. You will see her again, and you will give her a letter which, if you think proper, will explain to her as to yourself what is passing in my heart. Read it; I prepared it last night. Something told me I should see you today.' He held the letter out, and d'Artagnan read it.

The letter was a long rigmarole of his pardoning her and blaming himself. Returning it to him d'Artagnan remarked caustically,

'The letter is very well,' said the captain. 'I have only one fault to find with it.'

'Tell me what that is,' said Raoul.

'It is that it tells everything except the thing which exhales, like a mortal poison, from your eyes and from your heart; except the senseless love which still consumes you.'

Raoul grew paler, but remained silent.

'Why did you not write simply these words: "MADEMOISELLE, — Instead of cursing you, I love you and I die."'

'That is true,' exclaimed Raoul with a sinister joy.

And tearing the letter he had just taken back, he wrote the following words upon a leaf of his tablets: 'To procure the happiness of once more telling you that I love you, I commit the baseness of writing to you; and to punish myself for that baseness, I die.'

And he signed it.

'You will give her these tablets, Captain, will you not?'

'When?' asked the latter.

'On the day,' said Bragelonne, pointing to the last sentence, — 'on the day when you can place a date under these words.' And he sprang away quickly to join Athos, who was returning with slow steps.

Next day brought the final farewells.

'Till we meet again then, dear Athos: and the sooner you are home the sooner I shall embrace you.'

So saying, he put his foot in the stirrup, which Raoul held.

'Farewell!' said the young man, embracing him.

'Farewell!' said d'Artagnan, as he got into his saddle. His horse made a movement which divided the cavalier from his friends.

This scene had taken place in front of the house chosen by Athos, near the gates of Antibes, whither d'Artagnan, after his supper, had ordered his horses to be brought. The road began there, and extended white and undulating in the vapours of the night. The horse eagerly inhaled the salt sharp perfume of the marshes. D'Artagnan put him into a trot; and Athos and Raoul sadly turned towards the house. All at once they heard the rapid approach of a horse's hoofs, and at first believed it to be one of those singular echoes which deceive the ear at every turn in a road; but it was really the return of the horseman. They uttered a cry of joyous surprise; and the captain, springing to the ground like a young man, seized within his arms the two beloved forms of Athos and Raoul. He held them in a long embrace, without speaking a word, or suffering the sigh which was bursting his breast to escape him. Then, as rapidly as he had come back, he set off again, with a sharp application of his spurs to the sides of his fiery horse.

'Alas!' said the count, in a low voice, 'alas! alas!'

'Evil presage!' on his side said d'Artagnan to himself, making up for lost time. 'I could not smile upon them. Evil presage!'

* * *

I observed earlier that the novel might be said to resemble a classical symphony in its structure, with exposition — development — recapitulation — coda. With d'Artagnan's return to Paris to resume his normal duties we reach the last bars of the recapitulation and approach the final coda. The time of day is now that of sunset; brightness falls from the air; the shadows lengthen. The ageing principal characters see their star dimming and sinking, and prepare to leave the stage to a younger generation.

First Fouquet. Despite the fact that Louis owed his being still alive and king to the superintendent, with singular vindictiveness he had determined to crush him, to annihilate him, and he chose d'Artagnan as his agent, to the latter's chagrin and mixed emotions. For as we have already seen, the captain had a soft spot in his heart for the opulent but carelessly lavish and warm-hearted minister, now ageing and ailing and only too aware of his approaching *débâcle*. At first ordered by the king merely to keep the superintendent under surveillance, the Musketeer, moved by pity for the ailing man, ventured to drop broad hints of his future ruin at the hands of the king, thereby giving him the opportunity to make good his escape before it was too late. But Fouquet dithered and dallied — fatally, for from the moment when Louis at last brought himself to the sticking point of ordering Fouquet's arrest by his Captain of Musketeers, the latter's mind was cleared: the unwilling sympathizer of the finance minister became the disciplined and disciplinary soldier and defender of the king. Nevertheless, true to character, he had the audacity to confess his feelings regarding the order of arrest.

'I would have liked to save M. Fouquet at one time, Sire,' The king started.

'Because,' continued the captain, 'I had then a right to do so, having guessed Your Majesty's plan without your having spoken to me of it, and because I took an interest in M. Fouquet. Then, I was at liberty to show my interest in the man.'

'In truth, Monsieur, you do not reassure me with regard to your services.'

'If I had saved him then, I should have been perfectly innocent; I will say more, I should have done well, for M. Fouquet is not a bad man. But he was not willing; his destiny prevailed; he let the hour of liberty slip by. So much the worse! Now I have orders I will obey them, and M. Fouquet you may consider as a man arrested. He is at the Castle of Angers, is M. Fouquet.'

'Oh, you have not got him yet, Captain.'

'That concerns me; every one to his trade, Sire. Only, once more, reflect! Do you seriously give me orders to arrest M. Fouquet, Sire?'

'Yes, a thousand times, yes!'

'Write it, then.'

'I have already done so. Here it is.'

D'Artagnan read it, bowed to the king and left the room.

Too late now the belated attempt by Fouquet to escape; too late the white horse provided by his faithful Epicureans. For it was as he left the king with the order for Fouquet's arrest in his pocket that the Musketeer caught sight of the galloping white horse and its desperate rider. Remembering his vow to the king to see Fouquet arrested and taken to Angers prison, he hurriedly selected his best horse, a black one, and set off in pursuit. The race between the white horse of escape and the black horse of pursuit might have been written by Zane Grey!

At moments, when the wind cut his eyes so as to make the tears spring from them; when the saddle had become burning hot; when the galled and spurred horse reared with pain and threw behind him a shower of dust and stones, — d'Artagnan, raising himself in his stirrups, and seeing nothing on the waters, nothing beneath the trees, looked up into the air like a madman. He was losing his senses. A hoarse sigh broke from his lips as he repeated, devoured by the fear of ridicule, 'I! I! duped by a Gourville! I! They will say I am growing old; they will say I have received a million to allow Fouquet to escape!' It was an unheard-of spectacle, — this race between two horses which were only kept alive by the will of their riders. To the furious gallop had succeeded the fast trot, and then the slow trot; and the race appeared equally warm to the two fatigued athletes. D'Artagnan, in despair, seized his second pistol, and cocked it. 'At your horse! not at you!' he cried to Fouquet. And he fired. The animal was hit in the rump; he made a furious bound, and plunged forward. At that moment d'Artagnan's horse fell dead.

'I am dishonoured!' thought the Musketeer. Then he cried, 'For pity's sake, M. Fouquet, throw me one of your pistols so that I may blow out my brains!' But Fouquet rode on.

'For mercy's sake! For mercy's sake!' cried d'Artagnan; 'that which you will not do at this moment, I myself will do within the hour. But here upon this road I should die bravely, I should die esteemed; do me that service, M. Fouquet!'

Fouquet made no reply, but continued to trot on. D'Artagnan began to run after his enemy. Successively he threw off his hat, his coat, which embarrassed him, and then the sheath of his sword, which got between his legs as he was running. The sword in his hand even became too heavy, and he threw it after the sheath. From a trot the exhausted animal sunk to a staggering walk; the foam from his mouth was mixed with blood. D'Artagnan made a desperate effort, sprang towards Fouquet and seized him by the leg, saying in a broken, breathless voice, 'I arrest you in the king's name! Blow my brains out, if you like; we have both done our duty.'

Fouquet hurled far from him into the river the two pistols which d'Artagnan might have seized, and dismounting from his horse, 'I am your prisoner, Monsieur,' said he, 'will you take my arm, for I see you are ready to faint?'

'Thanks!' murmured d'Artagnan, who in fact felt the earth turning under his feet and the sky melting away over his head; and he rolled upon the sand without breath or strength. Fouquet hastened to the brink of the river, dipped some water in his hat, with which he bathed the temples of the Musketeer, and introduced a few drops between his lips. D'Artagnan raised himself, looking round with a wandering eye. He saw Fouquet on his knees, with his wet hat in his hand, smiling upon him. 'You are not gone, then?' cried he. 'Oh, Monsieur! the true king in loyalty, in heart, in soul, is not Louis of the Louvre or Philippe of Ste. Marguerite; it is you, the proscribed, the condemned!'

'I, who this day am ruined by a single error, M. d'Artagnan.'

'What in the name of heaven is that?'

'I should have had you for a friend!'

It was not d'Artagnan, then, who returned in triumph with Fouquet as his prisoner, but the reverse. And with that last typically generous quixotic gesture Fouquet disappears from the pages of the novel and from normal life.*

* * *

With Fouquet at last disposed of, Louis, now feeling himself coming into full plenitude of power and tolerating no rivals or opponents, was equally determined to lay revengeful hands on the two who had had the audacity to humiliate him beyond belief by abducting him and imprisoning him in his own Bastille for twelve mortal hours. So the scene shifts to Belle-Ile-en-Mer, where Aramis and Porthos are in hiding. And here at last, driven to his final defences and questioned by the puzzled Porthos, the former threw aside his cunning and deliberate falsification of his plot and confessed the truth, ending by declaring that he had done it with the best intentions, that he alone was guilty and would take all the blame and see that his friend would not be made to suffer.

'Did you deceive me for my good, Aramis?' Porthos asked.

'I thought so, Porthos; I thought so sincerely.'

'Then,' said the honest Seigneur de Bracieux, 'you have rendered me a service,

---

* See Brief Biographies.

and I thank you for it.'

Before this ingenuous greatness of spirit Aramis felt himself made small.

Eventually a boat arrived bearing d'Artagnan, who landed and hurried up the pier steps, closely followed by an officer ordered by Colbert not to let the captain out of his sight, thus making his idea of secretly proposing a truce with the Belle-Ile defenders and so the escape of his friends impossible — an impossibility further ensured by an order from the king commanding the captain to be relieved of any command and recalled to Paris, and the surrender of Belle-Ile along with the capture of the two rebels.

The duel is on, not only between the king and the two rebels, but between him and d'Artagnan. Events move rapidly. After exhorting the hopelessly outnumbered defenders, as their bishop and spiritual leader, to yield to the royal besiegers, Aramis and Porthos now aim to make good their escape via the grottos of Locmaria which lead by tortuous passages to the sea — and freedom. But catastrophically a fox, pursued by a posse of huntsmen and dogs, takes the same route, followed in turn by a brigade of soldiers searching for the two rebels. The chapter 'The Death of a Titan' narrates what ensued.

Porthos took refuge in the second compartment, which was absolutely black as pitch. Aramis glided into the third; the giant held in his hand an iron bar of about fifty pounds weight. Porthos handled this lever, which had been used in rolling the boat, with marvellous facility. During this time, the Bretons had pushed the boat to the beach. In the enlightened compartment, Aramis, stooping and concealed, was busied in some mysterious manoeuvre. A command was given in a loud voice. It was the last order of the captain. Twenty-five men jumped from the upper rocks into the first compartment of the grotto, and having taken their ground, began to fire. The echoes growled; the hissing of the balls cut the air; an opaque smoke filled the vault.

'To the left! to the left!' cried Biscarrat who in his first assault had seen the passage to the second chamber, and animated by the smell of powder, wished to guide his solders in that direction. The troop accordingly precipitated themselves to the left — the passage gradually growing narrower. Biscarrat, with his hands stretched forward, devoted to death, marched in advance of the muskets. 'Come on! come on!' exclaimed he, 'I see daylight!'

'Strike, Porthos!' cried the sepulchral voice of Aramis.

Porthos breathed a sigh; but he obeyed. The iron bar fell full and direct upon the head of Biscarrat, who was dead before he had ended his cry. Then the formidable lever rose ten times in ten seconds, and made ten corpses. The soldiers could see nothing; heard only sighs and groans; stumbled over dead bodies, but as they had no conception of the cause of all this, they came forward jostling one another. The implacable bar, still falling, annihilated the first platoon without a single sound having warned the second, which was advancing. But this second platoon, commanded by the captain, had broken a thin fir growing on the shore, and with its resinous branches twisted together, the captain had made a torch.

On arriving at the compartment where Porthos, like the exterminating angel, had destroyed all he touched, the first rank drew back in terror. No firing had replied to that of the guards, and yet their way was blocked by a heap of dead bodies — they literally walked in blood. Porthos was still behind his pillar. The captain, on lighting up with the trembling flame of the fir this frightful carnage, of which he in vain sought the cause, drew back towards the pillar behind which Porthos was concealed. Then a gigantic hand issued from the shade and fastened on the throat of the captain, who uttered a stifled rattle, his outstretched arms beating the air. The torch fell and was extinguished in blood. A second after, the corpse of the captain fell close to the extinguished torch and added another body to the heap of dead which blocked the passage.

All this was effected as if my magic. On hearing their captain's strangled gasps, the accompanying soldiers, turning, saw only his extended arms and his eyes starting from their sockets; then the torch fell, leaving them once more in darkness. By an instinctive, mechanical impulse the lieutenant cried 'Fire!' Immediately a volley of musketry flamed and thundered around the cavern, bringing down enormous fragments from the vaults. To this succeeded a profound silence broken only by the steps of a third brigade now entering the cavern.

It was then that Porthos felt a light touch on his arm, and heard Aramis's voice saying 'We are ready. Come along.' And amid the noise of the third brigade which continued its advance amid the imprecations of those guards still living, the two crept along the sides of the cavern. In the last grotto but one Aramis showed Porthos a barrel of powder to which he had just lit a match.

'*Mon ami*,' he said, 'I want you to take up this barrel and hurl it into the middle of our enemies. Can you do that?'

'*Pardieu!*' replied Porthos lifting it with one hand. 'Light it!'

'Wait,' said Aramis, 'until they are all massed together, and then, my Jupiter, hurl your thunderbolt.'

'Light it,' repeated Porthos.

'In the meantime I will join our Bretons and help them to get our boat to the sea and wait for you there. So now, throw it, and then join us.'

'Light it,' said Porthos for the third time. Aramis gave the burning torch to Porthos, and after giving his massive arm a friendly press, made his way to the outlet where the three rowers awaited them.

Left alone, Porthos applied the spark to the match, which shone in the engulfing darkness like a firefly. It was a brief but splendid spectacle of this giant, pale and bloody, his face lit up by the flame against the surrounding blackness. The spectacle lasted only a couple of seconds; but in that time the officer of the brigade gave the order for his men to fire. A sinister burst of laughter followed the aimless discharge which did nothing but spatter the ground and sides of the cavern.

Then Porthos swung his arm, sending through the air a train of fire. The barrel, clearing the barricade of dead bodies, fell among the group of shrieking soldiers who threw themselves on their faces. The rush of air made by the barrel only served to activate the match, and the infernal thing exploded. Furious vortices, hissings of sulphur and nitre, devouring ravages, rending the rocks, followed. The great walls of silex tottered, then fell upon the sand, and the sand itself, blown by the blast, riddled the place with its myriads of lacerating atoms. Cries, howlings, imprecations, lives — all were extinguished in one great crash, leaving nothing remaining of the three grottos.

With the chaos of rocks tumbling around him Porthos made his stumbling way towards the last grotto, from which in the distance he could see daylight, the sea,

Aramis and the boat. There were his friends; there was liberty; there was life beckoning. But suddenly, under the weight of the collapsing walls he felt his legs give under him.

'Quick! Quick!' Aramis called, bending forward as if to draw Porthos to him.

With a superhuman effort Porthos rose, a giant among these giants, and made a couple of strides forward. But as he moved, the double hedge of granite phantoms, toppling, crashed down over him. Porthos stretched his arms to right and left to repulse the falling rocks. A third granite mass pinioned him between his vast shoulders. For an instant he appeared in this frame of granite like the angel of chaos. But then the lateral rocks, held back for an instant, drew together again, adding their weight to that of the others. The giant fell without a cry: fell while uttering words of encouragement to his friend. But Aramis could only watch as by degrees the crushing block sank lower and lower.

On hearing the dying voice of his friend Aramis sprang from the boat, followed by two of the Bretons. Frenzied, animated with the energy of despair, he rushed towards the triple mass, and with his delicate hands by a miracle of strength raised a corner of the immense granite sepulchre wherein he caught the last light in the eyes of his friend. The two Bretons, pushing the levers they brought with them under the tiny gap, tried to lift the mass. All was useless. The men slowly gave way with exclamations of grief as the faint voice of Porthos came to them in a tone of banter, 'Too heavy for you!' Then the eye darkened and closed as the Titan breathed his last. The men dropped their levers. Breathless, pale, his brow covered with sweat, Aramis stood, listening, his heart ready to break.

Nothing more. The strong man slept his eternal sleep in the sepulchre made by death to his measure.

* * *

This death scene of Porthos has been generally discerned as being along with the slaughter of the suitors in the *Odyssey* and of the Normans at Bourne by Hereward in Kingsley's *Hereward the Wake* as the ultimate example. This being so, it can only be a matter for regret that Dumas thought fit to spoil the double inspired touch of Porthos's last words and, in the chapter narrating Aramis's escape to Spain as 'Porthos's Epitaph' with its 'first tears which had even fallen from the eyes of Aramis' by interpolating a lengthy over-sentimental passage almost biblical in its language. But the fact is that Dumas was so overcome by the killing off of a creation which had shadowed him through three novels and over a lustrum of time that his literary sense became temporarily unbalanced. How deeply it affected him is revealed in the three letters to Perée, editor of the *Siècle*, explaining why he was playing truant and for the break in the continuance of copy. He writes:

My dear Perée,
You scold me for having taken a rest for some days, and with reason, since that rest, at least you have the goodness to say so, is prejudicial to the pleasure of your subscribers. But how could it be otherwise? We cannot separate ourselves from a friend we have known for six years, with whom we have lived daily, and who kept

no secrets from us; from a friend whose goodness had become proverbial; we do not bury such a friend without its tearing one's heart and mind, and for a time enervating one's strength and compelling us to retire for consolation among friends who are still living.

By the dead friend, I mean poor Porthos. By the living, my good and dear friends of Villers-Cotterêts.*

Believe me, dear friend, the profession of novelist and dramatist undoubtedly has its pleasures, its joys, and above all its pride, but it also has its sorrows. One of these sorrows, which will be incomprehensible to many, but real and profound to me, is that of having given life to a personage, of having brought him up, seen him grow, loved him, and then, after having led him through the vicissitudes of an adventurous life, of facing the implacable necessity of sending it to oblivion...

I have, then, to my deep regret, lost Porthos, and my regret is so much the more poignant from this being so well known as the good and valiant, making it all the more hard for me never to allow this phantom of my imagination to don his old uniform, cover his head with his wide-spreading beaver, or wield his long rapier. Porthos is, then, surely dead, leaving no heir, no successor, no imitation in the future...

Sleep then, my good Porthos, in peace beneath the druidical rocks of Locmaria!

As for myself, I have retired to mourn your loss beneath the old trees of the forest of Villers-Cotterêts, near the graves of the friends of my youth, interred as you beneath earth perhaps still heavier that that which covers you...

The last letter concludes:

And now you have, dear friend, the story I wished to relate to you; and this, besides my three roebucks, is what I bring you from Villers-Cotterêts. Moreover, tomorrow you should receive the next chapters of our long history which you may resume without fear of further interruption.

Tout à vous.
Alexandre Dumas.

Although Dumas kept his promise and resumed the novel, one has the feeling that his heart had gone out of it. The true Dumas verve, with one or two exceptions, is lacking.

The exceptions are, as might be expected, those in which d'Artagnan is involved. Following the order from Louis for him to return from Belle-Ile the Musketeer, in a high state of frustration and fury, determined to have it out with the king for the last time, bend or break.

This was to be the fourth and last of his monumental interviews with his royal master. It is not only the last: it is uniquely different from the others. In those he had been the complainer, the accuser, the eloquent demander for justice and recognition. Now all that was changed. It was the turn of Louis to accuse, the Musketeer to be put on the defensive. After their ding-dong preliminary rounds of complaints, accusations, remonstrances, the king decides

---

* Dumas's birthplace.

to put an end to it all with

'Enough, M. d'Artagnan, enough of these dominating concerns which arise to keep the sun from my interest. I am founding a state in which there shall be but one master, as promised you formerly; the moment is come for keeping my promise. You wish to be, according to your tastes or your friendships, free to destroy my plans and save my enemies; I will break you, or I will abandon you. Seek a more compliant master. I know full well that another king would not conduct himself as I do, and would allow himself to be dominated over by you at the risk of sending you some day to keep company with M. Fouquet and the others; but I have a good memory, and for me, services are sacred titles to gratitude, to impunity. You shall only have this lesson, M. d'Artagnan, as the punishment of your want of discipline; and I will not imitate my predecessors in their anger, not having imitated them in their favour. And then, other reasons make me act mildly towards you: in the first place, because you are a man of sense, a man of heart, and you will be a good servant to him who shall have mastered you; secondly, because you will cease to have any motives for insubordination. Your friends are destroyed or ruined by me. These supports upon which your capricious mind instinctively relied I have done away with. At this moment, my soldiers have taken or killed the rebels of Belle-Ile.'

D'Artagnan became pale. 'Taken or killed!' cried he. 'Oh, Sire, if you thought what you tell me, if you were sure you were telling me the truth, I should forget all that is just, all that is magnanimous in your words, to call you a barbarous king and an unnatural man. But I pardon you these words,' said he, smiling with pride; 'I pardon them to a young prince who does not know, who cannot comprehend, what such men as M. d'Herblay, M. du Vallon, and myself are. Taken or killed! Ah, ah, Sire! tell me, if the news is true, how much it has cost you in men and money. We will then reckon if the game has been worth the stakes.'

As he spoke thus, the king went up to him in great anger and said, 'M. d'Artagnan, your replies are those of a rebel! Tell me, if you please, who is King of France? Do you know any other?'

'Sire,' replied the Captain of the Musketeers, coldly, 'I remember that one morning at Vaux you addressed that question to people who did not know how to answer it, while I, on my part, did answer it. If I recognized my king on that day, when the thing was not easy, I think it would be useless to ask it of me now, when Your Majesty is alone with me.'

At these words, Louis cast down his eyes. It appeared to him that the shade of the unfortunate Philippe passed between d'Artagnan and himself, to evoke the remembrance of that terrible episode. Almost at the same moment an officer entered and placed a despatch in the hands of the king, who, in his turn, changed colour while reading it.

'Monsieur,' said he, 'what I learn here you would know later; it is better I should tell you, and that you should learn it from the mouth of your king. A battle has taken place at Belle-Ile.'

'Oh! oh!' said d'Artagnan, with a calm air, though his heart beat enough to break through his chest. 'Well, Sire?'

'Well, Monsieur, I have lost a hundred and six men.'

A beam of joy and pride shone in the eyes of d'Artagnan. 'And the rebels?' said he.

'The rebels havĕ fled,' said the king.

D'Artagnan could not restrain a cry of triumph.

'Only,' added the king, 'I have a fleet which closely blockades Belle-Ile, and I am certain no boat can escape.'

'So that,' said the Musketeer, brought back to his dismal ideas, 'if these two gentlemen are taken.'

'They will be hanged,' said the king quietly.

'And do they know it?' replied d'Artagnan, repressing a shudder.

'They know it, because you must have told them yourself; and all the country knows it.'

'Then, Sire, they will never be taken alive, I will answer for that.'

'Ah!' said the king, negligently, taking up his letter again. 'Very well, they will be dead then, M. d'Artagnan, and that will come to the same thing, since I should only take them to have them hanged.'

D'Artagnan wiped the sweat from his brow. 'I have told you,' pursued Louis XIV, 'that I would one day be to you an affectionate, generous, and constant master. You are now the only man of former times worthy or my anger of my friendship. I will not be sparing of either to you, according to your conduct. Could you serve a king, M. d'Artagnan, who should have a hundred other kings, his equals, in the kingdom? Could I, tell me, do with such weakness the great things I meditate? Have you ever seen an artist effect solid work with a rebellious instrument? Far from us, Monsieur, those old leavens of feudal abuses! The *Fronde*, which threatened to ruin the monarchy, has emancipated it. I am master in my home, Captain d'Artagnan, and I shall have servants who, wanting perhaps your genius, will carry devotedness and obedience up to heroism. Of what consequence, I ask you, of what consequence is it that God has given no genius to arms and legs? It is to the head he has given it; and the head, you know, all the rest obey. I myself am the head.'

D'Artagnan started. Louis XIV continued as if he had seen nothing, although this emotion had not at all escaped him. 'Now, let us conclude between us two that bargain which I promised to make with you one day when you found me very small, at Blois. Do me justice, Monsieur, when you think that I do not make anyone pay for the tears of shame I then shed. Look around you: lofty heads have bowed. Bow yours, or choose the exile that will best suit you. Perhaps, when reflecting upon it, you will find that this king has a generous heart, who reckons sufficiently upon your loyalty to allow you to leave him, knowing you to be dissatisfied, and the possessor of a great state secret. You are a brave man, I know. Why have you judged me before trial? Judge me from this day forward, d'Artagnan, and be as severe as you please.'

D'Artagnan remained bewildered, mute, undecided for the first time in his life. He had just found an adversary worthy of him. This was no longer subterfuge, it was calculation; it was no longer violence, it was strength; it was no longer passion, it was will; it was no longer boasting, it was wisdom. This young man who had brought down Fouquet and could do without d'Artagnan, deranged all the somewhat headstrong calculations of the Musketeer.

'Come, let us see what stops you?' said the king, kindly. 'You have given in your resignation; shall I refuse to accept it? I admit that it may be hard for an old captain to recover his good-humour.'

'Oh!' replied d'Artagnan, in a melancholy tone, 'that is not my most serious care. If I hesitate to take back my resignation it is because I am old in comparison with you, and I have habits difficult to abandon. Henceforward, you must have courtiers who know how to amuse you — madmen who will get themselves killed to carry out what you call your great works. Great they will be, I feel; but if by chance I should not think them so? I have seen war, Sire; I have seen peace; I have served Richelieu and Mazarin; I have been scorched with your father at the fire of Rochelle, riddled with thrusts like a sieve, having made a new skin ten times, as serpents do. After affronts and injustices, I have a command which was formerly something, because it gave the bearer the right of speaking as he liked to his king. But your Captain of the Musketeers will henceforward be an officer guarding the lower doors. Truly, Sire, if that is to be the employment from this time, seize the opportunity of our being on good terms to take it from me. Do not imagine that I bear malice. No, you have tamed me, as you say; but it must be confessed that in taming me you have lessened me, — by bowing me, you have convicted me of weakness. If you knew how well it suits me to carry my head high, and what a pitifully mien I shall have while scenting the dust of your carpets! Oh, Sire, I regret sincerely, and you will regret as I do, those times when the King of France saw in his vestibules all those insolent gentlemen, lean, always swearing, — cross-grained mastiffs, who could bite mortally in days of battle. Those men were the best of courtiers for the hand which fed them, — they would lick it; but for the hand that struck them, oh, the bite that followed! A little gold on the lace of their cloaks, a little more portliness of figure, a little sprinkling of grey in their hair, and you will behold the handsome dukes and peers the haughty marshals of France! But why should I tell you all this? The king is my master; he wills that I should make verses; he wills that I should polish the mosaics of his antechambers in satin shoes. *Mordioux!* that is difficult; but I have got over greater difficulties than that. I will do it. Why will I do it? Because I love money? I have enough. Because I am ambitious? My career is bounded. Because I love the court? No; I will remain because I have been accustomed for thirty years to go and take the order of the king, and to have him say to me, "Good-evening, d'Artagnan," with a smile I did not beg for. That smile I will beg for! Are you content, Sire?' And d'Artagnan bowed his silvered head, upon which the king, smiling, proudly placed his white hand.

Stevenson was right. D'Artagnan the untameable is tamed at last. The coda to the scene shows his gain from his loss.

'Thanks, my old servant, my faithful friend,' said Louis. 'As reckoning from this day, I have no longer any enemies in France, it remains with me to send you to a foreign field to win your marshal's baton. Depend upon me for finding you an opportunity. In the meantime, eat of my best bread and sleep tranquilly.'

'That is all kind and well!' said d'Artagnan, much agitated. 'But those poor men at Belle-Ile, — one of them, in particular, so good and so brave?'

'Do you ask their pardon of me?'

'Upon my knees, Sire!'

'Well, then, go and take it to them, if it be still time. But do you answer for them?'

'With my life, Sire!'

'Go, then. Tomorrow I set out for Paris. Return by that time, for I do not wish you to leave me in future.'

'Be assured of that, Sire,' said d'Artagnan, kissing the royal hand. And with a heart swelling with joy, he rushed out of the castle on his way to Belle-Ile.

* * *

The scene is the last to have the true Dumasian verve. With the possible exception of the reading of Porthos's will the remainder of the novel tails off with a loss of heart. The close of that scene is moving. D'Artagnan is present, and though unable to restrain a tear himself, does his best to comfort the desolated, age-long faithful Mousqueton who had shared all his late master's perilous situations and adventures. The will ends

> 'Moreover, I bequeath to M. le Vicomte de Bragelonne my old servant and faithful friend, Mousqueton, already named, with the charge to the said viscount that he shall so act that Mousqueton shall declare when dying that he has never ceased to be happy.'
> On hearing these words, Mousqueton bowed, pale and trembling; his large shoulders shook convulsively; his countenance, impressed by a frightful grief, appeared from between his icy hands, and the spectators saw him stagger and hesitate, as if, though wishing to leave the hall, he did not know the way.
> 'Mousqueton, my good friend,' said d'Artagnan, 'go and make your preparations. I will take you with me to Athos's house, where I shall go on leaving Pierrefonds.'
> Mousqueton made no reply. He scarcely breathed, feeling as if everything in that hall would from that time be strange to him. He opened the door, and disappeared slowly.
> The procurator finished his reading, after which the greater part of those who had come to hear the last will of Porthos dispersed by degrees, many disappointed, but all with respect.
> As for d'Artagnan, left alone after having received the formal compliments of the procurator, he was lost in admiration of the wisdom of the testator, who had so judiciously bestowed his wealth upon the most necessitous and the most worthy, with a delicacy that none among the most refined and noble hearts could have displayed more becomingly.
> 'Porthos was all heart,' said d'Artagnan to himself with a sigh. As he made this reflection he fancied he heard a moan coming from the room above him, and he thought at once of poor Mousqueton and his need for some consolation. With this purpose he hastily left the room and went up the stairs to the next storey, where he found in Porthos's own room the worthy intendant lying on top of a pile of clothes of all colours and materials. These were now his, bequeathed to him by his late master, and more than master, friend. D'Artagnan approached. Then 'Mon Dieu!' he said. 'He has fainted!'
> But d'Artagnan was mistaken. Mousqueton was dead — like the dog who comes to die upon the cloak of his dead master.

* * *

After this we are left with the old age of Athos, slowly and inexorably fading out of existence following the return of Grimaud with news of the death of his son Raoul; the arrival of d'Artagnan too late to see Athos alive; the twin burial of father and son; the unexpected appearance of La Vallière remorsefully seeking for posthumous pardon, all leaving the Musketeer alone to make his poignant farewell.

> The captain watched the departure of the horses, horsemen and carriages; then crossing his arms upon his swelling chest, 'When will it be my turn to depart?' said he, in an agitated voice. 'What is there left for man after youth, after love, after glory, after friendship, after strength, after riches?... only that rock under which sleeps Porthos, who possessed all I have named; this moss, under which repose Athos and Raoul, who possessed still much more!' He hesitated a moment with a dull eye; then, drawing himself up, 'Forward! still forward!' said he. 'When it shall be my time, God will tell me, as he has told others.'
> He touched the earth, moistened with the evening dew, with the tips of his fingers, made a sign as if he had been at the *bénitier* of a church, and retook alone — ever alone — the road to Paris.

There is of course still Aramis, now in Spain. The final 'Epilogue' brings him back four years later as the Duc d'Alméda and ambassador from Spain guaranteeing that country's neutrality in the event of France going to war against the United Provinces for which Louis and Colbert were preparing. He and d'Artagnan meet. But the scene, like all the rest, is brief, a mere vignette, beset by an atmosphere of change, with old animosities laid; old affections too.

> 'And so,' said d'Artagnan, taking Aramis's arm, 'you, the exile, the rebel, are back in France?'
> 'Yes. And I shall be dining with you at the king's table,' said Aramis, smiling. 'You will be asking yourself what worth fidelity is in this world. Look! Let us allow poor La Vallière's carriage to pass. See how unhappy she is; how her tearful, jealous eye follows the king on horseback over there with Mademoiselle de Tonnay-Charente, now Mme de Montespan.'
> 'What! Is she deserted, then?'
> 'Not quite yet, but she soon will be.'

Nowhere is this change more emphasized than in the different characterization of Colbert. It was through Colbert that peace had been made between Louis and Aramis and for the latter's return as ambassador. As though to make amends for his earlier pro-Fouquet anti-Colbert stance, Dumas now lets him reveal himself to Aramis and D'Artagnan as he really was — that is to say as the king's chief minister and the political genius who was to reorganize the country's ruinous finances, its agriculture, commerce, industry, civil code, navy, to ensure generous support for science, art and literature — in short as the founder of a new epoch for France, making his country the most prosperous, powerful and feared in all Europe.*

The scene between him and d'Artagnan ends with the minister promising the baton of field-marshal.

---

* See Brief Biographies.

The next day Aramis, who was setting out for Madrid to negotiate the neutrality of Spain, came to take farewell of d'Artagnan. 'We have to love each for four,' said d'Artagnan as they embraced. 'There are only two of us now.'

'And perhaps we may never see each other again, dear d'Artagnan,' said Aramis. 'If only you knew how I have loved you! We are old, and I am extinguished and dead.'

'Mon ami,' said d'Artagnan, 'you will outlive me. Diplomacy commands you to live, but honour condemns me to die.'

'Bah! such men as we, M. le Maréchal, only die satiated with glory.'

'Ah!' replied d'Artagnan with a melancholy smile, 'I assure you, M. le Duc, I feel very little appetite for that.'

They embraced for the last time, and soon afterwards separated.

* * *

Colbert kept his word, as did the king. D'Artagnan was sent by them as commander of twelve thousand horse and infantry for the invasion of Holland, and took a dozen bastions within a month. On receiving news of the victories Louis ordered his first minister to keep their promise without delay. So, with orders to find the captain wherever he might be and to present him with his marshal's baton, their envoy sought him out on the field of battle.

D'Artagnan was holding out his hand to receive the coffer containing the baton when a ball from the bastion struck him full in the chest and knocked him down on a heap of earth. He tried to pick himself up. It was thought he was only wounded. But a cry broke out from the group of his frightened officers when they saw that the marshal was covered in blood. The pallor of death spread over his features. Leaning on the arms held out to support him he was just able to see the white flag on the walls of the bastion, his ears to catch feebly the drum roll announcing final victory. Then, clasping in his nerveless hand the baton with its ornamented fleurs-de-lis, he fell back murmuring strange words which seemed cabalistic to the officers — words which held so much meaning, and which only the dying man understood: 'Athos, Porthos, au revoir! Aramis, adieu!'

EPILOGUE

So this great epic of friendship ends. Paying tribute to it John Galsworthy, wiser than Mr Polly and the prefacers, writes:*

> ' — the great Musketeer trilogy places Dumas at the head of all writers of historical romance. *Le Vicomte de Bragelonne* is perhaps, for wealth of incident and character intricately woven, his greatest effort. Few, if any, characters in fiction inspire one with such belief in their individual existences, or their importance as types.'

Stevenson claimed he had read the novel six times, describing it as a book for the winter evenings and the log fire, for the mature-minded, the old and the not so young.

But although the book is a whole gallery of living portraits, it is d'Artagnan who stands out as the crowning triumph. By his words and actions the Captain of the Musketeers has become one of the archetypal universal figures of literature, a creation we feel we know, on closing the book, better than our own friends. And Dumas, who wept when Porthos died in the grottos of Locmaria, was past tears when this supreme creation of his fancy was crushed to earth by the fatal cannon ball. That is easy to understand. To destroy d'Artagnan was, for his creator, to destroy the companion and intimate of countless secret hours, the being into whom he had instilled every faculty of invention, expressed his human ideal: in fact to destroy a life.

But a character of fiction, once it has really lived, can never really die. And just as somewhere about the old lanes of England the shades of Mr Pickwick and his companions go driving, so in France a grey-headed Gascon Captain of Musketeers stands for ever guard over the perished royalty of the Louvre. For the *Mousquetaires'* cycle has become the saga of France no less than the *Odyssey* of Greece and *Don Quixote* of Spain; and d'Artagnan lives in its pages and in the literary world's heart more palpably and enduringly than in Doré's statue of him in the Place Malesherbes.

---

* v. *'Four Novelists in Profile'* — The English Review, vol. LVG, October 1932.

BRIEF BIOGRAPHIES

Louis XIV (1638–1715)

Son of Louis XIII and Anne of Austria and grandson of Henry IV, he became king on the death of his father in 1643 at the age of five. During the eighteen years of his minority, in the course of which occurred the civil riots of the *Fronde*, he and the country were governed by his mother and Mazarin; but on the death of the latter in 1661, and now married to the Infanta Maria Theresa, he took over the reins of kingship and government, and with Colbert as his brilliant finance minister, gradually made himself a despot to the extent of being able to say *Le'État, ce'est moi!*

His private life was dissolute, with first Louise de la Vallière, then Mme de Montespan, and finally Mme de Maintenon as his mistresses, who between them bore him a round dozen natural offspring. By the middle of his reign he and Colbert had made France the most prosperous and powerful nation in Europe. But after that minister's death in 1683, what with the scandalous dissipations of the court, costly wars of would-be conquest and religion under the Jesuit-dominated influence of Mme de Maintenon, his last years became exemplary of the Virgilian *Facilis descensus Averno*, and a bodement of the reigns of his grandson Louis XV, Louis XVI and the Revolution.

Jean Baptiste Colbert (1619–83)

In 1661 he entered the service of Mazarin, who so esteemed his capabilities that he is reported to have said to Louis XIV just before his death 'I pay my debt to Your Majesty by bequeathing you Colbert' — incident seized on by Dumas with all his sense of the dramatic. By 1662 he had become the King's first minister, and remained so until his death.

In the twenty-three years of his office he brought about a succession of reforms by which he raised France from being an almost bankrupt country to becoming the most powerful, civilized and envied nation in Europe. But with the advent and ascendancy of Mme de Maintenon and her bigoted Jesuitry, the revocation of the Edict of Nantes, the ruinous wars of colonialism and religion and the oppressive taxes to pay for them, he was to see his regeneration of his country wasted, and he died a bitter and disappointed man.

Nicolas Fouquet (1615–80)

Attaching himself closely to Mazarin, he was made *procureur-générale* in 1650, and superintendent of finance three years later, after which he lived a Monte-Cristoesque life of lavish hospitality and extravagant display to the extent of maintaining a small army in his marquisate of Belle-Ile.

Jealous of his wealth and popularity, and suspicious of his ambitions, the king and Colbert set about his downfall. He was arrested, and after a three-year trial put away for life in the fortress of Pignerol, where he died.

Sympathetic to his romantic and quixotic nature, Dumas, while keeping to historic fact, makes him a more benignant character than that of the more duteous Colbert.

Louise de la Vallière (1644–1710)

Brought to court and becoming one of the maids of honour to Madame Henrietta, she fell in love with the king, and by the simple charm of her manners and sweetness of her nature, caught his attention and became his first (at least official) mistress. She bore him four children; but although she and they received wealth and titles, she never lost her awareness to the dishonour of their birth. When he forsook her for Mme de Montespan she retired into a Carmelite nunnery in Paris where she spent her last years, dying there at the age of seventy.

Henrietta of England (1644–70)

Younger sister of Charles II, she became Duchesse d'Orléans by her marriage to Louis XIV's younger brother Philippe in 1661. Mercurial, beautiful, witty and wilful, in addition to Buckingham, half the young nobles of the French court fell for her charms, and even the king himself.

Her short but brilliant life ended mysteriously at the age of twenty-six, poisoned, it was bruited, by her jealous husband. Her seduction of Louis and his brief infatuation for her are among the highlights of the novel.

Charles II, King of England (1630–85)

During the English Civil War, the young prince Charles spent several years travelling around Europe, principally France and Holland. Following his father's execution he went into exile, trailing around France and the Low Countries in hope of raising support for his claim to his father's crown, 'needy everywhere, everywhere profligate'.* Finally, thanks to the fall of the Protectorate, the nation's dread of army and Puritan rule, and Monk, he achieved his aim and was crowned in May 1660.

It is during his French wanderings that Dumas presents him to us, stressing the neediness but omitting the profligacy, and so giving a somewhat idealistic portrait of him.

George Monk (1608–70)

'Soldier of fortune and restorer of the English monarchy.'* Fought brilliantly

*Quotation from *Chambers's Encyclopaedia*.

with Cromwell at Dunbar, then went on to complete the subjugation of Scotland. On Cromwell's death in 1658, seizing his chance to take control in the national confusion, he crossed the border with 6,000 men, marched on London and took the city virtually unopposed. For some time he played Brer Fox and lay low, watching events. At last, sensing the mood of the nation and its detestation of Puritan and army rule, he welcomed Prince Charles at Dover in May 1660.

His canny nature and secretive policies, making his conversion to the royal cause something of a mystery, gave Dumas his great opportunity to make Athos and d'Artagnan in their own way an influence towards his change of heart and mind, so persuasively and delightfully narrated.

Blois Castle

The castle of Blois, where the opening scene of the novel is set, has been the site of many dramatic events and is a part of French history. Within its walls Louis XII was born, Henri IV and Marguerite de Valois were married, the Duc de Guise and his brother the Cardinal de Guise were murdered at the instigation of Henri III, and the notorious Catherine de Medici died.

The Man in the Iron Mask

The identity of the above has long been one of the great historical mysteries. He has been named as being at least six different people; and the reasons for his imprisonment and his true name have still not been discovered. In chronological order the theories as to whom he was are:

1. The Duke of Vermandois, a natural son of Louis XIV and La Vallière — a theory accepted and bruited by Voltaire in his *Siècle de Louis XIV*.

2. A natural son of Anne of Austria and the Duke of Buckingham. Dumas treats the duke's passion for Anne as authentic in *The Three Musketeers*.

3. A son of Mazarin and Anne of Austria (who, it was claimed, were secretly married) and so elder brother of Louis XIV.

4. A twin brother of Louis XIV, by name Philippe — the theory adopted by Dumas for the novel.

5. A certain Count Matthioli, minister of the Duke of Mantua.

6. A 'soldier of fortune', de Marchiel(y).

In addition to the claims to the above, it is almost certain that the mask itself was not of iron but of black velvet. It was myth and legend, those incitements to mystery and romance, which transformed the 'velvet' into 'iron'.